The Mystery of Israel and the Church

Volume 3

The Messianic Kingdom of Israel

Lawrence Feingold

The Miriam Press

Imprimatur: †Most Reverend Robert J. Hermann
                Auxiliary Bishop of St. Louis
                St. Louis, MO
                August 4, 2010

Cover Design: Kelly Boutross
Cover Art: High altar of the Cathedral Basilica of St. Louis, MO. Photograph by Mark Abeln. Used with permission.

ISBN: 978-0-939409-05-1

The Mystery of Israel and the Church

A four-volume series

The Mystery of Israel and the Church

Dedicated to Mary,
Daughter of Zion,
Mother of the Messiah,
Mother of the Church

And now the Lord says, who formed me from the womb to be his servant, to bring Jacob back to him, and that Israel might be gathered to him . . . : "It is too light a thing that you should be my servant to raise up the tribes of Jacob and to restore the preserved of Israel; I will give you as a light to the nations, that my salvation may reach to the end of the earth. . . . Lo, these shall come from afar, and lo, these from the north and from the west, and these from the land of Syene."

Isaiah 49:5–12

As you looked, a stone was cut out by no human hand, and it smote the image on its feet of iron and clay, and broke them in pieces; then the iron, the clay, the bronze, the silver, and the gold, all together were broken in pieces, and became like the chaff of the summer threshing floors; and the wind carried them away, so that not a trace of them could be found. But the stone that struck the image became a great mountain and filled the whole earth.

Daniel 2:34–35

For I will take you from among the Gentiles, and will gather you together out of all the countries, and will bring you into your own land. And I will pour upon you clean water, and you shall be cleansed from all your filthiness, and I will cleanse you from all your idols. And I will give you a new heart, and put a new spirit within you, and I will take away the stony heart out of your flesh, and will give you a heart of flesh. And I will put my spirit in the midst of you, and I will cause you to walk in my commandments, and to keep my judgments, and do them.

Ezekiel 36:24–27

Table of Contents

Foreword

The Mystery of Israel and the Church: The Messianic Kingdom of Israel is the third volume in a series that seeks to present Catholic theology with an eye to the great importance of that mystery. Each volume contains the text of a series of lectures presented by Dr. Feingold, with each chapter corresponding to one lecture.

The various series of lectures, sponsored by the Association of Hebrew Catholics (AHC) at the Cathedral Basilica School in Saint Louis, Missouri, have been ongoing since the fall of 2007. We are very grateful for the wonderful gifts given by our Lord to Dr. Feingold and for his great generosity in sharing his gifts, at no cost, with all who have willing hearts and open minds.

Lawrence Feingold expertly weaves together Sacred Scripture, Magisterial teachings, the Church Fathers, St. Thomas Aquinas, Pope John Paul II, Pope Benedict XVI, and many others, along with the teaching that has come from Vatican II. What one especially appreciates about his presentations is his ability to present difficult and abstract material in an intelligible and digestible way. He also presents the story of Israel and her role in salvation history in a magnificent light that enables us to better appreciate all that God has brought to pass through His great fidelity, love, and mercy in fulfilling the promises He made to Israel.

Lawrence Feingold and his wife Marsha, both Hebrew Catholics, entered the Church in 1989. Dr. Feingold studied Philosophy and Theology at the Pontifical University of the Holy Cross in Rome, earning a doctorate in Systematic Theology in 1999. He spent a year studying Biblical Hebrew and Greek at the Studium Biblicum Franciscanum in Jerusalem in 1995–96. He then taught Philosophy and Theology in the House of Formation of Miles Christi in Argentina. Currently he is Assistant Professor of Theology for the Institute of Pastoral Theology of Ave Maria University. In addition to the AHC lectures, Dr. Feingold is also part of the RCIA team at the Cathedral Basilica Parish, has taught at Kenrick-Glennon Seminary, and finds time one evening a week to host a study session in his home on various aspects of the teaching of St. Thomas Aquinas.

In issue 85 of *The Hebrew Catholic*, Dr. Feingold gives his "Account of My Conversion."[1] As he relates his journey to faith in the Messiah and to His Church, Dr. Feingold writes:

---

[1]http://www.hebrewcatholic.org/TheHebrewCatholic/85winter-spring2.html.

So I set out to pray for the first time. I took the train to go to Florence to pray in the Duomo built by Brunelleschi. I was not definitively thinking of Christianity, but nor was I opposed to it. On the way, I was moved to make this prayer: *Teach me to love; teach me to be a light unto others.* I don't know why I prayed like this, but to this day I know of no better prayer.

God so wants us to pray, that if we do so, He pours His grace upon us. After making this prayer, I thought of the words of Psalm 2: *"You are my son; this day I have begotten you."* Although an atheist, I knew the Bible from studying art history and comparative religion. And in this moment of grace I understood that these words were addressed by God the Father to Jesus Christ His Son, and also to me (and all other human beings) *in Christ* the Son.

Not only did our Lord give Dr. Feingold the gift that enabled him to understand who Jesus Christ was and is, but He answered his initial prayer, giving him the grace *to be a light unto others,* a grace to which Dr. Feingold has so faithfully corresponded.

In the concluding paragraphs of his "Account," Dr. Feingold writes:

Many Jews who come to believe in Christ and the Church He founded feel anguish over what is perceived as a betrayal of the Jewish people. My wife and I never experienced this trial. On the contrary, I discovered a great attraction for things Jewish that I never experienced before. I had never learned Hebrew as a child, but I found great joy in learning it as a Christian, so as to pray the Psalms, for example, in the language of the Chosen People. This sense was clarified and stimulated by reading the book *Jewish Identity* by Fr. Elias Friedman, founder of the Association of Hebrew Catholics, which I came across not long after our entrance into the Catholic Church.

In the first years after our conversion, people often asked me why I "chose" Christianity or the Catholic Church, and not Judaism or Buddhism or Protestantism. The question is framed in the language of religious liberalism, as if religion were a matter of our personal sentiments, personal preferences, personal loyalties or choices. The experience of converts is not that we have chosen anything, but that it is God who has chosen to redeem us through the Incarnation and Passion of the Messiah, which is continued and made present in the Catholic Church, and it is God who called us to enter the ark of salvation. We who have been given the grace to hear, through no merit of our own, have the duty to pray for those who have not yet been given that gift.

If these lectures enable readers to grow in their understanding of the mysteries of God, they will find that they will also grow in their appreciation of the Jewish roots of their faith, in gratitude for all that God has done, and in the love of our Lord, *Yeshua haMashiach*.[2] May it be so!

Briefly stated, the mission of the Association of Hebrew Catholics is pastoral and educational: to preserve the identity and heritage of Jews within the Church, helping them to serve the Lord, His Church, and all peoples within the mystery of their irrevocable calling. Those who are interested may write to the AHC, 4120 W Pine Blvd., Saint Louis, MO 63108, for more information and a sample issue of our publication, *The Hebrew Catholic*.

Now we invite you to partake of a feast of the Spirit as you encounter the truths of our faith given by Jesus Christ, preserved by the Church, taught by the Magisterium, and here presented by Dr. Lawrence Feingold. May you be blessed.

David Moss, President
Association of Hebrew Catholics

---

[2] All of the lectures represented by the chapters of this volume, including question-and-answer sessions after each lecture, can be listened to or downloaded to your computer at no cost from the AHC website at http://www.hebrewcatholic.org/Studies/MysteryofIsraelChurch/mysteryofisraela.html.

Preface

This book grew out of a lecture series entitled "The Mystery of Israel and the Church: Themes of the Kingdom," organized by the Association of Hebrew Catholics and held in the fall of 2008 in the Cathedral Basilica of St. Louis. Three chapters (7, 12, and 14) have been added from subsequent lecture series on St. Paul and the early Fathers. Interest was expressed in bringing these talks to a wider public without losing their original character as oral presentations.

The principal focus of the lectures is the mystery of the Kingdom of God that Christ established in the Catholic Church and the relationship between Israel and the Church in God's plan. In our time many Jews are coming to recognize Jesus as the Messiah, while not yet recognizing the Catholic Church as the Kingdom founded by Him, in which believers have the fullness of access to Him. Indeed, Jesus cannot be fully understood or embraced apart from His Church, prefigured by Biblical Israel. Two goals of this work are to help those who do not yet recognize the true Church to come to that faith, and to help those who believe in the Church to understand and live its mystery more deeply, and to be able to communicate more effectively the reasons for our faith. So many of our contemporaries fail to understand the mystery of the Church, which they see as a purely human institution they logically have no obligation to embrace. St. Peter, in his first letter (3:15), tells believers to "always be ready to give a defense to everyone who asks you a reason for the hope that is in you, with meekness and fear." Catholics have to be prepared to defend their faith not only in Christ, but also in the Church, which is His Kingdom and Mystical Body.

A significant part of the task of apologetics is to make clear the relationship between Biblical Israel and the Church. A third goal of this book, therefore, is to help elucidate the complex and beautiful relationship between Israel and the Church in God's plan. It is hoped that this book may deepen the awareness of Catholics (and others) of the luminous teaching of the Second Vatican Council in *Nostra aetate* 4: "As the sacred synod searches into the mystery of the Church, it remembers the bond that spiritually ties the people of the New Covenant to Abraham's stock."

I would like to thank the President of the Association of Hebrew Catholics, David Moss, and his wife, Kathleen, for organizing and sponsoring the lecture series which were the origin of these volumes. Special thanks go to Archbishop Burke for welcoming the Association of Hebrew Catholics into the Archdiocese of St. Louis and supporting our work, and to Archbishop Carlson and Bishop Hermann for continuing that support. I also thank our pastor, Msgr. Pins, for his support and for allowing us to use the Cathedral Basilica School for the lecture series. Above all, I would like to thank my wife, Marsha, who is my editor, inspiration, and support, and who spent countless hours improving the text. I also thank everyone else who helped to edit these volumes, and all those who attended the series and contributed with their encouragement and their questions and comments.

I would also like to thank Ave Maria University's Institute for Pastoral Theology. This book and the other volumes in this series have been enriched by my teaching experience with this remarkable program. It is our conviction in the Institute for Pastoral Theology that deeper knowledge of Catholic doctrine, growth in holiness, the life of prayer, and pastoral activity are inseparably united. Greater knowledge of the truths of the faith should help us to love God more faithfully and to lead others to that same truth and love, thereby helping to build up the Church. I pray that a more perfect knowledge of the Catholic faith, including its Jewish roots, may lead the reader to a deeper encounter with the God of Abraham, Isaac, and Jacob—the Triune God glimpsed by these Patriarchs, in whose seed all nations have been blessed (Gen 22:18).

List of Abbreviations

Abbreviation of Sources

ANF   *The Ante-Nicene Fathers.* Peabody, MA: Hendrickson, 1994.

NPNF *Nicene and Post-Nicene Fathers.* Peabody, MA: Hendrickson, 2004.

CCC   *Catechism of the Catholic Church.*

D   Denzinger. *The Sources of Catholic Dogma.* Fitzwilliam, NH: Loreto, 2002.

DS   Denzinger-Schönmetzer. *Enchiridion Symbolorum, definitionum et declarationum de rebus fidei et morum* (1965).

DV   Second Vatican Council, Dogmatic Constitution on Revelation, *Dei Verbum.*

HV   Paul VI, encyclical *Humanae vitae*, 1968.

LG   Second Vatican Council, Constitution on the Church, *Lumen gentium.*

PG   *Patrologia graeca.* J.P. Migne, editor. Paris, 1857 ff.

PL   *Patrologia latina.* J.P. Migne, editor. Paris, 1844 ff.

ST   *Summa theologiae of St. Thomas Aquinas.* 2nd ed. Translated by Dominican Fathers of the English Province. London: Burns, Oates, & Washbourne, 1920–1932.

Other Abbreviations

a.   article

ch.   chapter

q.   question

n.   paragraph number

CHAPTER 1

People of God and Kingdom of God: Israel and the Church

Israel and the Church in God's Eternal Plan

Let us begin by reflecting on why God willed to choose one people, Israel, out of all the nations of the earth to be His people, and why He subsequently willed to form a new People and Kingdom of God from out of the bosom of Israel and to call all nations to enter into that new People and Kingdom.

What is God's eternal purpose in creating the world, and how do Israel and the Church figure into that plan? God could have no other purpose in creating the universe than to manifest and communicate His goodness outside of Himself. This is because God, being infinite goodness in Himself, needs nothing from creation and cannot be enriched by it. His only purpose in creating, therefore, is to give; He wills to give to beings outside Himself a share in His goodness.

All the levels of God's creation, even the lower levels such as rocks, plants, and bugs, manifest God's goodness. However, God can fully communicate His goodness only to rational creatures—human beings and angels—who have the ability to appreciate the gift they have received, and to return the gift back in love.

This communication of His goodness culminates in drawing His rational creatures into a union of love and intimate friendship with Himself. It follows that God created rational creatures for Himself, that they might know and love His Goodness and enter into friendship with Him. The other creatures on the face of the earth, by contrast, were created for man, in order to help man live and achieve his end of friendship with God.

The union that God wishes to establish with mankind has two dimensions: vertical and horizontal. First and foremost, the union is a vertical one by which the souls of men are united with the Blessed Trinity. However, by a necessary consequence, God wishes His rational creatures who are to be drawn into union with Him also to be drawn into a horizontal communion with one another in the bonds of charity.

1

All those who are called to union with God are also called to an intimate union of charity with one another.

The vertical union with God brings us into communion with the Blessed Trinity by making us sons of God in the Son. The horizontal communion is the supernatural fraternity and charity of all those who have been made sons and daughters of God.

This dual communion into which we are called has been eloquently presented by the Second Vatican Council in *Gaudium et spes* 24, a text cited time and again by John Paul II:

> Indeed, the Lord Jesus, when He prayed to the Father, "that all may be one . . . as we are one" (John 17:21–22) opened up vistas closed to human reason, for He implied a certain likeness between the union of the divine Persons, and the unity of God's sons in truth and charity. This likeness reveals that man, who is the only creature on earth which God willed for itself, cannot fully find himself except through a sincere gift of himself.

This text is very dense. God, who is a communion of Persons, willed to create human persons to enter into friendship and communion with Him. Thus human beings, alone among material beings, have been created for their own sake to be recipients of God's love and brought into union with Him. However, just as God loves man by giving a complete gift of Himself to man (by becoming incarnate, dying for us on the Cross, instituting the Eucharist, giving us the Holy Spirit), so man is called to find his fulfillment likewise in making a sincere gift of himself to God and to his fellow men. It follows that the union between man and God that is our salvation must also include the horizontal dimension of communion among men: "the unity of God's sons in truth and charity." This horizontal communion is meant to be a kind of mirror and "enlargement" of the ineffable communion of three divine Persons.

This mirroring of God's inter-Trinitarian love means that mankind achieves salvation and redemption not individually, but as a social body tied together with bonds analogous to the mysterious bond of eternal charity that unites the Blessed Trinity. God's plan was not for us to be redeemed and become sons of God independently from one another, as islands. We live in a society profoundly marked by the spirit of individualism, born in part by the Protestant rejection of the Catholic Church, and thus it costs us effort to overcome this individualistic mentality. Pope Benedict XVI recently alluded to this in his encyclical on hope.[1]

---

[1] Benedict XVI, encyclical *Spe salvi* 13–16.

Man is by nature a social creature, and since grace does not destroy nature but perfects it, it is necessary that grace also perfect man as a social and communal being. The redemption of man must have a fundamental social aspect, which is the Church, prepared for and prefigured in ancient Israel. Man cannot be redeemed without his social dimension being redeemed as well.

Furthermore, man's social nature can be seen in the fact that he naturally desires communion and fraternity, such that he cannot be completely happy without deep interpersonal relations. It follows that the perfect happiness of man, to be brought about by the Incarnation and Redemption, must culminate in the redemption and perfect restoration of a life of communion which is to be fully realized in the Kingdom of heaven, but also anticipated here in God's Kingdom on earth.

The Second Vatican Council expressed this truth in *Lumen gentium* 9:

> At all times and in every race God has given welcome to whosoever fears Him and does what is right. God, however, does not make men holy and save them *merely as individuals*, without bond or link between one another. Rather has *it pleased Him to bring men together as one people*, a people which acknowledges Him in truth and serves Him in holiness.

This plan of social redemption was first begun with the election of Israel as the People of God. *Lumen gentium* continues:

> He therefore chose the race of Israel as a people unto Himself. With it He set up a covenant. Step by step He taught and prepared this people, making known in its history both Himself and the decree of His will and making it holy unto Himself. All these things, however, were done by way of preparation and as a figure of that new and perfect covenant, which was to be ratified in Christ, and of that fuller revelation which was to be given through the Word of God Himself made flesh. . . . This was to be the new People of God.

In order to prepare for His Incarnation by which He would enter human history and take on the human condition, God chose one people from all the nations of the earth. He elected Abraham to be the father of this people and called him from his father's house to go into a land that God would show him. God revealed to Abraham that in his seed all nations of the world would be blessed. This was the first Messianic prophecy after that given to Adam and Eve upon their expulsion from Paradise.

The election of Israel as the People of God, therefore, was not an end in itself, but a preparation for and prefiguring of a universal blessing in the person of the Messiah and in the universal kingdom of God to be founded by the Messiah in Israel. This universal Kingdom would be a "new People of God" and a "new Israel."

The Incarnation of the Second Person of the Trinity was thus prepared for by God, two thousand years before that event, by His choosing one family and making them into a people: the Chosen People. The children of Abraham were joined to God by a covenant whose sign was circumcision, which marked them out from all other peoples as the one in which God would become incarnate. In view of this, the people was made the recipient of a whole series of marvelous privileges designed to make them fitted to receive the Incarnation of God.

In the broad sense of the word, we can already speak of the Chosen People as the Church present in germ in the long period of expectation of the Messiah. They lived by hope in the realization of the Messianic promises given to Abraham and the prophets: that all nations would be blessed in the future Messiah who would establish a universal and eternal kingdom—the Kingdom of God.

The People of God as God's Own Possession

In view of the coming Messiah, the Chosen People was constituted as the People of God, God's "own possession"[2] among the nations of the earth. This is expressed by God in Exodus 19:3–6, as Israel gathered at the foot of Mt. Sinai to receive the Law and the covenant. God said to them through Moses:

> Thus you shall say to the house of Jacob, and tell the people of Israel: You have seen what I did to the Egyptians, and how I bore you on eagles' wings and brought you to myself. Now therefore, if you will obey my voice and keep my covenant, you shall be *my own possession among all peoples*; for all the earth is mine, and you shall be to me a *kingdom of priests and a holy nation*.

As God's "own possession," Israel was made a priestly and prophetic People called to bear the progressive revelation of the Messiah and the Messianic age. Israel was prepared for this great role by the reception of the Law of Moses.

Another great text that speaks of Israel as God's own possession is Deuteronomy 7:6–14:

---

[2] See Deut 7:6; Ex 19:5.

For you are a people holy to the Lord your God; the Lord your God has chosen you to be a *people for his own possession*, out of all the peoples that are on the face of the earth. It was *not because you were more in number* than any other people that the Lord set his love upon you and chose you, for you were the fewest of all peoples; but it is *because the Lord loves you*, and is keeping the oath which he swore to your fathers, that the Lord has brought you out with a mighty hand, and redeemed you from the house of bondage, from the hand of Pharaoh king of Egypt. Know therefore that the Lord your God is God, the faithful God who keeps covenant and steadfast love with those who love him and keep his commandments, to a thousand generations, and requites to their face those who hate him. . . . You shall therefore be careful to do the commandment, and the statutes, and the ordinances, which I command you this day. And because you hearken to these ordinances, and keep and do them, the Lord your God will keep with you the covenant and the steadfast love which he swore to your fathers to keep; he will love you, bless you, and multiply you; . . . You shall be blessed above all peoples.

The identity of Israel in God's plan is perfectly set forth in these two texts. First of all, Israel is a people gratuitously chosen from all the peoples of the earth. They were not chosen because of their size, military prowess, intelligence, or any other natural gifts. The *only motive of God's election is His gratuitous love*, which is prior to any merits on man's part. This was true of Israel and it is true of all those who are called to enter the Catholic Church.

Secondly, Israel was chosen to be a people that would be the *unique possession of God*. After her election, Israel was not "her own," for she was consecrated to God. The dignity of Israel lay not in being autonomous—being a law unto herself—but rather in *losing her autonomy so as to be God's people*, entering into a covenant with Him and accepting the yoke of His Torah. This renunciation, nevertheless, involved a higher freedom, for Israel entered into the covenant with God by free choice (Ex 19:8) and was preserved by it from the bondage of idolatry and ignorance.

Third, since God is holy, the People of God must likewise be holy. This holiness has two dimensions. Israel is outwardly set apart from other peoples and consecrated to God by a holy liturgy and laws, as set forth in the Law of Moses. This outward holiness in turn is ordered to an interior moral and religious sanctity.

Finally, in order to realize this holiness in the liturgy ordained by God, the entire people of Israel is given a priestly dignity: "You shall be to me a *kingdom of priests*" (Ex 19:6), a people ordained to offer to God the sacrifice of obedience and praise. Even though only the descendants of Aaron were ministerial priests, the entire people of Israel exercised a "royal priesthood" (cf. 1 Pt 2:9) in that they were to offer the interior sacrifice of the heart through obedience to God, through faith, hope, and charity, and through interiorly offering themselves to God with the ritual victims.

The Church as People of God, Royal Priesthood, and Holy Nation

These characteristics of Israel—the gratuitous election to be God's holy and priestly People through a covenant established by Him—are applied also to the Church in the New Testament. Indeed, we cannot understand the identity of the Church except in relation to these characteristics of Israel, which the Church must possess in a still higher way.

St. Paul manifests the gratuitous election of the Church as the New Israel in numerous places. One of the most eloquent is the hymn at the beginning of the Letter to the Ephesians (1:3–10):

> Blessed be the God and Father of our Lord Jesus Christ, who has blessed us in Christ with every spiritual blessing in the heavenly places, even as he chose us in him before the foundation of the world, that we should be holy and blameless before him. He destined us in love to be his sons through Jesus Christ, according to the purpose of his will, to the praise of his glorious grace which he freely bestowed on us in the Beloved. In him we have redemption through his blood, the forgiveness of our trespasses, according to the riches of his grace which he lavished upon us. For he has made known to us in all wisdom and insight the mystery of his will, according to his purpose which he set forth in Christ as a plan for the fullness of time, to unite all things in him, things in heaven and things on earth.

Like Israel, the members of the Church were chosen gratuitously in Christ before the foundation of the world. This election is mysterious for it does not correspond to any human merit, but is freely bestowed on us in love "to the praise of His glorious grace" (Eph 1:6), in Christ, the Beloved.

Like Israel, the Church is the recipient of God's liberating mercy, through the blood of the paschal lamb. The Church has been redeemed, however, by an incomparably better sacrificial Lamb whose blood is able to work the forgiveness of all the sins of the world.

Like Israel, the Church does not belong to herself but to Christ, the Word of God, who has redeemed her with His Blood and lavished her with His grace. In consequence of this gratuitous election to be united to Christ, the members of the Church, like Israel, are called to be holy and blameless, and are called to be sons of God in the Son.

Like Israel, the Church is the recipient of the Revelation of God's wisdom. The Church, however, has received a still higher wisdom than ancient Israel, for she has received Christ, the incarnate Wisdom who has revealed the fullness of God's plans for mankind.

The Church, finally, like Israel, has been given a priestly dignity that is a participation in the priesthood of Christ. St. Peter explains this privilege by quoting the text of Exodus 19:6 in 1 Peter 2:9: "But you are a chosen race, a *royal priesthood*, a holy nation, God's own people, that you may declare the wonderful deeds of him who called you out of darkness into his marvelous light." The whole Church is spoken of as having a "royal priesthood" because Christ gave His sacrifice to the whole Church to be her dowry and greatest treasure. All the faithful share in Christ's priesthood in the sense that they are called to offer up the interior holocaust of their hearts in union with the sacrifice of the Sacred Heart of Christ made present on our altars in the holy Mass, and, together with the immaculate victim, to call down blessings upon men.

Visible and Invisible Aspects of the People of God

The fact that a people is chosen by God to be His own is a mystery with an invisible dimension. The People of God, in order to be a people, must be a visible, social, juridical, and institutional reality, like the other peoples on the earth. However, to be the People of God, this chosen people must have an invisible dimension of grace, faith, hope, and charity, by which they are consecrated to God. This conjunction of visible institutional elements and invisible charismatic elements is proper both to Israel and to the Church.

The Israel of the Old Testament thus already was endowed with visible and invisible aspects. On the one hand, Israel was a visible kingdom which reached its greatest visibility in the times of David and Solomon. It was ruled by the Davidic dynasty, and its religious life was presided over by the high priesthood of the line of Aaron. The high priests were aided by all the other priests and Levites who were set apart in Israel for the divine liturgy, celebrated in the glorious Temple of Solomon, in which all sacrifice was to be offered. Although this unity was shattered by the breaking away of the ten northern tribes and the setting up of a schismatic temple in Samaria (Mt. Gerazim), the ideal of unity under the Davidic line and the Temple in Jerusalem always remained.

Israel also had an invisible life of faith, hope, and charity. This invisible life was constantly being obscured by the public sins of many of the great and mighty in Israel. Nevertheless, this invisible life continued in all generations of Israel in her saints and prophets. At the dawn of the New Testament we can see this invisible life in Zachariah, Elizabeth, Simeon, Anna, John the Baptist, and above all in St. Joseph and the Blessed Virgin. Mary was the culmination of the entire faith of Israel, such that we can see her as the paradigmatic daughter of Zion mentioned frequently in the prophets.

Israel thus clearly prefigured the Church founded by Christ and was already the seed and germ of that Church. Let us briefly summarize the characteristics of the People of God of the Old Covenant insofar as it prefigures the Church of Christ.

1.   The Chosen People was adopted by God as His people through a gratuitous election.

2.   Israel was a visible kingdom endowed with a visible hierarchical authority that was the bearer of invisible supernatural gifts.

3.   Israel was meant to be one kingdom whose religious life centered on the Temple in Jerusalem. The schism of the Northern Kingdom was denounced again and again as a great infidelity, which ended in the almost complete loss of the ten northern tribes. The New Israel will likewise be one Kingdom with a center of religious unity: the rock of Peter.

4.   Israel was chosen through a covenant with God, sealed by the sacrificial blood of bulls. The New Israel will likewise be formed through a new covenant sealed with the sacrificial Blood of the Messiah.

Christ's Incarnation as the Model of the Two Dimensions of the Church

Christ's Incarnation is the model for the Church. Christ, we know, is one Person in two natures: human and divine. The human nature is visible to us, whereas the divine is invisible. However, through the visible human nature, the divine has entered our world and has become manifest through the humanity of Christ.

In an analogous way, the Church, like ancient Israel before her, has two natures, as it were.[3] On the one hand, the Church is a visible social body, with visible bonds of communion and hierarchical authority. She is visible above all through the human beings that enter her communion through the sacrament of Baptism, and through the common profession

---

[3] See Vatican II, Dogmatic Constitution on the Church *Lumen gentium* 8: "The society structured with hierarchical organs and the Mystical Body of Christ . . . form one complex reality which coalesces from a divine and a human element. For this reason, by no weak analogy, it is compared to the mystery of the incarnate Word."

of the Catholic faith, which is made visible in Magisterial documents. Her visible government and hierarchical structures derive from the sacrament of Holy Orders and ecclesiastical jurisdiction. She has a visible juridical system based on canon law. Even the life of prayer of the Church has a fundamental visible dimension through the public liturgy of the Church. The Church is also visible through her impact on human culture: her patronage of the arts, sciences, education, and her manifold works of charity. Most people only see the visible dimension of the Church.

The Church, however, has an *invisible life of grace that comes through her visible sacraments*. This life of grace is the soul of the Church, and consists in sanctifying grace and the theological virtues that flow from grace: faith, hope, and charity. All the "living" members of the Church—who are in a state of grace—share in this supernatural life. The Church, unfortunately, also has dead members in her bosom, the baptized who profess the Catholic faith, but who have fallen into mortal sin, but whom we hope will return to life through contrition and the sacrament of Penance. All the living members of the Church have one living faith, revealed by God and infallibly taught by the Church. They also have one hope for the beatific vision and union in the life of God in heaven. Likewise, all the living members of the Church share the same charity, which is the love for God above all things, as Father and Spouse, and love for our neighbor for God's sake.

The Church lives through the supernatural charity that flows in her "veins," infused through the power of the sacraments. This is the living water that Jesus spoke of to the Samaritan woman at the well in John 4:10–14: "If you knew the gift of God, and who it is that is saying to you, 'Give me a drink,' you would have asked him, and he would have given you living water. . . . The water that I shall give him will become in him a spring of water welling up to eternal life."

The invisible supernatural life of the Church also consists in our common sharing in the seven gifts of the Holy Spirit: wisdom, understanding, counsel, fortitude, knowledge, piety, and fear of the Lord. These gifts enable the living members of the Church to be moved by the secret impulses of God's grace and to be docile to divine inspirations. God rules His Church not just through the visible structures of ecclesiastical authority, but also and especially through the hidden impulses of the Holy Spirit which we receive through the seven gifts of docility, which are the seven gifts of the Holy Spirit.

Through the sacraments, beginning with Baptism and culminating in the Eucharist, the members of the Church are joined to Christ through mystical or sacramental bonds, which create a real supernatural union with Christ. This union has two dimensions: baptismal character and sanctifying grace. In virtue of baptismal character, all the faithful receive a share in Christ's priestly, prophetic, and kingly office.[4] This means that through Baptism we receive a spiritual power to participate in the priestly offering of Christ's redemptive sacrifice, in the prophetic office of professing the true faith, and in the kingly office of ordering of all temporal realities according to the Law of God, which is summarized in the bond of supernatural charity.

In virtue of sanctifying grace, not only are we joined to Christ's priestly, prophetic, and kingly mission, but we are also joined to Him in a real union of friendship and adopted sonship. All the members of Christ are thus made into one Mystical Body with Him.

St. Paul, in 1 Corinthians 12:12–13, speaks of this intimate union of Christ and the Church, and of the complementarity of members in the Body of Christ:

> For just as the body is one and has many members, and all the members of the body, though many, are one body, so it is with Christ. For by one Spirit we were all baptized into one body—Jews or Greeks, slaves or free—and all were made to drink of one Spirit.

The Body of Christ which results from our sacramental union with Him has both visible and invisible dimensions, in which the many members complement each other in a marvelous way. Visibly, the Church is hierarchically structured according to the sacrament of Holy Orders, according to the calling which some of the members of the Body have received. The Body is also structured by various spiritual charisms, such as the vocation to the consecrated or religious life, or the vocation of the laity, who also participate in complementary spiritual gifts for the building up of the Body of Christ, each according to his own circumstances, temporal activity, and apostolate.

Thus there is diversity of roles in the Body, but the Body remains one through its living connection with the one Head of the Body, which is Christ, and through the one soul animating the Body, which is the Holy Spirit.

Pius XII has written a beautiful encyclical on the Mystical Body of Christ (*Mystici Corporis* of 1943), in which he says: "If we would define and describe this true Church of Jesus Christ—which is the One, Holy, Catholic, Apostolic and Roman Church—we shall find nothing more noble, more sublime, or more divine than the expression 'the Mystical Body of Christ.'"[5]

---

[4] See *Lumen gentium* 31; John Paul II, Apostolic Exhortation *Christifideles laici* 14.
[5] Pius XII, *Mystici Corporis* 13.

Who are the members of this Mystical Body? Pius XII gives a brief and clear answer to this crucial question:

> Actually only those are to be included as members of the Church who have been baptized and profess the true faith, and who have not been so unfortunate as to separate themselves from the unity of the Body, or been excluded by legitimate authority for grave faults committed. . . . It follows that those who are divided in faith or government cannot be living in the unity of such a Body, nor can they be living the life of its one Divine Spirit.[6]

In other words, the members of the Mystical Body of Christ are the baptized faithful who have not become tragically separated through public schism, heresy, apostasy, or excommunication. Those visible members who have not separated themselves in any of those ways but are in a state of mortal sin are still members of the Body, but not living members.

Relation between the Visible and the Invisible Dimensions of the Church

What is the relation between the visible and the invisible aspects of the Church? Just as the two natures in Christ were never separated, so too the visible and invisible aspects of the Church are intimately united. The invisible life of faith, hope, charity, and the seven gifts of the Holy Spirit could not be maintained in the Church without her visible and institutional elements: her sacraments, which give supernatural life; her infallible Magisterium, which preserves the faith; and the sacred authority of the ecclesiastical hierarchy, which maintains unity, and thus protects charity. However, it takes faith to see the invisible dimension of the Church. As we know, so many of our contemporaries fail to see it.

Of the two dimensions, which is primary? We can ask the same question of Christ's two natures. Obviously, Christ's divine nature is primary. Likewise in the Church, the invisible dimension of grace, sanctity, and truth, is primary. The visible and external social body serves the invisible dimension, just as Christ's humanity was a living and free "instrument" of His divinity.

This principle has great importance. All of the visible and institutional aspects of the Church, like the visible and institutional aspects of ancient Israel, are divinely instituted *means* to help her to save souls and foster the supernatural communion of the sons and daughters of God. The ecclesiastical hierarchy is a means to sanctify souls, to conserve the truth of divine Revelation until the end of time, and to

---

[6] Ibid., 22.

constantly ensure and foster the unity of the People of God. Although the visible dimension of the Church is simply a means or instrument, this does not mean that it is unimportant or can be dispensed with! The visible Church is as important to the life of the Church as the body is important for the life of the human person. Just as the human body merits great respect for the sake of the person, so the visible and institutional dimension of the Church is to be venerated on account of the life of grace that she serves. Just as we love our own bodies, so we must also love the visible dimension of the Church, without which her (and our) supernatural life cannot subsist.

Errors with Regard to the Church

Just as there are two opposing ways to deny the mystery of the Incarnation, so too there are two opposing ways to deny the nature of the Church. One could exclusively recognize her visible dimension while forgetting or denying her supernatural dimension. This is called the error of naturalism.[7] Obviously, it is an error that is very common today, even among many who say they are Catholic. In this view, the Church is simply a human institution among others (even if it is held to be worthy of respect), like those who hold that Christ was merely a great moral teacher. This view is the natural outlook of all those who lack Catholic faith.

An opposing error is a kind of supernaturalism, denying the visible and institutional dimension of the Church. With regard to Christ, one can deny His Incarnation not only by denying His divinity, but also by denying His humanity. Strangely, the first Christological heresy to plague the Church was the denial of His true humanity. This heresy, called *docetism*, held that Christ's humanity and Passion were only an appearance or fiction.[8] A similar heresy can exist with regard to the Church, holding it to be an exclusively supernatural and invisible reality, without true visible and institutional aspects that belong to its divine constitution, such as the apostolic succession and the hierarchy.[9]

This type of view does not completely deny visible elements of authority in the Church, but regards them as merely organizational or

---

[7] See Pius XII, *Mystici Corporis* 9, which speaks of the error of "popular naturalism, which sees and wills to see in the Church nothing but a juridical and social union."

[8] It is interesting to note that the Gnostics who denied Christ's true humanity normally also denied His true divinity, seeing Him as a kind of archangel.

[9] *Mystici Corporis* 14 denounces this error as well: "Hence they err in a matter of divine truth, who imagine the Church to be invisible, intangible, a something merely 'pneumatological' as they say, by which many Christian communities, though they differ from each other in their profession of faith, are united by an invisible bond."

bureaucratic structures that do not belong to the essence of the Church, which remains exclusively invisible. These visible structures, being regarded as purely human institutions, could thus be changed at will.

This is really the essence of the Lutheran and Protestant view of the Church. The leaders of the Protestant Reformation did not deny the existence of the Church that we profess in the Creed. Martin Luther denied, however, that the Church professed in the Creed was in fact the same Church that is made visible in the Catholic Church through her seven sacraments, the visible hierarchy of the Church, her sacred authority, and her authentic Magisterial teaching. Luther thought he could continue to belong to the invisible Church while being excommunicated from its visible Body and indeed seeking to destroy that visible and institutional Body, and substituting for it a different organizational structure.

Luther's rejection of the visible Body of the Church is manifested in his rejection of the sacrament of Holy Orders, by which that Body is divinely structured and governed. Already in 1520, Luther denied the ecclesiastical hierarchy in his work *On the Babylonian Captivity of the Church*[10] and his *Address to the Christian Nobility of the German Nation.*[11] In its place he recognized only a priesthood of the faithful. In this view, the priest or pastor is not essentially or ontologically marked by a priestly character, but is simply one who fulfills a certain function in the Church: preaching and presiding. This function of preaching is not essentially different, in this view, from that of shoemaking, for example, for which no special hierarchical mission is needed. This was a heresy with incalculable consequences, for it led to the almost entire abolition of the sacramental system, leaving only Baptism and matrimony, for which the sacrament of Holy Orders is not necessary. This is so grave because the sacramental system is the divinely appointed means by which the Church is given both a *visible* dimension and an *invisible* and supernatural life! Thus the attack against the sacrament of Holy Orders and the Church's sacramental system was an attack on her visible life (directly), but also no less an attack on her supernatural life, which comes through her visible means of sanctification—the sacraments. Attacking the sacramental system leads one to lose key visible and invisible dimensions of the Church.

---

[10] *Luther's Works*, volume 36: *Word and Sacrament II*, ed. Abdel Ross Wentz (Philadelphia: Muhlenberg Press, 1959), 116: "Let everyone, therefore, who knows himself to be a Christian, be assured of this, that we are all equally priests, that is to say, we have the same power in respect to the Word and the sacraments."

[11] *Luther's Works*, vol. 44, *The Christian in Society I*, ed. James Atkinson (Philadelphia: Fortress Press, 1966), 127–130.

The denial of the visibility of the Church is incompatible not only with the model of the Incarnation, but also with the model of ancient Israel as the People of God. For ancient Israel was very clearly willed by God to be a kingdom endowed with both visible and invisible elements. Ancient Israel had a religious authority invested in Moses, Aaron, and the sons of Aaron who were entrusted with the high priesthood. Christ Himself acknowledges their rightful authority in Israel by saying: "The scribes and the Pharisees sit on Moses' seat; so practice and observe whatever they tell you, but not what they do" (Mt 23:2–3).

The Protestant conception thus ends up making Israel and the Church no longer parallel but antithetical. If this were the case, Biblical Israel would not have been a true preparation for and prefiguring of the Church, and God's plan of salvation would lose its continuity and harmony.

Unfortunately, today many Messianic Jews, following the conception of Luther, fail to understand the twofold nature of the Church as simultaneously visible and invisible.

Pope Leo XIII spoke of these two opposing errors with regard to the visible and invisible nature of the Church in an important encyclical on the Church called *Satis cognitum* (1896):

> From this it follows that those who arbitrarily conjure up and picture to themselves a hidden and invisible Church are in grievous and pernicious error: as also are those who regard the Church as a human institution which claims a certain obedience in discipline and external duties, but which is without the perennial communication of the gifts of divine grace, and without all that which testifies by constant and undoubted signs to the existence of that life which is drawn from God. It is assuredly as impossible that the Church of Jesus Christ can be the one or the other, as that man should be a body alone or a soul alone. The connection and union of both elements is as absolutely necessary to the true Church as the intimate union of the soul and body is to human nature. The Church is not something dead: it is the body of Christ endowed with supernatural life.[12]

As we have seen, this perennial doctrine of the Church was denied by the first Protestants, who tended to think of the Church as completely invisible, and thus without authoritative structures. It is also rejected by rationalist currents that see the Church as entirely visible, as nothing more than a human institution. Thus it is crucial to see the Church in the image of Christ, the Word Incarnate, and on the pattern

---

[12] Leo XIII, *Satis cognitum* 3.

of Biblical Israel, endowed with visible and invisible dimensions. The visible structure of the Church is the sign and instrument of the invisible communion in grace and charity that is realized by the Holy Spirit in the Church, as Christ's sacred humanity is the instrument and "sacrament" of His divinity. The Second Vatican Council expressed this idea in *Lumen gentium* 8:

> Christ, the one Mediator, established and continually sustains here on earth His holy Church, the community of faith, hope and charity, as an entity with visible delineation through which He communicated truth and grace to all. But, the society structured with hierarchical organs and the Mystical Body of Christ, are not to be considered as two realities, nor are the visible assembly and the spiritual community, nor the earthly Church and the Church enriched with heavenly things; rather they form one complex reality which coalesces from a divine and a human element. For this reason, by no weak analogy, it is compared to the mystery of the incarnate Word. As the assumed nature inseparably united to Him, serves the divine Word as a living organ of salvation, so, in a similar way, does the visible social structure of the Church serve the Spirit of Christ, who vivifies it, in the building up of the body.

The Church, therefore, like ancient Israel, is at once a visible hierarchical kingdom, and a spiritual communion in spiritual gifts.

The Visibility of the Church in the Post-Apostolic Age

In order to refute the Lutheran idea that the Church is only an invisible reality, we should look at the Church as established by Christ, and how she appears in the first century of her existence. Christ clearly built His Church on the rock of Peter and the twelve Apostles (Mt 16:18). The very fact that He chose twelve Apostles was a clear reference to the twelve tribes of Israel, in which the Chosen People of the Old Covenant lived as a visible society. The book of Acts shows us that the Apostles exercised a clear hierarchical authority in the Church after the death of Christ. The Church founded by Christ was the Church governed by the Apostles. The Acts of the Apostles also shows us that the Apostles ordained successors to govern the churches after their death, and they ordained bishops and presbyters (priests) in each city they evangelized.

By the end of the first century, the Church had the same visible structure that we see today, although obviously on a reduced scale. In each city, there was one bishop who represented Christ and governed the local church as a successor of the Apostles. He was aided by a college of presbyters or priests, together with a group of deacons who distributed the alms of the Church.

A beautiful witness of this visible structure of the Church is given by one of the greatest of the Apostolic Fathers, St. Ignatius Martyr of Antioch. As a direct disciple of St. John the Apostle, and bishop of Antioch after St. Peter, St. Ignatius is a crucial link in showing us the continuity between the Apostles and the post-apostolic age.

St. Ignatius was condemned to be eaten by the wild beasts in the Coliseum in Rome by the Emperor Trajan around the year 107 AD. On his way to Rome to be martyred he wrote a remarkable series of letters to other churches, in which he stresses again and again the theme of the unity of the Church, with one bishop in each diocese presiding over a college of presbyters and deacons dedicated to the works of charity. This is very valuable evidence that by the year 107 AD the hierarchical structure of the Church had exactly the same basic visible form that we know today (although in miniature). In the Letter to the Smyrnaeans, he writes:

> Flee from divisions as the beginning of evils. You must all follow the bishop as Jesus Christ followed the Father, and follow the council of presbyters as you would the apostles; respect the deacons as the commandment of God. Let no one do anything that has to do with the church without the bishop. Only that Eucharist which is under the authority of the bishop (or whomever he himself designates) is to be considered valid. Wherever the bishop appears, there let the congregation be; just as wherever Jesus Christ is, there is the catholic church. It is not permissible either to baptize or to hold a love feast without the bishop. But whatever he approves is also pleasing to God, in order that everything you do may be trustworthy and valid. . . . The one who honors the bishop has been honored by God; the one who does anything without the bishop's knowledge serves the devil.[13]

By the way, this is the first recorded use of the expression "Catholic Church" to denote the true Church of Christ, which is universal,[14] as foretold by the prophets and by Jesus Himself. The Catholic Church is present through communion with the bishops, the successors of the Apostles, who are in communion with one another and with the successor of Peter.

In the Letter to the Ephesians St. Ignatius exhorts the faithful:

---

[13] St. Ignatius, Letter to the Smyrnaeans 8–9, trans. Michael Holmes, *The Apostolic Fathers: Greek Texts and English Translations*, 3rd ed. (Grand Rapids, MI: Baker Academic, 2007), 255–57.

[14] "Catholic" means universal. Here it signifies the Church throughout the world.

Run together in harmony with the mind of God. For Jesus Christ, our inseparable life, is the mind of the Father, just as the bishops appointed throughout the world are in the mind of Christ.

Thus it is proper for you to run together in harmony with the mind of the bishop, as you are in fact doing. For your council of presbyters, which is worthy of its name and worthy of God, is attuned to the bishop as strings to a lyre. Therefore in your unanimity and harmonious love Jesus Christ is sung. . . . Let no one be misled: if anyone is not within the sanctuary, he lacks the bread of God. For if the prayer of one or two has such power, how much more that of the bishop together with the whole church! Therefore whoever does not meet with the congregation thereby demonstrates his arrogance and has separated himself. . . . Let us, therefore, be careful not to oppose the bishop, in order that we may be obedient to God.[15]

A similar exhortation is given in the Letter to the Magnesians:

Therefore as the Lord did nothing without the Father . . . (for he was united with him), so you must not do anything without the bishop and the presbyters. Do not attempt to convince yourselves that anything done apart from the others is right, but, gathering together, let there be one prayer, one petition, one mind, one hope, with love and blameless joy.[16]

Likewise in the Letter to the Trallians:

For when you are subject to the bishop as to Jesus Christ, it is evident to me that you are living not in accordance with human standards but in accordance with Jesus Christ, who died for us in order that by believing in his death you might escape death. It is essential, therefore, that you continue your current practice and do nothing without the bishop, but be subject also to the council of presbyters as to the apostles of Jesus Christ, our hope, in whom we shall be found, if we so live. Furthermore, it is necessary that those who are deacons of the mysteries of Jesus Christ please everyone in every respect. For they are not merely deacons of food and drink but ministers of God's church. . . . The one who is within the sanctuary is clean, but the one who is outside the sanctuary is not clean. That is, whoever does anything without the bishop and

---

[15] St. Ignatius, Letter to the Ephesians 3–5, *The Apostolic Fathers*, 185–87.
[16] St. Ignatius, Letter to the Magnesians 7, *The Apostolic Fathers*, 207.

council of presbyters and deacons does not have a clean conscience.[17]

The idea that the Church is essentially invisible and non-institutional, without juridical and hierarchical bonds, stands in *complete opposition to the picture of the Church that we find already in the first century*, as established by Christ, just as it is contrary to the reality of ancient Israel. To act against the legitimate hierarchical authority in the Church goes against the Catholic conscience, today as in the time of St. Ignatius of Antioch. The institutional dimension of the Church, however, was not instituted for its own sake, but to be the servant of the communion in faith, hope, and charity, which is the life of the Kingdom of God.

---

[17] St. Ignatius, Letter to the Trallians 2 and 7, *The Apostolic Fathers*, 215–19.

CHAPTER 2

Prophecies of the Messianic Kingdom

What picture do the Messianic prophecies paint of the future Church?[1] One of the main themes of these prophecies concerns the Kingdom that will be established by the Messiah. In many of these prophecies, the figure of the Messiah is portrayed as a King who will reign over a universal Kingdom that will have no end, and in which all nations shall be blessed.

All Nations Will Be Blessed in Abraham's Seed

The first implicit prophecy of the Messianic kingdom was given by God to Abraham at the very moment when He called him out of Ur in Mesopotamia and gave him the promise that he would be the founder of a great nation, as numerous as the sands of the sea and the stars of the sky. This promise first concerned the kingdom of Israel. However, the calling of Abraham concluded with the promise of a universal blessing: all nations would be blessed in Abraham's seed:

> And the Lord said to Abram: "Go forth out of thy country, and from thy kindred, and out of thy father's house, and come into the land which I will show thee. And I will make of thee a great nation, and I will bless thee, and magnify thy name, and thou shalt be blessed. I will bless them that bless thee, and curse them that curse thee, and *in thee shall all the kindred of the earth be blessed.*"[2]

Clearly the promise that a great nation would come from Abraham refers to the kingdom of Israel. The promise, however, that all the nations of the earth would be blessed in Abraham, refers to the Messiah that would come from Abraham's descendants, and the Messianic Kingdom He would establish which would come to include all nations.

---

[1] Much of the material in this chapter is drawn from an earlier lecture published in the first volume in this series, *The Mystery of Israel and the Church: Figure and Fulfillment*, chapter 4; it is included again here on account of its importance for the theme of the Church.

[2] Gen 12:1–3, Douay Rheims version.

19

It follows that the promise made to Abraham on his calling was a twofold promise, referring both to Israel and the Church. The promise concerning the nation that was to spring from his loins—Israel—was clearer and more direct, for its realization was soon to begin. However, the promise that he would be the father of a great nation was in itself ordered to the universal blessing to be given to all peoples through Abraham's seed. That is, the promise concerning Israel was in itself ordered to a larger and more universal promise, which we today understand is the Church of the Messiah.

This twofold promise that Abraham would be the forefather of a great nation and a universal blessing is then repeated in Genesis 18:18 and 22:18, and announced to Isaac and Jacob in Genesis 26:4 and 28:14.

This prophecy, repeated five times, is very significant. At the very dawn of Israel's existence, Israel is implicitly associated with a universal blessing, which we understand to be the universal Church. A synonym for the universal Church is the *Catholic* Church, for "catholic" in Greek means universal.

The Blessing of Jacob in Genesis 49

The next Messianic prophecy that also touches on the Church is the blessing of Jacob on his children before he dies in Genesis 49:8–11. When he blesses his fourth son Judah, Jacob says:

> Judah, your brothers shall praise you; your hand shall be on the neck of your enemies; your father's sons shall bow down before you. Judah is a lion's whelp. . . . The scepter shall not depart from Judah, nor the ruler's staff from between his feet, until he comes to whom it belongs; and to him shall be the obedience of the peoples. . . . He washes his garments in wine and his vesture in the blood of grapes.

According to this prophecy, the kingship in Israel shall be in the tribe of Judah, as shall the Messiah, who is presented as the one to whom the scepter and judgment rightly belong. The Messiah will therefore be the true King of Israel. His Kingdom, however, will not be limited to the twelve tribes, but be truly universal or *catholic*, for "to him shall be the obedience of peoples." The Messiah will thus be a king over a universal kingdom including the peoples of the earth.

The Blessing of Balaam: the Star of Jacob

The universal Kingdom of the Messiah is also alluded to in the next Messianic prophecy given in Numbers 24:17–19. In this curious prophecy, Balaam, a pagan soothsayer, is commanded by his king to curse Israel, but God makes him bless Israel instead. However, the blessing and prophecy is not confined to Israel, but also extends to the Messiah and His future universal Kingdom.

Balaam first foretells the greatness of Israel and its conquest of Canaan. He says: "How beautiful are thy tabernacles, O Jacob, and thy tents, O Israel!" However, he then passes on to a Messianic prophecy, which, as he specifies, concerns a much more distant future:

> I shall see him, but not now: I shall behold him, but not near. A star shall rise out of Jacob and a scepter shall spring up from Israel, and shall strike the chiefs of Moab, and shall waste all the children of Seth. . . . Out of Jacob shall he come that shall rule, and shall destroy the remains of the city.[3]

The scepter that shall spring up from Israel will have dominion not only over the chiefs of Moab, but also over "all the children of Seth." Who are the children of Seth? Seth is the third son of Adam and Eve mentioned in Scripture. It was in the line of Seth that the true religion was passed on from Adam and Eve, and Seth is perhaps used as a figure of the just of all ages.[4] Noah was of the line of Seth according to Genesis 5. Therefore, since the Flood eliminated the population of the earth except for the family of Noah, all peoples on the earth today are the children of Seth. The Messiah, therefore, is to conquer and exercise dominion not over one country, such as Canaan, but over all nations. Obviously, the type of conquest that is truly intended is spiritual: the conversion of the sons of Seth to the worship of the true God.

The Messianic Kingdom in the Book of Isaiah

The Messianic prophecies of Isaiah are extraordinarily rich. Isaiah gives us a picture of the Messiah in His birth, ministry, Passion, and in His Kingdom. The universal dimension of the Messianic kingdom is portrayed in Isaiah 2:2–4:

> It shall come to pass in the latter days that the mountain of the house of the Lord shall be established as the highest of the mountains, and shall be raised above the hills; and *all the nations shall flow to it*, and *many peoples shall come*, and say: "Come, let us go up to the mountain of the Lord, to the house of the God of Jacob;

---

[3] Num 24:17–19. Douay-Rheims translation.

[4] See Gen 4:25–26: "And Adam knew his wife again, and she bore a son and called his name Seth, for she said, 'God has appointed for me another child instead of Abel, for Cain slew him.' To Seth also a son was born, and he called his name Enosh. At that time men began to call upon the name of the Lord." Genesis speaks of the separate lineages of Cain and of Seth in Gen 4–5.

that he may teach us his ways and that we may walk in his paths."
For out of Zion shall go forth the law, and the word of the Lord
from Jerusalem. He shall judge between the nations, and shall
decide for many peoples; and they shall beat their swords into
plowshares, and their spears into pruning hooks.

This prophecy does not directly mention the Messiah, but rather
describes what He will achieve. In the "latter days," which refers to the
Messianic age, the glory of the "house of the Lord" will be established
on the highest of mountains, which means above all other things in the
sight of all nations, who shall flow to the house of the Lord, "that he
may teach us his ways" (Is 2:3). The law of God shall go out from Mt.
Zion in Jerusalem and shall become the law of the nations, teaching
peace.[5] This is fulfilled in the Church founded by Christ, into which the
nations have flowed in the course of the past twenty centuries. In this
way the nations worship the God of Jacob and revere the Ten
Commandments revealed on Mt. Sinai.

Isaiah 49:5–12 speaks of the Messiah as the light to the nations,
given so that the salvation of God "may reach the end of the earth,"
which is accomplished through the Church:

> And now the Lord says, who formed me from the womb to be his
> servant, to bring Jacob back to him, and that Israel might be
> gathered to him . . . : "It is too light a thing that you should be my
> servant to raise up the tribes of Jacob and to restore the preserved
> of Israel; I will give you as a *light to the nations*, that my salvation
> may reach to the end of the earth." Thus says the Lord, the
> Redeemer of Israel and his Holy One, to one deeply despised,
> abhorred by the nations . . . : "Kings shall see and arise; princes,
> and they shall prostrate themselves. . . . And I will make all my
> mountains a way, and my highways shall be raised up. Lo, these
> shall come from afar, and lo, these from the north and from the
> west, and these from the land of Syene."

The mission of the Messiah is certainly ordered to the restoration,
conversion, and fulfillment of the People of Israel, for the Messiah was
sent "to bring Jacob back to Him," which implies conversion of the
heart to God. However, God says that this would be too little. The
supernatural communion of Israel is to be enlarged so as to reach the

---

[5] On the basis of Is 2:2–4 and similar texts, the rabbinical tradition recognizes
that in the Messianic Age the entire world will unite to learn Torah and convert to
the doctrine of Judaism. See Shlomo Riskin, "Conversion in Jewish Law," in *The
Conversion Crisis* (Rabbinical Council of America, 1990), 70.

ends of the earth. The Messiah will first be the light of Israel, and then become the light of all nations, bringing salvation to them.

Another beautiful Messianic text, Isaiah 60:1–11, further develops the reference in Isaiah 49 to the Messiah as the light to the Gentiles:

> Arise, shine, for your light has come, and the glory of the Lord has risen upon you. For behold, darkness shall cover the earth, and thick darkness the peoples; but the Lord will arise upon you, and his glory will be seen upon you. And nations shall come to your light, and kings to the brightness of your rising. Lift up your eyes all around, and see; they all gather together, they come to you; your sons shall come from afar; . . . the wealth of the nations shall come to you. A multitude of camels shall cover you; . . . all those from Sheba shall come. They shall bring gold and frankincense, and shall bring good news, the praises of the Lord. . . . For the islands shall wait for me, the ships of Tarshish first, to bring your sons from far, their silver and gold with them, for the name of the Lord your God. . . . Foreigners shall build up your walls, and their kings shall minister to you. . . . Your gates shall be open continually; day and night they shall not be shut; that men may bring to you the wealth of the nations, with their kings led in procession.

At the coming of the Messiah, the nations will be in great darkness, but the glory of the Lord will arise on Zion (in the person of the Messiah), and the nations will come to the light of the revelation made to Israel. They shall come into the Church, which is the fullness of Israel, and shall bring their wealth with them. This refers not just to gold, but especially to their cultural patrimony, which shall enrich the universal Church, and give glory to God. The gates of the Church will be continually open through the centuries to receive the peoples into her bosom through her missionary activity.

Prophecies concerning a New Covenant in Jeremiah and Ezekiel

In Jeremiah and Ezekiel we are told that the Messiah will inaugurate a new Law and a new covenant, written not on tablets of stone, but in the hearts of men. This prophecy concerns the gift of sanctifying grace and the gifts of the Holy Spirit in Baptism and Confirmation, by which the law of God is written in our hearts through the ministry of the Church.

This prophecy of a new covenant is given in Jeremiah 31:31–34:

> Behold, the days are coming, says the Lord, when I will make a *new covenant* with the house of Israel and the house of Judah, not like the covenant which I made with their fathers when I took them by

the hand to bring them out of the land of Egypt, my covenant which they broke, though I was their husband, says the Lord. But this is the covenant which I will make with the house of Israel after those days, says the Lord: I will put my law within them, and I will write it upon their hearts; and I will be their God, and they shall be my people. And no longer shall each man teach his neighbor and each his brother, saying, "Know the Lord," for they shall all know me, from the least of them to the greatest, says the Lord; for I will forgive their iniquity, and I will remember their sin no more.

The New Covenant is compared to the covenant established with Israel on Mt. Sinai, and is promised to be superior. The Old Covenant was written upon tablets of stone, by which the Law was given. The New Covenant is said here to consist in the forgiveness of sins and the writing of God's law on our hearts, which occurs through the gift of grace and charity by means of the sacraments. Just as the Old Covenant established Israel as the People of God, so it follows that the New Covenant spoken of by Jeremiah must imply the new establishment of the People of God, which is the Catholic Church.

By speaking of a "new covenant," this prophecy is of extreme importance, so much so that the Letter to the Hebrews quotes it twice, in 8:8–12, and 10:16–17. The expression, "new covenant," was taken up by Jesus on Holy Thursday in the solemn moment of the institution of the Eucharist, in which He says over the chalice: "This cup which is poured out for you is the new covenant in my Blood."[6]

A similar prophecy is given in Ezekiel 36:24–27. Although the expression "new covenant" is not used, the content of the promise coincides:

> For I will take you from among the Gentiles, and will gather you together out of all the countries, and will bring you into your own land. And I will pour upon you clean water, and you shall be cleansed from all your filthiness, and I will cleanse you from all your idols. And I will give you a new heart, and put a new spirit within you, and I will take away the stony heart out of your flesh, and will give you a heart of flesh. And I will put my spirit in the midst of you, and I will cause you to walk in my commandments, and to keep my judgments, and do them.

This text refers to the interior cleansing worked by the sacrament of Baptism. The members of the new Israel, taken also from among the Gentiles and from all countries, are incorporated into the People of God by means of the water of Baptism, by which we are cleansed from the

---

[6] Lk 22:20. See also 1 Cor 11:25: "This cup is the new covenant in my blood."

stain of original sin and all personal sins. Baptism confers the inestimable gift of sanctifying grace and infused charity, which enable us to follow the Law of God consistently, as long as we cooperate with that grace. The reference to being brought back "into your own land" should be understood to signify incorporation into the People of God, which is the Body of Christ, spoken of by St. Paul as the "Jerusalem which is above . . . , which is our mother" (Gal 4:26).

Outpouring of the Holy Spirit

In Joel 2:28–32 there is a prophecy of the outpouring of the Holy Spirit on all humanity in the Messianic Age:

> And it shall come to pass afterward, that I will pour out my spirit on all flesh; your sons and your daughters shall prophesy, your old men shall dream dreams, and your young men shall see visions. Even upon the menservants and maidservants in those days, I will pour out my spirit. And it shall come to pass that all who call upon the name of the Lord shall be delivered.

The prophecy shows that the Messianic period will be marked by an outpouring of the Holy Spirit that is superabundant and universal in scope. This outpouring of the Holy Spirit—the source of all holiness—will not be limited to the learned, for it will fall upon the simple: menservants and maidservants. Nor will it be limited to Israel, but will extend to "all flesh," "all who call upon the name of the Lord."

In conformity with the prophetic text, the rabbinic tradition affirms that the Holy Spirit will be "poured out equally upon Jews and pagans, men and women, freemen and slaves."[7]

On the first Christian Pentecost in Acts 2, St. Peter quoted this text and proclaimed that it was realized in the Church, beginning on that day. This shows that one of the key marks of the Church must be holiness—the work of the Holy Spirit—manifested among men and women of all social classes and cultural backgrounds.

The Messianic Kingdom in Nebuchadnezzar's Dream

Two of the most important prophecies of the universal Messianic Kingdom are given in dreams in the book of Daniel.

Daniel 2:32–45 recounts the prophetic dream of King Nebuchadnezzar of Babylon, in which a colossal statue made of gold, silver, bronze, and iron was destroyed by a stone not cut by human

---

[7] "Holy Spirit," in *Jewish Encyclopedia*, vol. 6 (New York: Ktav Publ. House, 1964), 449, citing the midrash *Tanna debe Eliyahu*.

hands that then grew into a mountain. The king commanded his native Chaldean sages to interpret the dream, and in order to test the truth of the interpretation, he insisted that they tell him the dream itself first—which he had not revealed to them—and then its interpretation. Needless to say, they were all unable to do this and were put to death. The king then condemned to death every other man in Babylon reputed to be a sage, such as Daniel. Both the dream and its interpretation, however, were revealed by God to Daniel.

He tells the king that the colossal statue made of four different metals corresponded to four world empires which would succeed one another. Nebuchadnezzar himself, king of the Babylonian empire, is the head of gold. Babylon would be followed by three other world empires, of which the last would be "strong as iron, because iron breaks to pieces and shatters all things; and like iron which crushes, it shall break and crush all these" (Dan 2:40). Nevertheless, the last world empire would have an internal weakness represented by feet and toes partly of iron and partly of clay. Intermarriage would not sufficiently bond the peoples of this empire.

Daniel does not identify these empires, but the identification is fairly clear. The second empire is that of the Persians, who, under Cyrus, conquered Babylon in 539 BC. It was Cyrus who allowed the exiled Jews to return from Babylon to Jerusalem and begin the rebuilding of the Temple. The third empire is that of the Greeks established by Alexander the Great in 330 BC. The fourth empire, strong as iron, is that of Rome, which had the longest life of the world empires and the most stable dominion.[8]

Finally, Daniel relates that during the time of the fourth world empire, another kingdom would arise that would take the place of the earlier empires and fill the entire earth, being still more universal than its predecessors:

> As you looked, a stone was cut out by no human hand, and it smote the image on its feet of iron and clay, and broke them in pieces; then the iron, the clay, the bronze, the silver, and the gold,

---

[8] St. Jerome, in his commentary on Daniel 2, gives this interpretation of the four empires. See *Jerome's Commentary on Daniel*, trans. Gleason L. Archer, Jr. (Grand Rapids, MI: Baker Book House, 1958), 31–32. With regard to the fourth empire, he writes: "Now the fourth empire, which clearly refers to the Romans, is the iron empire which breaks in pieces and overcomes all others. But its feet and toes are partly of iron and partly of earthenware, a fact most clearly demonstrated at the present time. For just as there was at the first nothing stronger or hardier than the Roman realm, so also in these last days there is nothing more feeble, since we require the assistance of barbarian tribes both in our civil wars and against foreign nations."

all together were broken in pieces, and became like the chaff of the summer threshing floors; and the wind carried them away, so that not a trace of them could be found. But the stone that struck the image became a great mountain and filled the whole earth.[9]

The fact that this fifth kingdom grows out of a stone not cut by human hands signifies that its founder is God Himself. In his interpretation of the dream, Daniel says that this fifth kingdom will not be temporal, like the other kingdoms, but will remain and grow without end:

And in the days of those kings the God of heaven will set up a kingdom which shall never be destroyed, nor shall its sovereignty be left to another people. It shall break in pieces all these kingdoms and bring them to an end, and it shall stand for ever; just as you saw that a stone was cut from a mountain by no human hand, and that it broke in pieces the iron, the bronze, the clay, the silver, and the gold.[10]

In hindsight, we can see that this rock is the Messiah, and the mountain that grew out from it and has filled the whole earth is the Catholic Church. St. Jerome writes:

However, at the final period of all these empires of gold and silver and bronze and iron, a rock (namely, the Lord and Savior) was cut off without hands, that is, without copulation or human seed and by birth from a virgin's womb; and after all the empires had been crushed, He became a great mountain and filled the whole earth.[11]

The Church realizes the prophecy of Daniel in four ways. Unlike the temporal kingdoms that preceded it, the Church is of supernatural origin, founded by God made man on the rock of Peter and the other Apostles. Second, it is truly universal in scope. Although the Babylonian, Persian, Greek, and Roman empires were relatively universal, the Catholic Church is truly universal, existing in every continent and culture.

Third, the universality of the Church is something that is developing in time, as the stone not cut by human hands gradually grew into a mountain filling the earth. The 2,000-year history of the Church is a history of gradual growth, in which losses sustained in one region are compensated for by the conversion of new cultures and nations. For

---

[9] Dan 2:34–35.
[10] Dan 2:44–45.
[11] *Jerome's Commentary on Daniel*, 32.

example, while much of northern Europe was lost by the Catholic Church in the sixteenth century, the Gospel was brought to the Americas, Africa, and the Orient.

Finally, as the supernatural kingdom in Nebuchadnezzar's dream was given a sovereignty that would never be destroyed, the Church has now withstood the ravages of time for twenty centuries, as she has watched nations rise and fall around her. Her adversaries have often deemed her doomed to extinction, but she has risen from each crisis stronger than before.

The Messianic Kingdom in Daniel's Dream

Another great prophecy regarding the Church is given in chapter 7 of Daniel. This also concerns a dream—this time dreamt by Daniel himself. He dreams about four great beasts who successively appear: a lion, a bear, a leopard, and a fourth beast with no name—"terrible and wonderful, and exceeding strong, and it had great iron teeth. . . . And it had ten horns" (Dan 7:7). These four beasts apparently correspond to the four empires in the dream of Nebuchadnezzar.[12]

After this vision, the scene changes, and Daniel sees the heavenly court of the eternal God—the Ancient of Days—to whom myriads of angels minister. Before Him comes "one like the son of man":

> I saw in the night visions, and behold, with the clouds of heaven there came one like a son of man, and he came to the Ancient of Days and was presented before him. And to him was given dominion and glory and kingdom, that all peoples, nations, and languages should serve him; his dominion is an everlasting dominion, which shall not pass away, and his kingdom one that shall not be destroyed.[13]

Who is this "son of man"? We know that Christ made a direct reference to this text when He was questioned by Caiaphas before the Sanhedrin on the eve of His Passion. Caiaphas asked Him, in the name of the living God, if He was the Christ (Messiah), the Son of God. He responded affirmatively: "You say that I am."[14] He then adds: "'But I tell you, hereafter you will see the Son of man seated at the right hand of Power, and coming on the clouds of heaven.' Then the High Priest rent

---

[12] See *Jerome's Commentary on Daniel*, 72–76.

[13] Dan 7:13–14.

[14] This is an idiomatic way in Aramaic of affirming the truth of the question, corresponding to our "it is as you say," as we see many times in the Gospels. Mark (14:62) translates the idiom for his Gentile audience, telling us that Jesus says: "I am."

his garments, and said, 'He has uttered blasphemy'" (Mt 26:63–65). Christ was referring to His second coming at the end of history, in which He shall appear glorious in the clouds of Heaven.

This affirmation of Christ brought on His Passion. However, it is one thing for Christ to say that the text of Daniel applies to Him. It is another thing to realize the further prophecy contained in the text of Daniel: "All peoples, nations, and languages should serve him; his dominion is an everlasting dominion, which shall not pass away, and his kingdom one that shall not be destroyed." We today see that this prophecy is fulfilled, and that this fulfillment has been going on for many centuries. Indeed, the Church has members in every tribe, and every tongue serves Christ in the liturgy as He gives glory to God the Father in the Mass, which makes the sacrifice of Calvary present in every altar on which it is celebrated, in every corner of the world.

It is true that the Kingdom of the Messiah has two principal stages: the Church militant on earth and the Church triumphant.[15] On both levels, all nations and tongues serve Christ, to the glory of God the Father. However, on earth that service is incomplete and mixed with constant rebellion and infidelity. We have to wait for the second coming of the Messiah for the complete manifestation of His triumph, in which there shall no longer be any infidelity, but only the pure glorification of God by all His elect.

Psalm 72

The prophecy of Christ as an eternal ruler of a universal Kingdom is confirmed also in Psalm 72:5–17:

> And he shall continue with the sun. . . . In his days shall justice spring up, and abundance of peace, till the moon be taken away. And he shall rule from sea to sea, and from the river unto the ends of the earth. Before him the Ethiopians shall fall down, and his enemies shall lick the ground. The kings of Tharsis and the islands shall offer presents; the kings of the Arabians and of Saba shall bring gifts. And all kings of the earth shall adore him; all nations shall serve him. . . . And in him shall all the tribes of the earth be blessed; all nations shall magnify him.[16]

The Messiah is here foretold to have dominion over a kingdom that shall stretch from sea to sea, that will last as long as the sun and moon endure. The kings of the remotest nations shall give tribute and serve

---

[15] The souls expiating their sins in purgatory are also members of the Church: the Church suffering.

[16] Douay Rheims translation (numbered as Ps 71).

Him. In other words, all the cultural riches of the globe shall be given in tribute to build up the Messianic Kingdom that shall be universal in time and space. We see this prophecy fulfilled today in the Catholic Church.

Psalms 2 and 110

Another Messianic psalm that concerns the Kingdom is Psalm 2. The psalm begins with the rebellion of the nations who rage against God and His Messiah. God laughs at their insurrection and responds by establishing the Messianic King as His own Son, to whom He has given the nations as his inheritance:

> Then he will speak to them . . . saying, "I have set my king on Zion, my holy hill." I will tell of the decree of the Lord: He said to me, "You are my son, today I have begotten you. *Ask of me, and I will make the nations your heritage, and the ends of the earth your possession.* You shall break them with a rod of iron, and dash them in pieces like a potter's vessel."[17]

The Messiah will thus be the Son of God, universal King by right, and He who vindicates the glory of God from the rebellion of mankind, and overcomes the glory of the temporal kingdoms, as in Daniel 2. Nevertheless, the psalm shows us that the Messianic Kingdom will involve continual combat with those among all nations who do not wish to take on the easy yoke of the Lord and His Messiah.

A similar image is given in Psalm 110:1–2:

> The Lord says to my lord: "Sit at my right hand, till I make your enemies your footstool." The Lord sends forth from Zion your mighty scepter. Rule in the midst of your foes!

This psalm, quoted by Jesus in Matthew 22:43–45, goes on to speak of the Messianic King also as "a priest forever after the order of Melchizedek" (Ps 110:4). The Messianic Kingdom, therefore, will be not only universal but also a priestly people like Israel,[18] endowed with an eternal priesthood.

The Church of the Gentiles in Malachi 1:11

A brief but very significant prophecy concerning the Church is given in Malachi 1:11. According to this text, the Messianic age will be marked by the fact that a fitting sacrifice is offered to God throughout the world, among the Gentiles: "For from the rising of the sun to its setting

---

[17] Ps 2:5–9.
[18] See Ex 19:6.

my name is great among the nations, and in every place incense is offered to my name, and a pure offering; for my name is great among the nations, says the Lord of hosts."

This prophecy is realized in the sacrifice of the Mass, by which the pure offering of Christ's sacrifice on Calvary is offered up every day in every Catholic church in the world, from the rising of the sun to its setting. This is no exaggeration.

A related prophecy is given in Zephaniah 3:9–10:

Yea, at that time I will change the speech of the peoples to a pure speech, that all of them may call on the name of the Lord and serve him with one accord. From beyond the rivers of Ethiopia my suppliants, the daughters of my dispersed ones, shall bring my offering.

In the Messianic Kingdom, all nations will call on the Lord with a pure speech, with one accord, and with an acceptable offering offered far beyond the physical borders of Israel. The Messiah will establish a unity of accord—a communion—among the children of God dispersed among the nations.

Prophecies in the New Testament

The prophecies of the Messianic Kingdom culminate in the New Testament, in the revelation made to Mary, Joseph, Simeon, and John the Baptist.

In the Annunciation to Mary, the angel Gabriel announces that "the Lord God will give to him the throne of his father David, and he will reign over the house of Jacob for ever; and of his kingdom there will be no end" (Lk 1:32–33). This prophecy is a clear echo of the prophecies of the Messianic Kingdom that we have seen in the Old Testament, such as Daniel 2:44 and Psalm 72:5.

In the Presentation in the Temple, Simeon calls Christ "a light for revelation to the Gentiles, and for glory to thy people Israel" (Lk 2:32). He thus identifies Jesus as the servant of the Lord spoken of in Isaiah 49:6, who is given two missions: to raise up Israel and to be a light to the Gentiles, extending Israel's salvation to the ends of the earth by establishing a universal Messianic Kingdom.

Above all, however, it is John the Baptist who performs the sublime role of pointing out Jesus as the Messiah who comes to inaugurate the Messianic Kingdom. He begins by proclaiming himself as the precursor of the one who will baptize with the Holy Spirit:

I baptize you with water for repentance, but he who is coming after me is mightier than I, whose sandals I am not worthy to carry; he will baptize you with the Holy Spirit and with fire. His winnowing fork is in his hand, and he will clear his threshing floor and gather his wheat into the granary, but the chaff he will burn with unquenchable fire.[19]

The reference to Baptism with the Holy Spirit alludes to the prophecy of Ezekiel 36:24–27 about Baptism, as well as the outpouring of the Spirit foretold in Joel 2:28–29. The Baptism with the Holy Spirit means that Jesus will establish a sacramental means of communicating the life of God through a washing with water.

John the Baptist also speaks of Jesus as the *Judge* who will gather the wheat into the granary and judge all men as wheat is separated from chaff. The gathering of the wheat into the granary refers to the definitive constitution of the Messianic Kingdom in the Church triumphant. By referring to Jesus as the Judge of the Last Judgment, John has implicitly identified Him with God, to whom alone it belongs to judge all men.

A third aspect of John the Baptist's prophecy is the identification of Jesus as the one who will make atonement for Israel as the true paschal *Lamb*. When John sees Jesus coming to be baptized, he proclaims him as "the Lamb of God, who takes away the sin of the world!" (Jn 1:29). This phrase identifies Jesus with the Servant of the Lord spoken of in Isaiah 53 who establishes the Kingdom through bearing our sins and atoning for them.

Finally, John the Baptist proclaims that Christ is the *Bridegroom* of Israel, whereas John himself is merely the "friend of the Bridegroom," who rejoices to hear His voice:

> You yourselves bear me witness, that I said, I am not the Christ, but I have been sent before him. He who has the bride is the bridegroom; the friend of the bridegroom, who stands and hears him, rejoices greatly at the bridegroom's voice; therefore this joy of mine is now full. He must increase, but I must decrease.[20]

The reference to the bride and the Bridegroom has a clear ecclesiological significance in the Biblical context, for God frequently presents His relationship with Israel as that of Bridegroom to bride.[21] Israel is the bride that God has espoused by entering into a covenant with her and establishing her as His people. By identifying Christ as the Bridegroom, John the Baptist has implicitly identified Christ as God,

---

[19] Mt 3:11–12. See the parallel texts: Mk 1:7–8, Lk 3:16–17, Jn 1:26–27. The prophecy recalls Mal 3:3, in which the Messiah is spoken of as coming to purge the sons of Levi.

[20] Jn 3:28–30.

[21] See Ezek 16; Hos 2.

who comes to restore and consummate His spousal relationship with the People of God through a new and eternal covenant.

Value of the Prophecies of the Messianic Kingdom

These prophecies concerning the formation of the Church from all the nations are a tremendous motive of credibility whose realization still stands before our eyes today. In this case no one can say that the realization of the prophecy perhaps did not really occur, as in the case of the division of the vestments of Christ (Ps 22:18) or other prophecies of the Old Testament. Here we ourselves are witnesses of the realization of the prophecies. For this reason, the formation, miraculous expansion, and continuity of the Catholic Church in history is a great sign of its being truly founded by the Messiah, and thus by God.

Perhaps this is the most impressive aspect of the prophecies. Who could have imagined, in the centuries before Christ, that the pagan nations would come to believe in one God, the God of Israel, and become incorporated into one *spiritual kingdom*—the New Israel—and share the faith of Israel in the Jewish Messiah? Who could have imagined that this spiritual kingdom formed from among the Gentile nations would last until the end of time and be universal in scope? This is a prophecy of enormous magnitude.

Rabbinical Interpretation of the Messianic Kingdom

How does the rabbinical tradition tend to view the prophecies of the Messianic Kingdom? The Messianic Kingdom is generally seen to be a glorious age in which the Messiah restores the temporal kingdom of David and Solomon, gathers the Jewish people in Israel, restores their religious fervor and study of the Torah, rebuilds the Temple and restores its worship, defeats the temporal power of the Gentiles, and establishes a period of world peace under the hegemony of Israel.

The great medieval scholar Moses Maimonides gave an authoritative and sober description of the Messianic Kingdom:

> King Messiah will arise in the future and will restore the kingship of David to its ancient condition, to its rule as it was at first. And he will rebuild the Temple and gather the exiled of Israel. And in his days all the laws will return as they were in the past. They will offer up sacrifices, and will observe the Sabbatical years and the jubilee years with regard to all the commandments stated in the Torah. . . . And think not that the Messiah must perform signs and portents and bring about new things in the world. . . . And if there should arise from the House of David a king who studies the Torah and occupies himself with the commandments as his father

David had, according to the written and the oral Torah, and if he forces all Israel to follow the Torah and observe its rules; and if he fights the wars of the Lord—then he must be presumed to be the Messiah. And if he succeeds in his acts, and rebuilds the Temple in its place, and gathers the exiled of Israel—then he certainly is the Messiah. And he will repair the whole world to serve the Lord together. . . . It should not come to one's mind that in the days of the Messiah anything in the customary order of the world will be annulled, or that there will be something new in the order of creation. For the world will continue in its path. . . . The sages said that the only difference between this world and the days of the Messiah will be with regard to the enslavement to the kingdoms.[22]

As we can see from the New Testament, these expectations were common among the people at the time of Christ, and the Apostles themselves shared the expectations of a temporal restoration of Israel.

The problem with such an interpretation is that it falls far too short. The Messiah is not a great warrior or political genius, nor can His Kingdom be established by political and military means. He came to inaugurate a Kingdom that is *supernatural* in aim and truly universal in scope. The Messianic Kingdom is not simply a restoration of the kingdom of Solomon, but something immeasurably more universal and supernatural. It is a spiritual rather than a temporal and political society.

The Four Marks of the Church

These prophecies concerning the Messianic Kingdom that we have examined here give us a clear indication of what the Church of Christ should look like through the centuries. The prophecies show us crucial distinguishing marks to be manifested by the Church which defy all human expectation.

The first of these marks is that the Church of the Messiah will gather her members from all peoples and nations. She will thus be universal, or Catholic. All tongues and cultures will serve her and be incorporated in her.

Secondly, the prophecies show us that the Church will be *one* universal kingdom, like the Kingdom of David, and thus will have the mark of unity.

Third, this kingdom will have no end, and will grow continually until it becomes a mountain filling the whole earth. It will be universal in time as well as geography, and its sovereignty will not fail.

---

[22] *Yad haHazaqa*, also known as the *Mishne Torah* (the Second Torah), quoted in Raphael Patai, *The Messiah Texts: Jewish Legends of Three Thousand Years* (Detroit: Wayne State Univ. Press, 1979), 323–25.

Finally, the prophecies also show us that this kingdom will be endowed with holiness, with God's Law written on the heart of its children. It will have a power capable of transforming hearts of stone into hearts responsive to the will of God, and it will offer a pure offering to the Lord in all nations.[23]

Thus if we look out into the world today to see whether the prophecies concerning the Messianic Kingdom have been realized and whether there exists today among the competing religious denominations one that corresponds to the prophecies, we must look for a Church that is (a) Catholic or universal, (b) one, (c) holy, and (d) showing continuous growth and expansion through history, on the one foundation of the rock not cut by human hand. These characteristics coincide with the four marks of the Church that we proclaim in the Nicene Creed: one, holy, catholic, and apostolic.

---

[23] For a fuller exposition of the mark of holiness, see chapter 8 below.

CHAPTER 3

The Parables of the Kingdom of God

We have seen in the last chapter how the Kingdom has been prophesied by the prophets. Here we shall look at how Jesus proclaims the Messianic Kingdom in the Gospels, focusing on the following questions: What are the principal marks of the Kingdom that Jesus proclaimed? Does Jesus' idea of the Kingdom correspond to the Messianic prophecies of the Old Testament? Does that Kingdom correspond to a reality that we can see in human history? Does it correspond to the Catholic Church or to something else? Is it a new reality distinct from the Kingdom of Israel?

The Kingdom of God as Proclaimed by Jesus in the Gospels

The earliest mention of the Messianic Kingdom in the Gospels occurs in the Annunciation, in which the angel Gabriel announces to Mary that "the Lord God will give to him the throne of his father David, and he will reign over the house of Jacob forever; and of his kingdom there will be no end" (Lk 1:32–33). This is in perfect harmony with the prophets.

When Jesus undertakes His public ministry some thirty years later, He begins (as John the Baptist did before Him in Mt 3:2) by calling people to conversion and with the proclamation that the Kingdom of God is at hand (Mt 4:17). The fact that Jesus' preaching is summarized in this way shows that the Kingdom is at the very heart of Jesus' mission.

In the Gospel of Matthew, Jesus uses the expression "Kingdom of heaven," whereas in Mark and Luke, Jesus says "Kingdom of God." It seems that both of these expressions translate the same Aramaic (or Hebrew) expression actually spoken by Jesus (*malkut shmaya*). Matthew, who seems to have been writing principally for Jewish Christians in Israel, gives a more literal version of the original phrase. Jews of that time and earlier avoided using the name of God (*Elohim*) as Orthodox Jews still do today (writing G-d), and substituted other words, such as Heaven, or Most High, etc. Mark and Luke rightly translated the meaning of the phrase as "Kingdom of God." As we shall see, it seems that the expression (in either form) refers to the Church, in her dual dimension of earthly and heavenly kingdom.[1]

The parables of the Kingdom show us that the Kingdom has two dimensions: within human history and beyond human history. Indeed, the Church has three levels or dimensions: the Church militant on earth, the Church suffering in purgatory, and the Church triumphant in heaven. Most of the parables of the Kingdom refer first to its earthly dimension and then to its heavenly consummation. (The Church in purgatory is not directly mentioned in the parables of the Kingdom.)

Many people (ordinary Christians and scholars) mistakenly think of the "Kingdom of heaven" as referring to a completely eschatological reality—a kingdom literally in heaven to be set up only after the Second Coming. Other scholars recognize that the Kingdom of heaven/Kingdom of God must have a historical and earthly dimension, but they dissociate it from the Church, as if the Kingdom had no ecclesiastical and institutional dimension. The Modernist theologian Alfred Loisy summed up this view by saying: "Jesus came preaching the Kingdom, and what arrived was the Church,"[2] as if the Kingdom and the Church were two very different realities. As we shall see, this view also cannot be reconciled with Jesus' teaching.

The Second Vatican Council (*Lumen gentium* 5) speaks of the relation of the Church and the Kingdom as follows:

> The Church, equipped with the gifts of its Founder, . . . receives the mission to proclaim and to spread among all peoples the Kingdom of Christ and of God and to be, on earth, the initial budding forth of that kingdom. While it slowly grows, the Church strains toward the completed Kingdom and, with all its strength, hopes and desires to be united in glory with its King.[3]

---

[1] There has been a great deal of discussion about the identification of the Kingdom with the Church. *Lumen gentium* (the Dogmatic Constitution on the Church of Vatican II) generally seems to use the term "Kingdom" as synonymous with the Church (militant or triumphant). However, the issue was taken up in the Declaration of the Congregation for the Doctrine of the Faith, *Dominus Jesus* (2000).

[2] Loisy, *L'Évangile et l'Église* (Paris: Picard, 1902), 155.

[3] See also the Declaration of the Congregation for the Doctrine of the Faith of 2000, *Dominus Jesus* 18: "On the one hand, the Church is 'a sacrament—that is, sign and instrument of intimate union with God and of unity of the entire human race.' She is therefore the sign and instrument of the kingdom; she is called to announce and to establish the kingdom. On the other hand, the Church is the 'people gathered by the unity of the Father, the Son and the Holy Spirit'; she is therefore 'the kingdom of Christ already present in mystery' and constitutes its *seed* and *beginning*. The kingdom of God, in fact, has an eschatological dimension: it is a

The Parables of the Kingdom

Matthew 13 and Mark 4 recount a series of parables about the Kingdom of heaven/Kingdom of God. The setting is magnificent. Jesus, pressed by the crowd on the shore of the Sea of Galilee, gets into a boat and begins to teach the crowd from there. The very setting shows the transcendence of Jesus and His message about the Kingdom.

Why does Christ teach in parables? The purpose of the parables, paradoxically, is twofold: to disclose and to hide. It discloses the mystery to those who are "inside" as Jesus says, and rightly disposed to understand. It conceals the meaning from those who are not privy to the interpretation given by the Master. When He began to preach in parables, the disciples asked Him why He preached in this way. Mark (4:11–12) gives His answer as follows:

> And he said to them, "To you has been given the secret of the kingdom of God, but for those outside everything is in parables; so that they may indeed see but not perceive, and may indeed hear but not understand; lest they should turn again, and be forgiven."

In other words, the parables are not meant to be self-explanatory, but require the aid of an interpretation that is not given to all, but only to the Apostles and disciples. They are "inside." Inside what? Inside the Kingdom/Church, because they have an intimate friendship with Jesus, the Founder and Life of the Kingdom, who reveals to them the mysteries that are hidden to those outside.

The Sower

The first parable of the Sower (Mt 13:19–23) is about conversion, by which one enters the Kingdom interiorly. As Jesus Himself explains, the Sower is he who preaches the "word of the Kingdom":

> When any one hears the word of the kingdom and does not understand it, the evil one comes and snatches away what is sown in his heart; this is what was sown along the path. As for what was sown on rocky ground, this is he who hears the word and immediately receives it with joy; yet he has no root in himself, but endures for a while, and when tribulation or persecution arises on account of the word, immediately he falls away. As for what was sown among thorns, this is he who hears the word, but the cares of the world and the delight in riches choke the word, and it proves

---

reality present in time, but its full realization will arrive only with the completion or fulfilment of history. . . . One may not separate the kingdom from the Church."

unfruitful. As for what was sown on good soil, this is he who hears the word and understands it; he indeed bears fruit, and yields, in one case a hundredfold, in another sixty, and in another thirty.

This parable shows that entrance into the Kingdom involves conversion and depends on the interior disposition of the heart. It is not a Kingdom determined by birth or ethnicity, but by a person's response to the proclamation of that Kingdom. The good soil refers to the disposition of the heart by which one cooperates with God's grace, with greater or lesser generosity.

In Matthew 18:3–4, Jesus specifies that the proper disposition to enter the Kingdom is humility. The Kingdom is not a club for those with influence, power, talent, or means, but for all who humble themselves before the grace of God.

The Kingdom in Its Growth in Human History Includes Sinners

Since Jesus shows that entrance into the Kingdom and its fruitfulness depends on conversion and cooperation with grace, one might get the impression that the Kingdom is limited to the just who are compared to good soil and yield a harvest of thirty-, sixty-, or a hundredfold. This view was that of Luther, Calvin, other Protestant leaders, and precursors such as Wycliffe, who held that the Church was the congregation of the predestined or true believers. They also held that sinful bishops and priests were not really members of the Church at all.

If this were the case, the Church would be an essentially invisible Kingdom, because one would not know who its authentic members were, nor its authentic ministers. The Church, in this view, would not be a visible institution that could be recognized in human history, but essentially a spiritual collection of righteous individuals present only in certain places at certain times. In such a view, it would not be important to enter the Church in any formal or institutional way at all. Such is the view of the Church according to the original principles of Protestantism, and shared generally by Messianic Jews today.

This view, however, is not correct, for it is contradicted by many other parables. Immediately after showing that entrance into the Kingdom and its fruitfulness depends on conversion and the cooperation of human dispositions with grace, Jesus tells the parable of the wheat and the tares (Mt 13:24–30) to ward off this false impression. Here He shows that the Kingdom is not limited to the righteous, just as the Kingdom of Israel included sinners as well as the just. Jesus then gives an explanation of the parable in Matthew 13:37–43:

He who sows the good seed is the Son of man; the field is the world, and the good seed means the sons of the kingdom; the weeds are the sons of the evil one, and the enemy who sowed them is the devil; the harvest is the close of the age, and the reapers are angels. Just as the weeds are gathered and burned with fire, so will it be at the close of the age. The Son of man will send his angels, and they will gather out of his kingdom all causes of sin and all evildoers, and throw them into the furnace of fire; there men will weep and gnash their teeth. Then the righteous will shine like the sun in the kingdom of their Father. He who has ears, let him hear.

The full separation of the good seed and the weeds cannot take place until the harvest at the end of the world. The clear implication is that the visible Kingdom, or visible Church, will always include members who are evil and give scandal, until the Last Judgment. Only in the Church triumphant is the Kingdom a pure communion of righteous members. Any claim on the part of the Church militant to be a pure collection of the righteous is thus shown to be false. It is true that only the righteous are properly said to be "sons of the Kingdom," for they are the only ones who live according to her Spirit and cooperate with her grace. Nevertheless, grave sinners are still members of her visible structure, although without being united to her Spirit, nor persevering as "sons of the Kingdom" through sanctifying grace.

The same basic point is made in Matthew 13:47–50 in the parable of the net that catches good and bad fish. It is very clear here that the Kingdom includes the bad fish, for the Kingdom is likened to the net which "was thrown into the sea and gathered fish of every kind" (Mt 13:47). Only at the end of the world will the good and evil be separated so that Christ will be able to "present the church to himself in splendor, without spot or wrinkle or any such thing, that she might be holy and without blemish" (Eph 5:27).

It follows from these parables that we cannot expect the Church to be the congregation of the righteous alone. The Church is certainly called to be holy, for Jesus says: "You, therefore, must be perfect, as your heavenly Father is perfect" (Mt 5:48). Likewise, He says, "For I tell you, unless your righteousness exceeds that of the scribes and Pharisees, you will never enter the kingdom of heaven" (Mt 5:20). Nevertheless, even though all are called to be perfect, Christ foretells that not all the visible members of the Church will actually correspond to that vocation. On the contrary, many among her visible members will give great scandal.

Parables of the Growth of the Kingdom

Several parables show that the Kingdom of heaven gradually grows in human history until it fills the world. In Matthew 13:31–32, Jesus compares the Kingdom of heaven to a mustard seed planted in the field, which is the least of all seeds, but which becomes a tree such that the birds can make their nests in its branches. Likewise, it is compared to leaven mixed in the dough till it was all leavened (Mt 13:33).

In other words, the kingdom of heaven will have a development of slow, continual, and organic expansion in history. This expansion will reach the point of leavening the whole dough and becoming a tree capable of hosting the birds of the air so that they can make their nests in it.

This picture of the gradual expansion of the Kingdom matches the picture given in Daniel 2:35 of the Messianic Kingdom which is pictured as a stone that "became a great mountain and filled the whole earth," taking the place of the four great world empires symbolized by the statue made of gold, silver, bronze, and iron.

It follows from this that the Kingdom of heaven/Kingdom of God cannot be simply identified with heaven, or with a kingdom beginning with the Second Coming of Christ. On the contrary, the Kingdom of heaven is something that develops continually in history.

It was (and remains) common among Liberal Protestants and Modernist theologians of the later nineteenth and twentieth centuries to hold that Christ was mistaken about the timing of the Second Coming, which He expected to be imminent.[4] These parables clearly show this to be false. Christ clearly knew and taught that the Kingdom of God—which is the Church—has to grow slowly in human history until it comes to reach all nations. Only then could the end come.

The gradual growth of the Kingdom is also shown in the parable of the wheat and the tares. The growth of the Kingdom is compared to the growth of the seed sown by the Son of Man, until the time of the final harvest at the end of the world. The Kingdom therefore is in a constant process of development from the preaching of Jesus until the end of the world.

It also follows from these parables of the growth of the Kingdom that the Church must be a visible structure that can be clearly seen and

---

[4] This thesis was condemned in the decree *Lamentabili* of the Holy Office of 1907 condemning the errors of Modernism. The thirty-third condemned proposition reads: "Everyone who is not led by preconceived opinions can readily see that either Jesus professed an error concerning the immediate Messianic coming or the greater part of His doctrine as contained in the Gospels is destitute of authenticity."

identified in the world, like the mustard tree, or the leavened loaf, or the net filled with fish (both good and bad), or the field sown with wheat and tares. All of these images of the Church are visible realities. The Church that grows gradually in history cannot be a purely spiritual and invisible reality. If Christ had wished us to consider the Church as an essentially invisible reality, He could have spoken of it using images that are naturally invisible, like the wind that we feel but do not see (Jn 3:8), which He used when speaking of the Spirit.

The Catholic Church perfectly realizes these images of the mustard seed that grows into a tree, or leaven that gradually leavens the whole loaf, or the stone that gradually becomes a mountain that fills the whole earth. No other Christian denomination, however, fulfills these images. It is clear that the Protestant churches do not fulfill the image of the mustard seed, for they were not sown directly by Christ and His Apostles, nor have they gradually grown since Pentecost so as to come to include all nations and tongues, as does the Catholic Church.

Perhaps one could think that the Eastern Orthodox churches fulfill this image of the growth of the mustard seed or the leaven. However, even they fall short, for they have not grown so as to include the whole earth. They lack the full mark of catholicity, which is possessed by the Catholic Church alone.

The Parables of the Value of the Kingdom

In Matthew 13:44–46, Jesus gives two parables showing the value of the Kingdom—the hidden treasure and the priceless pearl. These parables show that communion in the Kingdom of God, which is the Church, is of greater value than any other earthly reality, and that one should be prepared to sacrifice everything so as to take one's place in the Kingdom. We see this parable realized in the martyrs and saints, and all those who have made great sacrifices to enter the Church and live her interior life. Often a great price is exacted of Hebrew Catholics, who risk being disowned by their families and communities. A still greater price is sometimes asked of Muslim converts, who risk the death penalty for conversion.

The New and the Old

At the end of the parables of the Kingdom in Matthew 13, Jesus stresses the continuity between Israel and the Church. He says: "Every scribe who has been trained for the kingdom of heaven is like a householder who brings out of his treasure what is new and what is old" (Mt 13:52). The Messianic Kingdom does not annul the wisdom of Israel but builds something new on it. As Jesus will say later, the Eucharist, from which the Church is born, is the "new covenant in my Blood" (Lk 22:20). Nevertheless, Jesus shows here that the Old Testament revelation to Israel is to remain an abiding patrimony for the Church that is forever valid.

Closely related to this parable are Jesus' words about the abiding value of the Mosaic Law in the Sermon on the Mount (Mt 5:17–20):

> Think not that I have come to abolish the law and the prophets; I have come not to abolish them but to fulfill them. For truly, I say to you, till heaven and earth pass away, not an iota, not a dot, will pass from the law until all is accomplished. Whoever then relaxes one of the least of these commandments and teaches men so, shall be called least in the kingdom of heaven; but he who does them and teaches them shall be called great in the kingdom of heaven. For I tell you, unless your righteousness exceeds that of the scribes and Pharisees, you will never enter the kingdom of heaven.

The Kingdom or Church involves a fulfillment and perfection of the divine Law, which is summed up in the double commandment of charity. The greatest in the Kingdom—which means the greatest saints in the Church—are those who excel through the grace of God in the commandment of charity and everything that derives from it.

In order to understand Christ's words about fulfilling the Law, it is very helpful to distinguish three aspects of the Mosaic Law: (a) the moral law summed up in the Ten Commandments and the double commandment of charity, (b) the ceremonial law involving divine worship and ritual purity, and (c) the judicial precepts giving particular judicial procedures and penalties. Jesus is speaking here principally with regard to the moral law, which He fulfills in the perfect sanctity of His life and through the outpouring of grace to the disciples. However, the Church also perfects the ceremonial law in her liturgy, centering on the Eucharist and the other sacraments. Jesus does not give new judicial precepts, parallel to those of the Mosaic Law, but He gives, through the Magisterium of the Church, the principles that ought to govern the civil laws of nations.

Parable of the Laborers in the Vineyard

Another parable concerning the relation between Israel and the Church is that of the laborers in the vineyard, recounted in Matthew 20:1–16. Here the Church/Kingdom is likened to a householder hiring laborers for his vineyard. Evidently the householder is Christ Himself and His Church (for Christ and the Kingdom always go together). This shows us that Christ and His Church are constantly seeking laborers who will work through human history to build up the Kingdom of God. It is never too late to enter the great work of building up the Church. Even at the eleventh hour workers are still hired and receive the same wage (although reproached for having stood idle all the day).

This parable, like many others, has two applications: individual and social. The work day can be compared to the human life, and it can be compared to the larger scale of human history. It is never too late to enter the Church, both for individuals and nations. Nevertheless, it is a human tragedy to come late, having wasted one's day in "idleness." St. Augustine lamented in his *Confessions*: "Too late have I loved thee."[5]

With regard to nations, the history of the Church shows us how the evangelizing mission of the Church has reached different nations at different times. What formerly were pagan territories separated from knowledge of the true God have later become the strength and bulwark of the Church. It matters not when a society enters the Church, but how deeply it allows itself to be permeated by the Church's life.

There is also a clear reference to Israel and the Gentiles here. The first laborers in the vineyard were the Jews. This was a great privilege, for they were thus able to work to build up and prepare for the Kingdom for 2,000 years while the Gentiles were left in great darkness. This privilege, however, could lead Israel to think that their privileged status was not meant to be shared with all the other laborers who were to be hired later in the day of human history, and to overlook the fact that their longer service was its own reward and privilege.

Hierarchy of the Kingdom — Built on Peter

The continuous growth of the Kingdom of God in human history, as we have seen in various parables, also involves an institutional and hierarchical element, which guarantees the continuity of the growth and serves as its foundation. This key aspect of the Kingdom is manifested to us in the crucial text of Matthew 16:15–19. Jesus had just asked the disciples to tell Him who people say that He is and who they themselves think that He is. As we know, Peter answered: "You are the Christ, the Son of the living God." Christ answered: "Blessed are you, Simon, son of Jonah! For flesh and blood has not revealed this to you, but my Father who is in heaven" (Mt 16:16). Christ then goes on to tell Simon bar-Jonah who *he* is—he has now become *Cephas*, which is Aramaic for "rock," which in Greek is *Petros*, and *Petrus* in Latin. Hence our English "Peter": "And I tell you, you are Peter, and on this rock I will build my Church, and the gates of hell shall not prevail against it. I will give you the keys of the kingdom of heaven, and whatever you bind on earth

---

[5] St. Augustine, *Confessions* 10.27.

shall be bound in heaven, and whatever you loose on earth shall be loosed in heaven" (Mt 16:18–19).

In this text, instead of the phrase, "Kingdom of heaven," Jesus uses the word "Church," which literally means "convocation." The Church is the society of those who respond to the call to enter the Kingdom preached by Jesus and founded by Him as a supernatural society in this world. However, when He speaks of the keys, Jesus refers to them as "keys of the kingdom of heaven." This seems to show that the two terms—"Church" and "Kingdom"—are being used as synonyms to refer to the same reality built on Peter and entrusted to His authority to bind and loose.[6]

This Church will be built by Christ on a foundation which He declares to be none other than Peter the rock. To this Kingdom/Church He promises that it shall never fail, in accordance with the Messianic prophecies of an eternal kingdom. This is what is meant by saying that the gates of hell shall not prevail over it.

Authority in the Church is represented by the "keys of the kingdom of heaven." The keys to a city were a traditional symbol of the power given to a viceroy or vicar to open and shut the gates of the city and to govern it in peace and war.[7] These keys, entrusted to Peter by Christ, are then connected to a loosing and binding of sins, and with the power to declare authoritatively the true contents of Revelation.

Jesus' prophecy that the gates of hell would not prevail over His Church founded on Peter was confirmed later before His Ascension into heaven when He gave His disciples the missionary mandate, telling them to go into all the world and preach the Gospel to all creation. In Matthew 28:18–20, Christ says:

> All authority in heaven and on earth has been given to me. Go therefore and make disciples of all nations, baptizing them in the name of the Father and of the Son and of the Holy Spirit, teaching them to observe all that I have commanded you; and lo, I am with you always, to the close of the age.

---

[6] There may be this difference, however, that the word "Church" is being used by Jesus to refer to the Church militant, whereas the "kingdom of heaven" includes both dimensions (earthly and heavenly). Only the church militant is built on Peter, for only on earth does the Church have a sacramental dimension, including the sacrament of Holy Orders, the episcopate, and the primacy of Peter. In the Church triumphant, all sacraments will pass away, and Christ will be "all in all" (1 Cor 15:28).

[7] See Is 22:20–22: "In that day I will call my servant Eliakim the son of Hilkiah, and I will clothe him with your robe, and will bind your girdle on him, and will commit your authority to his hand. . . . And I will place on his shoulder the *key of the house of David; he shall open, and none shall shut; and he shall shut, and none shall open.*"

The Church is to make disciples of all nations, and Christ promises to be present in His Church until the Second Coming.

Here we have a magnificent prophecy that we can test today, almost two thousand years later. Has this Church/Kingdom survived the vicissitudes of time? Has it stood the test of Roman persecution, barbarian invasion, Muslim threat, rebellion from within, the armies of Napoleon, Stalin, Hitler, the forces of Western secularism, etc.?

Is there still a kingdom on earth built on Peter, claiming the authority to bind and unbind in the name of Jesus Christ? Has it spread as leaven in the dough and as the mustard seed growing into a tree?

Here we have the most astounding combination of prophecy and realization. We have a series of Old Testament prophecies about the Messiah, son of David, founding an eternal kingdom that would come to rule over the Gentiles, over the ends of the earth. We have One who claimed to be that son of David, son of Man, Son of God, who claimed to found that kingdom which the gates of hell shall not overcome, on St. Peter. And today two thousand years later we still see that Church/Kingdom, governing over a billion souls, including all nations and tongues! And this has occurred with an uninterrupted series of 264 successors of that Peter, placed by Jesus to be the rock with the power to bind and unbind, to forgive and to teach. Perhaps Pharaohs or kings or Caesars or caliphs hoped that they would found an eternal kingdom, but none of them exist today.

The Parable of the Vineyard and the Wicked Tenants

The fact that Jesus builds His Church on Peter rather than on the Aaronic priesthood, and on the twelve Apostles rather than the twelve tribes, shows that the Kingdom is distinct from Israel in its institutional structure. This distinction between Israel and the Church is the subject of some of the parables of the Kingdom. One of these is Matthew 21:33–39, concerning the vineyard and the wicked tenants:

> There was a householder who planted a vineyard, and set a hedge around it, and dug a wine press in it, and built a tower, and let it out to tenants, and went into another country. When the season of fruit drew near, he sent his servants to the tenants, to get his fruit; and the tenants took his servants and beat one, killed another, and stoned another. Again he sent other servants, more than the first; and they did the same to them. Afterward he sent his son to them, saying, "They will respect my son." But when the tenants saw the son, they said to themselves, "This is the heir; come, let us kill him and have his inheritance." And they took him and cast him out of the vineyard, and killed him.

The vineyard, like that described in Isaiah 5, at first represents Israel. God the Father is the planter of the vineyard. The servants sent to get the fruit of the harvest represent the prophets. The fruits of the harvest would appear to represent fruits of righteousness and sanctity. The maltreatment of the servants represents the maltreatment suffered by the great prophets,[8] such as Elijah at the hands of Jezebel and Isaiah and Jeremiah at the hands of the leaders of Israel, who failed to heed the prophetic message.[9]

The son who is finally sent to get the fruit of the harvest clearly represents Christ, the Son of God, who is put to death outside the vineyard. This refers to Calvary, outside the walls of Jerusalem, or to the fact that Christ is put to death by the Roman authorities. Christ then connects this with the prophecy of Psalm 118:22. He is the "head of the corner" rejected by the builders, who represent those invested with juridical authority in Israel: Caiaphas, the other high priests, and the other members of the Sanhedrin.

After the killing of the son, Christ then asks His audience what will happen to the vineyard. They respond that the owner will turn it over to other tenants who will give him the fruits thereof (Mt 21:41). What is this vineyard? In case there was any doubt, Christ then explains that it refers to the Kingdom of God, saying with authority: "I tell you, the kingdom of God will be taken away from you and given to a nation producing the fruits of it" (Mt 22:43).

What does this mean? It is clear from these words that the Kingdom of God has a twofold existence: first in Israel, and then in the Church to be built up by the Apostles. The People of God and the Kingdom of God are twofold: Israel and the Church, which is the new Israel.

This parable therefore clearly shows that there is an essential continuity, but at the same time a no less important discontinuity. The Kingdom of God is to be given to a new people or nation, who become the new People of God.

However, it would be a mistake to think that the "new people" refers simply to the Gentiles. On the contrary, the new People of God

---

[8] See Leopold Fonck, *The Parables of the Gospel: An Exegetical and Practical Explanation*, trans. E. Leahy (New York: F. Pustet, 1915; reprinted under the title: *The Parables of Christ*, Fort Collins, CO: Roman Catholic Books [199?]), 352: "According to the unanimous interpretation of all commentators, the servants sent by the owner of the vineyard are the Prophets of the Old Covenant up to John the Baptist."

[9] Jeremiah was subjected to many indignities, such as being lowered into a dry well filled with mud (Jer 38:6). According to tradition, Isaiah was sawn in half under the impious king, Manasseh.

—the Church—is composed both of Jews and Gentiles. The first and principal members of this new People of God were all Jews: Mary, the Apostles, the seven deacons, St. Paul and Barnabas, and all the first disciples, such as Mary Magdalene, Martha, etc. The new People of God mentioned in Matthew 21:43 cannot be understood in an ethnic sense! The entrance into this people does not come through birth, but through Baptism and ecclesial communion.

This new People of God is endowed also with a new hierarchical structure and a teaching and governing authority which is sacramental, based on the sacrament of Holy Orders. The new hierarchy is constituted by the Apostles chosen by Jesus, and their successors, headed by the successor of Peter. Authority over the People of God has passed, therefore, from the High Priests and Sanhedrin to the Apostles and their successors. We see this already in the Gospels, and it is confirmed in the first chapters of the Acts of the Apostles, in which the new Kingdom and People of God—the Church—is governed by the teaching authority of the Apostles.[10]

Parable of the Wedding Feast

Immediately after the parable of the vineyard, St. Matthew recounts the parable of the wedding feast (Mt 22:2–14):

> The kingdom of heaven may be compared to a king who gave a marriage feast for his son, and sent his servants to call those who were invited to the marriage feast; but they would not come. Again he sent other servants, saying, "Tell those who are invited, Behold, I have made ready my dinner, my oxen and my fat calves are killed, and everything is ready; come to the marriage feast." But they made light of it and went off, one to his farm, another to his business, while the rest seized his servants, treated them shamefully, and killed them. The king was angry, and he sent his troops and destroyed those murderers and burned their city. Then he said to his servants, "The wedding is ready, but those invited were not worthy. Go therefore to the thoroughfares, and invite to the marriage feast as many as you find." And those servants went out into the streets and gathered all whom they found, both bad and good; so the wedding hall was filled with guests.

In this parable, the Kingdom/Church is shown in its Eucharistic dimension. The king's son who is to be married is clearly the Son of God. A first group of people is invited to the wedding, many of whom

---

[10] See Acts 2:42: "They devoted themselves to the apostles' teaching."

declined to come. The invitation was then extended to all those who could be found in the thoroughfares.

This twofold invitation seems to correspond to the preaching of the Kingdom first to the children of Israel, and then also to the Gentiles, represented by those found in the streets.

A curious detail is then given. One of the wedding guests lacks a wedding garment. This lack makes the guest unworthy to participate in the feast. He is then thrown out:

> But when the king came in to look at the guests, he saw there a man who had no wedding garment; and he said to him, "Friend, how did you get in here without a wedding garment?" And he was speechless. Then the king said to the attendants, "Bind him hand and foot, and cast him into the outer darkness; there men will weep and gnash their teeth." For many are called, but few are chosen.[11]

The wedding garment appears to indicate sanctifying grace and the possession of charity. One cannot celebrate the wedding feast of the Lamb without the wedding garment of charity.[12]

The wedding feast would appear to have two dimensions: Eucharistic communion in the Church militant and entrance into the full feast of the Lamb in the Church triumphant in heaven. Without the wedding garment of the state of grace, one cannot enter into the celebration of the wedding feast, either in its sacramental realization or in heaven when the sacramental veils are taken away.

Parable about the Unforgiving Debtor

Unworthiness for the Kingdom is also illustrated in the parable about the unforgiving debtor (Mt 18:23–35). Jesus begins by saying:

---

[11] Mt 23:11–14.

[12] See St. Augustine, *Sermon 40*, Nicene and Post-Nicene Fathers, series 1, 6:394: "What is that 'wedding garment' then? This is the wedding garment: 'Now the end of the commandment,' says the Apostle, 'is charity out of a pure heart, and of a good conscience, and of faith unfeigned' [1 Tim 1:5]." See also St. Jerome, *Commentary on Matthew*, trans. Thomas Scheck (Washington DC: Catholic Univ. of America Press, 2008), 250: "The wedding garments are the Lord's commands and the works that are fulfilled from the Law and the Gospel. These become the clothing of the new man. If anyone with the name of Christian, therefore, is found at the time of the judgment who does not have the wedding clothing, that is, the garment of the heavenly man from above, but has a polluted garment, that is, the hide of the old man, he is immediately reprimanded."

The kingdom of heaven may be compared to a king who wished to settle accounts with his servants. When he began the reckoning, one was brought to him who owed him ten thousand talents; and as he could not pay, his lord ordered him to be sold, with his wife and children and all that he had, and payment to be made. So the servant fell on his knees, imploring him, "Lord, have patience with me, and I will pay you everything." And out of pity for him the lord of that servant released him and forgave him the debt.[13]

The parable shows that the Kingdom of heaven, which is the Church, is a Kingdom of mercy in which God remits the sins of those who ask forgiveness. However, the parable goes on to show that that forgiveness of sins can be lost if one fails to exercise mercy and forgive one's neighbor in turn. Jesus goes on to relate how that same servant refused to forgive a fellow servant who owed him a mere fraction of what he had owed. Jesus concludes: "And in anger his lord delivered him to the jailers, till he should pay all his debt. So also my heavenly Father will do to every one of you, if you do not forgive your brother from your heart."[14]

The Kingdom of God Is Not a Kingdom of This World

Another fundamental aspect of the Kingdom is revealed by Jesus not in parables, but in His responses to questions of the Pharisees and of Pontius Pilate concerning the relation of the Kingdom to political authority. Here we learn that the Kingdom of God will be distinct from a political kingdom. It can exist under the political dominion of Caesar or any other monarch. This is declared to us when Jesus was asked if taxes should be paid to Caesar, and He gave the simple and luminous answer: "Render therefore to Caesar the things that are Caesar's, and to God the things that are God's" (Mt 22:21). The Kingdom of God exists to render unto God the glory that is due to Him, and so to save our souls and seek for sanctity in a society dedicated to that purpose. To be a citizen of the Kingdom of God—the Church—does not mean that we are not also citizens of a temporal society as well, subject to the temporal authority of Caesar or the president.

When Pilate asked Christ whether He was a king, He answered: "My kingdom is not of this world. If my kingdom were of this world, my servants would certainly strive that I should not be delivered to the Jews: but now my kingdom is not from here."[15] This does not mean that the Kingdom of Christ is something purely spiritual. Rather it means that it

---

[13] Mt 18:23–27.

[14] Mt 18:34–35.

[15] Jn 18:36 (Douay Rheims).

does not come from *merely* human agency. It is a supernatural kingdom based on purely supernatural means. These supernatural means are principally the seven sacraments established by Christ, and the preaching of the Word of the Gospel.

Before Pilate, Jesus referred to the Kingdom as "His," for He is its King and Head. Another text that connects Christ and the Kingdom still more closely is given in Luke 17:20–21:

> Being asked by the Pharisees when the kingdom of God was coming, he answered them, "The kingdom of God is not coming with signs to be observed; nor will they say, 'Lo, here it is!' or 'There!' for behold, the kingdom of God is in the midst of you."

The Greek text of the concluding words can be interpreted in two ways: "in the midst of you," or "within you." Although Jesus may have intended both aspects, the former seems to be the better reading and is more suited to the context. Jesus says that the Kingdom is in their midst for He is in their midst, and communion with Jesus is the essential content of the Kingdom. For this reason the Kingdom is Christ's Mystical Body.[16]

The Kingdom and the Church

After seeing various parables of the Kingdom, can we confirm our initial hypothesis that the Kingdom of heaven/Kingdom of God is indeed essentially the Roman Catholic Church? Let us summarize what we have seen. The parables show us the following features of the Kingdom. It is a visible although supernatural kingdom that will grow gradually in time, becoming ever more universal. The Kingdom therefore is shown to be *catholic*. Second, the Kingdom is not a collection of saints and the predestined, but includes sinners in her bosom. Nevertheless, it is still *holy*, for those sinners do not correspond to her inner life, nor do they spring from the sowing of the Sower. The tares, however, and those who lack the wedding garment of grace will finally be excluded from the consummation of the Kingdom in the Church triumphant.

Third, the Kingdom has a value greater than any human value. Fourth, the Kingdom is in continuity with Israel, whose mystery it continues, but also perfects and makes new. Fifth, the Kingdom is

---

[16] If we take the other interpretation—the Kingdom of God is "within you"—this would refer to the interior and supernatural dimension of the life of the Church. The Kingdom is governed by the principles given in the Sermon on the Mount, which presupposes the moral law given by Moses, and brings it to a higher ideal of holiness which goes beyond the strength of unaided human nature, but which is possible through the aid of the gifts of the Holy Spirit.

portrayed as a wedding feast of the Son of God. This dimension of the Kingdom is most fully realized in the Eucharist. It is God's vineyard which has been given to a new People of God which is the new Israel.

Sixth, the Church is a Kingdom whose keys were given to Peter. The Kingdom has an authority established by Christ on Peter and the other Apostles. The Kingdom, therefore, is *apostolic* and Petrine. Finally, in all the parables of the Kingdom, it is portrayed as *one*. The Kingdom is not a collection of churches, but one Kingdom with one authority built on Peter.

It follows, therefore, that the Kingdom of God as portrayed in the parables of the Kingdom corresponds essentially to the Roman Catholic Church, with her four marks: one, holy, catholic, and apostolic. Nevertheless, as the Second Vatican Council (*Lumen gentium* 8) observes, "many elements of sanctification and of truth are [also] found outside of its visible structure."

CHAPTER 4

The Church Is Catholic: The Ingathering of the Nations

The prophecies concerning the Church and Jesus' teaching on the Kingdom give us a clear indication of what the Church of Christ should look like through the centuries. These prophecies and parables show us crucial distinguishing marks to be manifested by the Church, which defy all human expectation: that she will be one, holy, catholic, and apostolic.

In this chapter we shall examine the mark of catholicity, or universality. We have seen how the prophets foretell that the Messiah will establish a Kingdom that is not restricted to Israel according to the flesh, but will extend to all nations. This is one of the four crucial marks of the true Church of Christ, the Messiah. The true Church must embrace all peoples and be truly universal, which is the etymological meaning of the word "catholic," the Greek term for universal.

The true Church cannot remain merely in one corner of the world and be restricted to one nationality, as Israel had been. This is an obvious consequence of the fact that Christ is the Savior and Redeemer of all men, the Way, the Truth, and the Life. The Word became man for all men, and thus it would be unfitting if divine Providence and the Holy Spirit did not aid the Church to become truly universal. The Way, the Truth, and the Life could not remain the spiritual property of one people or nation or region.

The universal nature of the Church was prophesied by Jesus before the Passion (Jn 12:32) when He said: "And I, when I am lifted up from the earth, will draw *all men* to myself." Some seven hundred years earlier the catholicity of the Church was prophesied by Isaiah in one of the canticles of the Suffering Servant (Is 49:6): "It is too light a thing that you should be my servant to raise up the tribes of Jacob and to restore the preserved of Israel; I will give you as a *light to the nations*, that my salvation may reach to the end of the earth." It was also shown in the dream of Nebuchadnezzar interpreted by Daniel, in which the Kingdom was symbolized as a rock cut by no human hand which grew into a mountain that "filled the whole earth" (Dan 2:35).

The catholic or universal nature of the Church also concerns the temporal dimension. The Church must extend not only to all nations, but also to all succeeding centuries, in accordance with Christ's promise (Mt 28:20): "I am with you always, to the close of the age." This was also prophesied in Daniel's interpretation of the dream of Nebuchadnezzar (Dan 2:44): "The God of heaven will set up a kingdom which shall never be destroyed, nor shall its sovereignty be left to another people. It shall break in pieces all these kingdoms and bring them to an end, and it shall stand for ever."

The Universality of the Church as the Mystery Hidden through All Ages

St. Paul speaks repeatedly of the catholicity/universality of the Church as a "mystery hidden for ages in God" (Eph 3:9). In Ephesians 3:4–6, he speaks of his "insight into the *mystery of Christ*, which was not made known to the sons of men in other generations as it has now been revealed to his holy apostles and prophets by the Spirit; that is, *how the Gentiles are fellow heirs, members of the same body, and partakers of the promise* in Christ Jesus through the Gospel." The same point is made in Colossians 1:26, in which he mentions again the "the mystery hidden for ages and generations but now made manifest to his saints. To them God chose to make known how great among the Gentiles are the riches of the glory of this mystery, which is Christ in you, the hope of glory."

To St. Paul, the Pharisee called to be Apostle to the Gentiles, the most mysterious work of God in his time in salvation history was the superabundance of God's mercy shown in the ingathering of the Gentiles into the new Israel, which is the Church. We tend to take it for granted today as something natural. However, for St. Paul, the engrafting of the Gentiles into the new Israel—constituted as the Body of Christ—is anything but natural: it is the "*mystery* hidden for ages and generations." It is a miracle of God greater than any other, for it is a miraculous catch, not of fish but of peoples formerly separated from the true faith, as St. Paul says in Ephesians 2:12, "strangers to the covenants of promise, having no hope and without God in the world." Although the ingathering had been foretold by the prophets and Christ Himself, the realization of the prophecy astounds the Apostle as he labors to bring it about.

The sheer universality of God's plan of salvation in Christ—which is to include all nations—was an absolutely new thing, and a fitting consequence of the Incarnation of the Word. Thus the calling of the Gentiles shares in the mystery of the Incarnation, as its fruit and purpose.

Pentecost and the Universality of the Church

The mark of universality was first adumbrated in the feast of Pentecost, the birth of the Church.[1] In order to fully understand this feast, it is useful to understand the Old Testament feast of the same name, for it was not by chance that the Lord chose to send the Holy Spirit on this day of the Jewish Pentecost to inaugurate the apostolic preaching and give full birth to the Church.

The Jewish Pentecost was primarily a celebration of the giving of the Mosaic Law and the Mosaic covenant at Mt. Sinai, recounted in Exodus 19–20, for this occurred exactly seven weeks—that is, fifty days—after the first Passover, when the Israelites left Egypt. Hence the Greek-speaking Jews called it "Pentecost," which means fifty,[2] while in Hebrew it was called the feast of "weeks" (*Shavuot*), for the seven weeks which separate the Passover from the solemn covenant on Mt. Sinai.

The Israelites were commanded to celebrate a feast in commemoration of this central event of their existence, and also in thanksgiving for the first harvest of the year. For this reason, they were to offer to the Lord the first fruits of their crops.[3] The Jewish feast of Pentecost is in a certain way the completion of what was begun in the Passover and the Exodus. It marks the end of the season of Passover, just as for Christians it marks the end of the season of Easter. Thus the feast has two principal aspects: thanksgiving for the gift of the Ten Commandments and the Covenant of Sinai, and thanksgiving for the first fruits of the land.

These two aspects of the Jewish Pentecost correspond perfectly with the event of the first Christian Pentecost. Just as the giving of the written Law of the Ten Commandments and the sealing of the Covenant with Israel occurred fifty days after Passover, so too the New Law of the Holy Spirit was given to the infant Church fifty days after Easter.[4]

---

[1] Although in one sense the Church was born on Good Friday as Christ merited man's redemption, her birth was completed on Pentecost with the gift of the Holy Spirit, which is essential to the New Covenant.

[2] See Tob 2:1; 2 Mac 12:32.

[3] See Lev 23:15–21 and Ex 34:22: "And you shall observe the feast of weeks, the first fruits of wheat harvest." This feast is also mentioned in Ex 23:16: "You shall keep the feast of harvest, of the first fruits of your labor."

[4] St. Thomas Aquinas identifies the essence of the New Law of Christ with the giving of the Holy Spirit. See *Summa of Theology* I-II, q. 106, a. 1: "That which is preponderant in the law of the New Testament, and whereon all its efficacy is based, is the grace of the Holy Spirit, which is given through faith in Christ. Consequently the New Law is chiefly the grace itself of the Holy Spirit."

As seen above, the giving of a new covenant written on our souls rather than on tablets of stone had been announced by the prophets—especially Jeremiah 31:31–33 and Ezekiel 36:24–27—some six centuries before its fulfillment. This promise was fulfilled first in a manifest and public way on the day of Pentecost, when three thousand Israelites were baptized, as recounted in Acts 2:41.[5] By the way, this was the first "celebration" of the sacrament of Confirmation. In this case, it was not administered by ministers of the Church, but by God Himself on the Apostles.

The Christian Pentecost also corresponded mystically to the Jewish feast of the first fruits, offered on that same day. The material first fruits of the harvest correspond to the spiritual first fruits of the apostolic preaching: a harvest of three thousand adult converts. These first fruits also include the gifts and fruits of the Holy Spirit in the souls of the disciples. Thus the first fruits of the Church offered to God on her first Pentecost were those of grace, preaching, and conversion.

The Apostles' speaking in tongues on Pentecost (Acts 2:5–11) was a prophetic indication of the universality of the Church, called to be the ark of salvation of the whole human race and thus to speak all languages and be understood by all. The event of Pentecost was thus the antitype of Babel with its confusion and pluralism of tongues. Although nations still speak different languages, and will doubtless continue to do so until the end of time, in the Church the original harmony is recomposed in the unity of faith. And although materially there continue to be many languages, they are one in proclaiming the same Creed.

St. Augustine on the Note of Catholicity

St. Augustine has a beautiful commentary on the significance of the miracle of tongues at Pentecost:

> At the beginning the Church was not yet spread throughout the entire world, making it possible for Christ's members to speak among all nations, and therefore the miracle happened in each person as a presage of what would later be true of all. Today the whole body of Christ does speak in the languages of all peoples, or, rather, if there are any tongues in which it does not yet speak, it will. The church will grow until it claims all languages as its own....
> I dare to say to you, "I speak in the tongues of all men and women. I am in Christ's body, I am in Christ's Church. If Christ's body today speaks in the languages of all, I too speak in all languages. Greek is mine, Syriac is mine, Hebrew is mine. Mine is the tongue

---

[5] "So those who received his word were baptized, and there were added that day about three thousand souls."

of every nation, because I am within the unity that embraces all nations."[6]

If St. Augustine could say around the year 400 that the Church already "speaks nearly all languages," how much more that is true today!

Since the Church is the Bride of Christ, it would be unfitting if the Bride were restricted to one "corner" of the world, whatever it may be. Such a condition would make it seem that God's providence had not been able to realize a wedding with mankind, that is, with all mankind that responds to His call.

St. Augustine develops this theme beautifully in his sermons against the Donatist schism. The Donatists were a sect originating in Carthage in the fourth century that went into schism over a dispute about episcopal succession. Even though an investigation which included the bishop of Rome declared them to be schismatic, they continued to spread and claimed to be the true Church of Christ, even though they were restricted to the region of North Africa. The most powerful and providential opponent of this schism was St. Augustine, who wrote:

> Christ is therefore the Bridegroom of the Church proclaimed in all nations, propagated and extended to the ends of the earth, beginning with Jerusalem. Of such a Church Christ is the Bridegroom. And you, what do you think? Of whom is Christ the Bridegroom? The Donatists? No, a million times no! . . . Let us consider the marriage, let us read the contract, and let us not argue. If you think that Christ is the spouse of the Donatist sect, I will reread the contract, and I will see that it is the *Church, which is dispersed throughout all the earth*.[7]

Another saying of St. Augustine against the Donatists was that "the judgment of the whole [Catholic] world is certain" against any portion thereof which secedes.[8] It was this sentence that moved the Anglican John Henry Newman decisively towards conversion to the Catholic Church in the mid-nineteenth century. Newman wrote:

> "Securus judicat orbis terrarum" ["The judgment of the whole world is certain"]. . . . They kept ringing in my ears. . . . What a light was hereby thrown upon every controversy in the Church!

---

[6] St. Augustine, *Exposition of Psalm 147*, n. 19, in *Expositions of the Psalms 121–150*, trans. Maria Boulding, *The Works of Saint Augustine*, part 3, vol. 20 (Hyde Park, NY: New City Press, 2004), 464.

[7] St. Augustine, Sermon 183.11, quoted in Charles Card. Journet, *Theology of the Church* (San Francisco: Ignatius Press, 2004), 31.

[8] St. Augustine, *Contra Epistolam Parmeniani* 3.24: "*Securus judicat orbis terrarum.*"

Not that, for the moment, the multitude may not falter in their judgment—not that, in the Arian hurricane, Sees more than can be numbered did not bend before its fury, and fall off from St. Athanasius—not that the crowd of Oriental Bishops did not need to be sustained during the contest by the voice and the eye of St. Leo; but that the deliberate judgment, in which the whole Church at length rests and acquiesces, is an infallible prescription and a final sentence against such portions of it as protest and secede. Who can account for the impressions which are made on him? For a mere sentence, the words of St. Augustine, struck me with a power which I never had felt from any words before.[9]

The universality of the Catholic Church and her deliberate judgment on the Protestant Reformation at the Council of Trent was sufficient witness that the Anglican church, restricted to British dominions and out of communion with Rome, could not be Christ's Bride.

Gradual Realization of the Promise of Catholicity

The prophetic promise of Catholicity has been progressively and continuously realized in the history of the Church, as can be seen from an objective study of the history of the Church.

Already in the first century, St. Paul speaks of the Gospel being preached in all the world and marveling at the rapid expansion to which his own missionary voyages gave rise.[10] In the second century we find the anonymous letter to Diognetus saying: "What the soul is to the body, Christians are to the world. The soul is dispersed through all the members of the body, and Christians throughout the cities of the world. The soul dwells in the body, but is not of the body; likewise Christians dwell in the world, but are not of the world."[11]

At the end of the second century, St. Irenaeus speaks of the Church having the same faith throughout the world:

Neither do the Churches that have been established in Germany believe otherwise, or hand down any other tradition, nor those among the Iberians, nor those among the Celts, nor in Egypt, nor in Libya, nor those established in the middle parts of the world. But as God's creature, the sun, is one and the same in the whole

---

[9] John Henry Newman, *Apologia Pro Vita Sua* (London: J M Dent, 1993), 174 (part 5, ch. 3).

[10] See Rom 10:18; 1 Thess 1:8.

[11] Letter to Diognetus 6, in *The Apostolic Fathers: Greek Texts and English Translations*, trans. Michael W. Holmes, 3rd ed. (Grand Rapids, MI: Baker Academic, 2007), 703–5.

world, so also the preaching of the truth shines everywhere, and illumines all men who wish to come to the knowledge of truth.[12]

At the time of Constantine in the first part of the fourth century, Eusebius described the state of the Catholic Church:

> Truth asserted herself, and with the march of time shone with increasing light. For by her activity the machinations of her foes were promptly shown up and extinguished, though one after another new heresies were invented, the earlier ones constantly passing away and disappearing, in different ways at different times, into forms of every shape and character. But *the splendor of the Catholic and only true Church, always remaining the same and unchanged, grew steadily in greatness and strength, shedding on every race of Greeks and non-Greeks alike* the majestic, spotless, free, sober, pure light of her inspired citizenship and philosophy.[13]

Towards the end of the fourth century, St. Augustine recounts in his *Confessions* that before he came to faith and was baptized, the universality of the Church made such an impression on him that it enabled him to banish doubts on the immortality of the soul. He responded to the materialistic thesis that death might be the end of everything, with the reflection:

> Or does death perhaps cut off and end all care along with our bodily sense? . . . But God forbid that it should be so. It is not for nothing or any mere emptiness that the magnificence of the authority of the Christian Faith is *spread over all the world.* Such great and wonderful things would never have been wrought for us by God, if the life of the soul were ended by the death of the body.[14]

With the fall of the Roman Empire in the West in the fifth century, and the ravages of the barbarian invasions, it might have seemed as if the Catholicity of the Church would be reduced once again and limited to what remained of the Eastern Roman Empire. However, contrary to all possible expectation, the barbarian invaders were gradually converted to the Catholic faith, and Christianity was consolidated in the new Europe forming during the early Middle Ages.

Later when it seemed as if Christendom had self-destructed in the Protestant Reformation, once again the Catholic nature of the Church

---

[12] St. Irenaeus, *Against Heresies* 1.10.2, *ANF* 1:331.

[13] Eusebius, *History of the Church* 4.7, trans. G.A. Williamson (London: Penguin Books, 1989), 110.

[14] Augustine, *Confessions* 6.11.19, trans. F. J. Sheed, *The Confessions of St. Augustine* (New York: Sheed & Ward, 1943), 122.

showed herself, as Catholicism was carried to the New World, and also to the Far East through the efforts of St. Francis Xavier and many others.

Three centuries later, the French Revolution and Napoleon sought to destroy the Catholic Church, imprisoning Pius VI and Pius VII. In 1848, Pius IX had to flee from Rome to save his life. However, the Catholic Church and the papacy grew immensely in prestige and popularity precisely through these great crises. We can see the same in our time, with the immense popularity of all the popes of the twentieth century, culminating in that of John Paul II, who manifested the Catholic nature of the Church in his evangelizing activity in every part of the globe.

All Cultures Are Called to Contribute to the Catholic Church

The Catholicity of the Church does not merely concern geography. Since the Church is destined to be the Bride of the Word Incarnate, a Bride uniting in herself the contributions of all mankind, it is fitting that all the cultures and languages of the world unite in serving the Bridegroom.

The Bride of Christ is to incorporate all the valid contributions of human culture to present them to Christ and have them serve for Christ's glory, according to the words of the prophet Daniel (7:13): "All peoples, tribes, and tongues shall serve him." Or in the words of Psalm 72:10, "May the kings of Tarshish and of the isles render him tribute, may the kings of Sheba and Seba bring gifts!" The gifts and tribute that figure in these prophecies rightly refer to the cultural riches of all nations, which are called to be used for the service of the glory of God and for His *Catholic* Church.

Among the treasures of the human cultural heritage, a principal place goes to philosophy, as the queen of the human sciences. Other aspects of culture which are to serve the Church include all the arts: literature, painting, architecture, music, etc., as well as the human and empirical sciences. Indeed, everything which serves human life and enhances its dignity is called to be put in the service of the mission of the Church and is part of her dowry in the broad sense of the word.

In order for this to occur, the cultural riches of the peoples of the earth need to be purified and elevated by being engrafted into God's cultivated olive tree, which, in the metaphor used by St. Paul in Romans 11, is the new Israel. In other words, the cultural riches of the Gentiles need to be "baptized" and come to partake of the "rich sap"[15] of Israel in order to be put in the service of Christ.

---

[15] Rom 11:17.

This idea—that the cultural heritage of the peoples is to be baptized and put into the service of God in the Church—is found in the Old and New Testaments, in the Fathers of the Church, in the life of the Church through the ages, and it has been recently emphasized by the Second Vatican Council.

Catholicity of the Church and Christian Philosophy

St. Justin Martyr

The idea that the patrimony of Hellenic culture was to be put in the service of Christ was a theme developed by St. Justin Martyr in the middle of the second century. St. Justin converted to Christianity while seeking the meaning of life through philosophy. After trying various schools of classical philosophy, he encountered a Christian who introduced him to revealed truth. Nevertheless, he did not repudiate the classical wisdom which failed to completely satisfy him. On the contrary, he saw Christ as the answer to the philosopher's quest for true wisdom and Christianity as the *true philosophy*: the true wisdom. As a Christian he continued to wear the distinctive dress of a philosopher, the philosopher's *pallium*, or cloak. Christian Revelation provided the answers to the most fundamental questions that had motivated the philosopher's quest. Furthermore, St. Justin saw that all that is true in the philosophers is properly the property of the Catholic Church, for Christ is the Wisdom and Light that illumines all those who have thought truly in every culture. Since Christ is the *Logos*, which means not only "Word," but also "reason," "order," or "rationality," all that shares in right reason is rightly the patrimony of the Church of the Logos Incarnate and is a "seed of the Logos." St. Justin says: "Whatever things were rightly said among all people are the property of us Christians. For next to God we worship and love the logos."[16]

St. Clement of Alexandria

St. Clement of Alexandria (c. 150–215), the head of the catechetical school of Alexandria, continued the theme of Christ as the true philosopher, or tutor of mankind, and the Church as the school of the *true wisdom*. He even took it a step further and defended the idea that *Greek philosophy served as a kind of indirect providential preparation for the Gospel*. Just as the Old Testament prepared for the New, by which it is completed but not abrogated, likewise Greek philosophy prepared in a different way for the fullness of wisdom which comes to us in Christ,

---

[16] St. Justin, *Second Apology*, ch. 13, trans. Leslie Bernard, *Ancient Christian Writers* 56 (New York: Paulist Press, 1997), 84.

which immeasurably perfects but does not abrogate the contribution of philosophy.[17] Just as the Old Testament preparation is incorporated into Christianity, the same ought to be the case for the true and valid contributions of Greek philosophy. He writes:

> So, before the Lord's coming, philosophy was an essential guide to righteousness for the Greeks. At the present time it is a useful guide towards reverence for God. It is a kind of preliminary education for those who are trying to gather faith through demonstration. . . . God is responsible for all good things: of some, like the blessings of the Old and New Covenants, directly; of others, like the riches of philosophy, indirectly. Perhaps philosophy too was a direct gift of God to the Greeks before the Lord extended his appeal to the Greeks. For philosophy was to the Greek world what the Law was to the Hebrews, a tutor escorting them to Christ. So philosophy is a preparatory process; it opens the road for the person whom Christ brings to his final goal.[18]

Here we see the Catholic character of the Church in its ability to harmoniously incorporate and elevate all that is naturally good in the human culture of the nations, especially its highest philosophical patrimony.

Typological Interpretation of the Despoiling of the Egyptians

The Fathers of the Church defend the use of pagan philosophy and culture in the service of the Gospel by giving an allegorical interpretation of an interesting passage in Exodus 12:35–36. Just before the Exodus, Moses told the Israelites to borrow "of the Egyptians jewelry of silver and of gold, and clothing; and the Lord had given the people favor in the sight of the Egyptians, so that they let them have what they asked. Thus they despoiled the Egyptians."[19]

It is surely a strange passage. It seems as if God were commanding the Israelites to commit theft, by borrowing items that they would not

---

[17] Pope Benedict XVI has expressed a similar idea in his Regensburg Lecture of Sept. 12, 2006, no. 19: "The encounter between the Biblical message and Greek thought did not happen by chance. The vision of Saint Paul, who saw the roads to Asia barred and in a dream saw a Macedonian man plead with him: 'Come over to Macedonia and help us!' (cf. *Acts* 16:6–10) - this vision can be interpreted as a 'distillation' of the intrinsic necessity of a rapprochement between Biblical faith and Greek inquiry."

[18] Clement of Alexandria, *Stromateis*, 1.5.28, trans. John Ferguson, (Washington DC: Catholic Univ. of America Press, 1991), 41–42.

[19] This episode was also foretold in Moses' vision of the burning bush in Ex 3:21–22.

be able to return. The Fathers of the Church see in the Egyptian gold and jewelry a symbol or type of cultural goods existing outside the Church, which the members of the Church are called to appropriate and use in the service of the Church. It is neither "theft" nor corruption of the Gospel because all that is good in every culture belongs ultimately to God, its source, and should be used to give Him glory.

The Fathers of the Church applied this allegory above all to Greek philosophy, which although born outside the Church, was born from the Logos, and is thus by right the property and patrimony of the Logos Incarnate and His Church. And so it is fitting that Catholic theology use classical philosophy as a handmaid or servant.

The same can be said of other cultural treasures, such as classical literature, art and architecture, jurisprudence, the sciences and practical arts, and the noble cultural traditions of all peoples. For example, the early Christian basilicas and mosaics took from classical culture their form of expression and put it in the service of Christ. The same was done throughout the centuries. Before the Church, ancient Israel had done likewise. King Solomon took wood and craftsmen from Tyre to work on the holy Temple in Jerusalem. The adorning of the Temple was entrusted to the sculptor Huram-abi of Tyre, the son of an Israelite mother and a father from Tyre, educated in the then-famous Phoenician artistic tradition.[20]

It is part of the Catholic nature of the Church that all that is true, good, and beautiful should find a noble place in the Church: in her doctrine and in her worship. The Church is open to all that is true and has a power of absorption (through her supernatural "rich sap") such that she can receive different cultural patrimonies without losing her own identity and her own truth.

Leo XIII speaks of this allegorical interpretation of Exodus 12:35–36 in his great encyclical *Aeterni Patris* on the restoration of Christian philosophy, and particularly that of St. Thomas Aquinas. He writes:

> But it is most fitting to turn these truths, which have been discovered by the pagan sages even, to the use and purposes of revealed doctrine, in order to show that both human wisdom and the very testimony of our adversaries serve to support the Christian faith—a method which is not of recent introduction, but of established use, and has often been adopted by the holy Fathers of the Church. What is more, those venerable men . . . recognize a certain form and figure of this in the action of the Hebrews, who, when about to depart out of Egypt, were commanded to take with them the gold and silver vessels and precious robes of the

---

[20] See 1 Kgs 7:13–14; 2 Chr 2–4.

Egyptians, that by a change of use the things might be dedicated to the service of the true God which had formerly been the instruments of ignoble and superstitious rites.[21]

Alluding to this allegorical interpretation of Exodus 12:35–36, St. Gregory of Nyssa says that Christ

commands someone who "borrows" from wealthy Egyptians to receive such things as moral and natural philosophy, geometry, astronomy, dialectic, and whatever else is sought by those outside the Church, since these things will be useful when in time the divine sanctuary of mystery must be beautified with the riches of reason.

Those who treasured up for themselves such wealth handed it over to Moses as he was working on the tent of mystery, each one making his personal contribution to the construction. . . . It is possible to see this happening even now. For many bring to the Church of God their profane learning as a kind of gift: Such a man was the great Basil, who acquired the Egyptian wealth in every respect during his youth and dedicated this wealth to God for the adornment of the Church, the true tabernacle.[22]

St. Augustine likewise says:

Any statements by those who are called philosophers, especially the Platonists, which happen to be true and consistent with our faith should not cause alarm, but be claimed for our own use, as it were from owners who have no right to them. . . . Similarly all the branches of pagan learning contain not only false and superstitious fantasies and burdensome studies . . . but also studies for liberated minds which are more appropriate to the service of the truth, and some very useful moral instruction, as well as the various truths about monotheism to be found in their writers. . . .

We can see, can we not, the amount of gold, silver, and clothing with which Cyprian, that most attractive writer and most blessed martyr, was laden when he left Egypt; is not the same true of Lactantius, and Victorinus, of Optatus, and Hilary, to say nothing of people still alive, and countless Greek scholars? This is what had been done earlier by Moses himself, that most faithful

---

[21] Leo XIII, encyclical *Aeterni Patris* 4 (1879).

[22] Gregory of Nyssa, *Life of Moses* 2.112–16, *PG* 44:359, trans. Abraham Malherbe and Everett Ferguson (New York: Paulist Press, 1978), 81.

servant of God, of whom it is written that he was trained in "all the wisdom of the Egyptians."[23]

The "gold, silver, and clothing" are metaphors for the use that they made of Greek philosophy and literature.

By appropriating the treasures of non-Christian cultures, such as Greek philosophy, the Church realizes the prophecies according to which all nations would bring precious offerings to Jerusalem in the Messianic period. All nations are bringing offerings to the Church of what they have that is noble and capable of being purified and put to holy use.

This use of what is noble in other cultures serves many purposes. On the one hand, it serves God by allowing those elements to be elevated so as to be used for the glory of God. Secondly, it serves theology, philosophy, and the arts themselves, because it allows them to progress and be elevated through a harmony of faith and reason collaborating fruitfully. Third, it helps the Gospel to be profoundly accepted and incorporated as a formative element into other cultures, as happened in the Greek and Roman world of the Patristic period.

It has frequently been objected throughout the history of the Church that this "borrowing" of classical philosophy is an adulteration of the pure Gospel, a diluting of the wine of the Gospel with water (or poison). In effect, Luther held this position and raged against what he saw to be the excessive influence of Aristotle in scholastic theology. Luther's position, however, destroys the harmony between faith and reason that is one of the essential characteristics of the Catholic Church and the Catholic Tradition.

Nevertheless, when appropriating elements from other cultural patrimonies, it is necessary that critical discernment be used. One can appropriate the riches of Egypt, but not their cultural poverty or religious or philosophical error! It has always been necessary to maintain a delicate balance in this appropriation and enculturation. The purpose of this appropriation is to elevate the elements that are adopted in the service of God by imbuing them with the faith of Israel, and not to lower the service of God to the level of other cultures.

It is also instructive to see what happened to much of that gold and silver that the Israelites took out of Egypt. Within the space of a few months, it was turned into the golden calf which the Israelites made while Moses was speaking with God on Mt. Sinai. However, the problem did not lie with the treasures themselves, but in the idolatrous use which was made of them.

---

[23] Augustine, *De doctrina christiana*, 2.40.144–46, trans. R. P. H. Green (Oxford: Clarendon Press, 1995), 125–127.

A contemporary example of such an abuse would be trying to take Marxist philosophy as a handmaid of theology, and put it into the service of the Gospel, as was attempted in Liberation Theology.[24] In reality, Marxism and the Gospel are incompatible for Marxism is based on radical materialism and the postulate of the necessity of class warfare. What actually occurred in Liberation Theology was not putting Marx in the service of God, but rather putting the resources of the Church in the service of Marxism, as the Israelites put their gold in the service of an idol.

St. Thomas Aquinas

St. Thomas Aquinas is perhaps the greatest example of this type of Catholicity: imbuing the riches of "Egypt" with the faith of Israel and putting them in the service of the Church. The Thomistic synthesis took the patrimony of Aristotelian philosophy, without taking its errors, and "baptized" it by putting it in the service of the greatest and most comprehensive synthesis of Catholic theology.

This Catholic attitude is summarized in one of the great principles of Thomism: grace does not destroy nature but elevates and perfects it. St. Thomas wrote: "Since therefore grace does not destroy nature but perfects it, natural reason should minister to faith."[25] Faith, which comes from grace, does not destroy reason, or lie in opposition to it, but perfects our intellect, as grace perfects nature. Thus faith can collaborate with the perennial philosophy of mankind, as found among all nations, and use reason and man's cultural patrimony in its service.

Whereas the Protestant and heretical principle is generally *either/or*—either faith or reason—the Catholic principle is inclusive: *both/and*—both faith and reason.

Benedict XVI's Regensburg Lecture

A very different attitude toward appropriating elements from other cultural patrimonies was exhibited in Islam at various moments during its history. A paradigmatic example concerned the Muslim attitude to the great library of Alexandria after the Muslims had conquered that great city in about 640 AD. The story is told that the conquering general asked Caliph Omar for instructions on what to do with the great library, which was the greatest in the world. He is quoted as saying that the works in the library "will either contradict the Koran, in which case they

---

[24] For an explanation and critique of Liberation Theology, see the Congregation for the Doctrine of the Faith, *Instruction on Certain Aspects of the "Theology of Liberation,"* August 6, 1984.

[25] St. Thomas Aquinas, *ST* I, q. 1, a. 8, ad 2.

are heresy, or they will agree with it, so they are superfluous." So the order was given to destroy it.[26]

To be fair, this story may well be legendary, and many great works of classical antiquity were indeed preserved by the Muslims while Christian Europe was in the dark ages. Nevertheless, on the whole, the Muslim attitude towards philosophy has not had the same *catholic* character and the appreciation of the contribution of human reason and culture as that which we find in the Catholic Church.[27] On the contrary, Islam has generally been marked by a certain suspicion of human reason, which philosophers refer to as an attitude of *fideism*: rejecting the contribution of human reason with regard to the faith. The same is generally true of Protestantism.

Benedict XVI has brought this point out very courageously in his famous Regensburg lecture, in which he spoke of the danger of *fideism* (the rejection of the Catholic attitude of harmony between faith and reason) in the Islamic world, in the Protestant world, and in the modern secular world. With regard to Islam, he aroused the ire of the Islamic world by citing the comments of a Greek Byzantine emperor (Manuel II):

> "Show me just what Mohammed brought that was new, and there you will find things only evil and inhuman, such as his command to spread by the sword the faith he preached."[28] The emperor, after having expressed himself so forcefully, goes on to explain in detail the reasons why spreading the faith through violence is something unreasonable. Violence is incompatible with the nature of God and the nature of the soul. . . . "Faith is born of the soul, not the body. Whoever would lead someone to faith needs the ability to speak well and to reason properly, without violence and threats. . . . To convince a reasonable soul, one does not need a strong arm, or weapons of any kind, or any other means of threatening a person with death."[29]

Benedict comments on this as follows:

---

[26] This story comes from Bishop Gregory Bar Hebræus, and may be legendary. Another translation is: "If what is written in them agrees with the Koran, they are not required; if it disagrees, they are not desired. Destroy them therefore."

[27] Exceptions to this dominant trend in the Muslim world were the medieval Muslim philosophers Avicenna and Averroes.

[28] In the footnote of the official text, Benedict explains: "In quoting the text of the Emperor Manuel II, I intended solely to draw out the essential relationship between faith and reason. On this point I am in agreement with Manuel II, but without endorsing his polemic."

[29] Manuel II, Controversy VII, 3 b–c.

The decisive statement in this argument against violent conversion is this: not to act in accordance with reason is contrary to God's nature. . . . For the emperor, as a Byzantine shaped by Greek philosophy, this statement is self-evident. But for Muslim teaching, God is absolutely transcendent. His will is not bound up with any of our categories, even that of rationality.[30]

Such an attitude makes it impossible to offer to God what St. Paul (Rom 12:1) calls our "reasonable service" or worship.[31] Benedict goes on to quote this text: "Consequently, Christian worship is, again to quote Paul—'λογικη λατρεία,' worship in harmony with the eternal Word and with our reason." The Catholic conviction that every culture is to offer to God through the Church whatever is valid in its philosophy and culture only makes sense if one has the conviction that God is the *Logos*, the Word that is the source of all rationality, whose seeds have been scattered among all the sons of men.

After securing the attention of the world with this introduction concerning Islam, Benedict then focuses on the Catholic understanding of the harmony of faith and reason, especially as manifested by the patrimony of classical Greek philosophy. Like St. Clement of Alexandria, he sees the conjunction of Biblical faith and Greek philosophy as a providential event which was clearly part of God's plan for the entire life of the Church. He points out an interesting symbol of the providential nature of this harmony in a curious event narrated in the Acts of the Apostles (16:9–10), during St. Paul's second missionary voyage, in which the Holy Spirit barred him from speaking the Word of God in Asia Minor (Turkey) and called him to pass over into Macedonia:

And a vision appeared to Paul in the night: a man of Macedonia was standing beseeching him and saying, "Come over to Macedonia and help us." And when he had seen the vision, immediately we sought to go on into Macedonia, concluding that God had called us to preach the gospel to them.

As a result, St. Paul brought the Gospel to Greece for the first time. Benedict comments:

This vision can be interpreted as a "distillation" of the intrinsic necessity of a rapprochement between Biblical faith and Greek

---

[30] Benedict XVI, Regensburg Lecture, September 12, 2006.

[31] Douay-Rheims translation. The Neo-Vulgate has: "*rationabile obsequium vestrum.*" The RSV translates this difficult text rather inadequately as "spiritual worship."

inquiry. . . . *This inner rapprochement between Biblical faith and Greek philosophical inquiry was an event of decisive importance* not only from the standpoint of the history of religions, but also from that of world history—it is an event which concerns us even today. Given this convergence, it is not surprising that Christianity, despite its origins and some significant developments in the East, finally took on its historically decisive character in Europe. We can also express this the other way around: this convergence, with the subsequent addition of the Roman heritage, created Europe and remains the foundation of what can rightly be called Europe.

The thesis that the critically purified Greek heritage forms an integral part of Christian faith has been countered by the call for a dehellenization of Christianity—a call which has more and more dominated theological discussions since the beginning of the modern age.[32]

Benedict goes on to critique the attempt to de-hellenize Christianity. In effect, such an attempt to de-hellenize Christianity would paradoxically take away its truly *Catholic* character. The Church is Catholic by its openness to reason as such, wherever it is found functioning uprightly. For the supernatural faith of the Church is the true answer to the philosopher's quest for the full meaning of life. Thus the Church is called to be the Bride of the *Logos*, a Bride comprising all the nations and cultural patrimony of the earth.

Through God's providence, the Church has grown from the engrafting of the patrimony of Greek philosophy and its respect for reason, inserted into the cultivated olive tree of Israel's Biblical faith. As John Paul II stated at the beginning of his encyclical *Fides et ratio*, faith and reason are the two wings by which the mind ascends to God. The catholicity of the Church and her continual expansion in history are rooted in her respect for both of these wings.

---

[32] Benedict XVI, Regensburg Lecture (my italics).

CHAPTER 5

The Church Is One

Why Should the Church Be One?

Today it is fashionable and politically correct to celebrate pluralism and diversity. Why should the Church be one? Why would God not want there to be many churches and religions? Why is the oneness of the Church a mark of the true Church founded by Jesus Christ?

Within the one body of the Church there is room for great diversity, as we have seen in the last chapter concerning the mark of Catholicity. But diversity is not the same as division. What the unity of the Church precludes is division, not diversity. The supernatural society, in which Catholic diversity is to be contained, must be one in order to unite men with God and with one another.

Simply from the natural point of view, it is easy to see that division is an evil, and goes together with corruption, death, and war. At death the different parts of an individual lose their unity and come apart: the soul separates from the body, and the different parts *de-compose*. A corpse is not really one being anymore, but a pile of decomposing organic parts. The soul gives unity just as it gives life. Unity is a consequence of being and life. But a house divided will fall, as Jesus says.

Just as a living animal seeks to avoid division and to maintain the unity of its bodily life, so human societies seek to avoid division and maintain unity. Unity in a society is a sign of its life, just as unity in the body is a sign of health. Nevertheless, this social unity presupposes diversity of members, just as we find in an animal body. However, social health and wellbeing mean that the different members are bound together in union by having one final end, as in a living animal body. The bond of union in society is charity, just as the cause of division is pride and the hatred it engenders.

If we look at the origin of the division of nations, languages, and cultures, we find that it is the consequence of sin: the sin of pride. This is the great lesson of Babel. As death divides a living being, so pride divides societies into warring and dissident factions.

However, even human pride seeks unity in society, but under one's own domination (uniting all under love of self). Thus every country would like to make itself a universal empire (which, of course, is a major source of war). Civil war is always considered by everyone to be the greatest of disasters. This shows us that there is a natural desire for social union, just as there is for happiness, life, and health.

Human happiness can only lie in society, and that social happiness can only lie in social union: a union of diverse members complementing each other in harmony through charity.

The family is the great natural model for the Church, and it is very easy to see that union in the family is the greatest of blessings, and division within the family is a terrible tragedy. The union of the family does not preclude diversity and complementarity, but rather presupposes it. What it precludes is division and schism.

Ancient Israel was formed by God to be one spiritual kingdom. The religious separation of the ten northern tribes after the death of Solomon was a great calamity, constantly denounced by the prophets, which ended with the deportation of the ten northern tribes and their disappearance as a people.

Leaving aside these analogies, the ultimate reason for the oneness of the Church comes from her end, or purpose. God entered into human history in order to bring men into union with Him and, through that, into union with one another in a supernatural society which is to culminate in the heavenly communion of saints: the Church triumphant.

This is made clear above all in Christ's priestly prayer after the Last Supper (Jn 17:11, 20–23), in which He prayed to the Father:

> And now I am no more in the world, but they are in the world, and I am coming to thee. Holy Father, keep them in thy name, which thou hast given me, *that they may be one, even as we are one.* . . . I do not pray for these only, but also for those who believe in me through their word, that they may all be one; even as thou, Father, art in me, and I in thee, that they also may be in us, *so that the world may believe that thou hast sent me.* The glory which thou hast given me I have given to them, *that they may be one even as we are one, I in them and thou in me, that they may become perfectly one, so that the world may know that thou hast sent me and hast loved them even as thou hast loved me.*

Christ prays for unity among His disciples for four principal reasons. The first reason is that the Church is founded to participate in the communion of the Blessed Trinity. Therefore Christ prays that the members of the Church be one, as He is one with the Father. We are to be one so as to be brought into the communion of the divine life and to have that intra-Trinitarian communion "extended" and glorified by our participation in it.

We cannot participate in the intra-Trinitarian communion in a purely individualistic way, each man separately from others. That would be contradictory! *We can enter the divine communion only in communion* with one another and with Christ, the Mediator between man and God. Our entrance into the divine communion is to be a glorification of that communion by extending it to the human community elevated to the order of grace. Just as there is no strife in the divine intra-Trinitarian communion, so *no strife can enter into it with us, but all must be made one so as to enter into the perfect union* that is the divine life.

Secondly, the divine life consists in charity, for God is Love. But charity is the bond of unity and oneness. Where charity reigns, division can find no place (although diversity and complementarity are most welcome). The Church is the kingdom of charity, and so it must be one. As Christ says, "that the love with which you have loved me may be in them, and I in them" (Jn 17:26).

Third, the Church lives the life of Christ and thinks with the mind of Christ according to His Revelation, and Christ is one. Therefore the Church must be one to continue Christ's life. It would be monstrous to think that Christ's life could be perfectly lived and manifested by thousands of divided religious bodies in strife.

Fourth, the Church must be one *as a sign* to the rest of the world that she is a supernatural society founded by God to share in the divine intra-Trinitarian communion and live the life of Christ, as His Mystical Body. We can see in Jesus' priestly prayer that the oneness of the Church is *the sign* that she is His Mystical Body.

The oneness of the Church can function as a sign of her supernatural origin because the human tendency, after the Fall, is division and schism on account of pride. A society that maintains its living unity over a significant time—for two millennia—clearly transcends the limitations of fallen human nature left to itself. A sobering example is the division of the Protestant world in the wake of the Reformation, which has become divided into some 10,000 different ecclesial communities which disagree on essential points of doctrine, worship, and government.

The Unity of the Church Prophesied and Prefigured in the Old Testament

The unity of the Messianic Kingdom is shown in two ways in ancient Israel: through prophecy and through the figure of the Temple. The prophecies of the Messianic Kingdom examined in chapter two speak of the Kingdom as having one head and one flock. In Daniel 2:34–35, King Nebuchadnezzar has a dream about a statue made of gold, silver, bronze, and iron, which is shattered by a stone not cut by human hands, which grows into a mountain filling the whole earth. Daniel interprets this dream as signifying four world empires which succeed one another. However, in the time of the fourth world empire, a new supernatural kingdom (not formed by human hands)—the Messianic kingdom—will appear (Dan 2:44–45). The earthly kingdoms are many, and they rise and fall. The Messianic Kingdom is one kingdom whose unity and identity shall never be destroyed, but which shall grow continually throughout human history. This prophecy clearly corresponds to the reality of the Catholic Church.

Furthermore, the unity of the Messianic Kingdom is clearly seen in the fact that the Messiah is to rule over His Kingdom forever, as David ruled over all Israel. The prophet Ezekiel speaks of this in Ezekiel 34:23: "And I will set up over them one shepherd, my servant David, and he shall feed them: he shall feed them and be their shepherd."

He returns to this theme in Ezekiel 37:21–28:

> Thus says the Lord God: Behold, I will take the people of Israel from the nations among which they have gone, and will gather them from all sides, and bring them to their own land; and I will make them *one nation* in the land, upon the mountains of Israel; and *one king shall be king over them all*; and they shall be no longer two nations, and *no longer divided into two kingdoms.* . . . My servant *David shall be king over them; and they shall all have one shepherd.* They shall follow my ordinances and be careful to observe my statutes. . . . *David my servant shall be their prince for ever.* I will make a covenant of peace with them; it shall be an everlasting covenant with them; and I will bless them and multiply them, and will *set my sanctuary in the midst of them for evermore.* My dwelling place shall be with them; and I will be their God, and they shall be my people. Then the nations will know that I the Lord sanctify Israel, when my sanctuary is in the midst of them for evermore.

In the Catholic Tradition, this text is interpreted as a prophecy of the Messianic Kingdom, which is the Church. This Kingdom shall be one, led by one king. The king, spoken of as David, is Christ the son of David, who reigns forever through His vicars on earth. This Kingdom will no longer be divided into two kingdoms, as Israel unfortunately had been.

The one sanctuary that the Lord promises to put in their midst "for evermore" refers to the Eucharist, by which the presence of God made man is perpetuated on earth in every Holy Mass and in every tabernacle where a consecrated host is kept.

The unity of the Church's sacrifice was prefigured in the Mosaic Law which stipulated that all sacrifice was to be done in the Temple in Jerusalem. This commandment, on the one hand, was a great difficulty for the Jewish people, requiring them to travel to Jerusalem three times a year. After the destruction of the Temple in 70 AD, this commandment meant that the entire sacrificial system of Mosaic Judaism could no longer be observed.

Why did God command that all sacrifice had to be offered in the Temple? First of all, it was a visible symbol of the unity that God wanted in His liturgy. Secondly, it helped preserve the unity of faith and worship in Israel, since all sacrifice was offered in one place under the oversight of the High Priest. Beyond these reasons, however, the precept that all sacrifice had to be offered in the Temple was a great symbol prefiguring the unity of worship in the New Covenant.

Although sacrifice is offered everywhere in the Catholic world, from the rising of the sun to its setting,[1] nevertheless, the worship of the Church is even more unified than that of Israel. Everywhere in the Catholic Church, *one and the same sacrifice*—the sacrifice of Calvary—is offered until the end of time in the Holy Mass. In Israel, many animal sacrifices were offered in only one place (the Temple), whereas in the Church, one and the same sacrifice is offered in every place under the sun.

Unity of the Church in the Teaching of Christ and the Apostles

Whenever Christ speaks about the Church, the mark of unity is always central. The most important text is Matthew 16:18–19: "And I tell you, you are Peter, and on this rock I will build my Church, and the powers of death shall not prevail against it. I will give you the keys of the kingdom of heaven, and whatever you bind on earth shall be bound in heaven, and whatever you loose on earth shall be loosed in heaven."

Christ said that He would found His Church on the rock of Peter, and not His "churches." The Church is to be one in that it is built on one rock—Peter—who has the ministry of unity in the Church. Peter and his successors in the episcopate are the supernatural means instituted by Christ for maintaining the supernatural life and unity of the Church.[2] The promise that the gates of hell, or the powers of death, will not prevail against it means that the supernatural life of the society of

---

[1] See Mal 1:11: "For from the rising of the sun to its setting my name is great among the nations, and in every place incense is offered to my name, and a pure offering; for my name is great among the nations, says the Lord of hosts."

[2] Apostolic succession is a supernatural means for maintaining unity because it is based on the grace of the sacrament of Holy Orders and Christ's promise of assistance.

the Church will never be lost through corruption and division, as happens in other social bodies.

If we look at the other times in which Christ speaks of His future Church, we always see the mark of unity. For example, when He later entrusts the actual primacy to Peter after the Resurrection by the Sea of Galilee (Jn 21:15–17), He tells Peter three times: "Feed my sheep." *All* of His sheep are entrusted to Peter. He does not tell Peter to feed his *portion* of the flock, but *all* of Christ's sheep. The clear implication is that if someone is not under the custody of Peter as shepherd of the Lord's flock, he is not one of the Lord's sheep, for the whole flock has been entrusted to Peter.

Furthermore, the parables of Christ all speak of the Church as one body which expands in time, like the mustard seed which grows into a tree where all the birds may come to perch; and as one Kingdom, the Kingdom of God, which is always spoken of in the singular. Christ never proclaimed the kingdom*s* of God, but one Kingdom which was at hand.

Finally, the oneness of the Church in the intention of Christ is perfectly clear from the fact that He formed one college of Apostles to be the foundation of the Church. If He had simply preached the Gospel throughout Israel without forming a unified college of Apostles under one head, which is Peter, then the Church would not have been able to be one after His death. Yet the Gospels show us that the principal concern of Jesus in His public ministry was precisely in forming the Apostles, who shared most intimately in His life and teaching for three years.

The Acts of the Apostles gives a beautiful witness to the unity of the Church beginning with Pentecost. Here we see a unity under the leadership of the Apostles, in faith, sacraments and prayer, government, and charity. In Acts 4:32–33 we read:

> Now the company of those who believed were of *one heart and soul,* and no one said that any of the things which he possessed was his own, but they had everything in common. And with great power the apostles gave their testimony to the resurrection of the Lord Jesus, and great grace was upon them all.[3]

Unity in the primitive Church was so great that it extended to the economic sphere in charity. The source of this unity is clearly shown to be unity in faith, founded on the witness and teaching of the Apostles.

---

[3] See also Acts 2:42–44.

St. Paul speaks of the unity of the Church in many places. In 1 Corinthians 1:11–13, he speaks of the report that has reached him of factions in the church at Corinth:

> For it has been reported to me by Chloe's people that there is quarreling among you, my brethren. What I mean is that each one of you says, "I belong to Paul," or "I belong to Apollos," or "I belong to Cephas," or "I belong to Christ." Is Christ divided?

The gravity of schism can be seen from the fact that it is the first of the many problems that he addresses in the church in Corinth. Since schism strikes against the unity of Christ's Mystical Body, it is radically incompatible with the life of the Church.

In Ephesians 4:4–6, St. Paul exhorts Christians to ecclesial unity on the foundation of the unity of God: "There is one body and one Spirit, just as you were called to the one hope that belongs to your call, one Lord, one faith, one baptism, one God and Father of us all, who is above all and through all and in all."

In What Sense Is the Church One?

In what sense do Catholics understand this unity in the Church? It is not a unity in any natural sense, based on sentiment, ethnicity, temporal government, etc. Indeed, the Church is full of diversity: of states of life (priesthood, consecrated life, the lay state), rites, languages, cultures, nations, liturgical practices, religious families, artistic styles, and legitimate differences of opinion in all kinds of matters, etc.

The unity of the Church is understood in three fundamental aspects: the Church is one in faith and doctrine (prophetic office), in sacraments (priestly office), and in government (kingly office). In addition, there is the unity in charity which is the very life of the Church, and which the unity in faith, worship, and government serve to maintain and nourish.

The Credo of the People of God promulgated by Paul VI in 1968 states:

> We believe that the Church founded by Jesus Christ and for which He prayed is indefectibly one in faith, worship and the bond of hierarchical communion. In the bosom of this Church, the rich variety of liturgical rites and the legitimate diversity of theological and spiritual heritages and special disciplines, far from injuring her unity, make it more manifest.

As will be seen more fully in the following chapter, the unity of the Catholic Church in faith, worship, and government is maintained by the office of St. Peter and his successors. The Church is one in government through the supreme authority of the successor of St. Peter over the whole Church. The Church is one in her liturgical practice, insofar as it is the task of the successors of St. Peter to have the supreme regulatory power over the sacraments and liturgy of the Church. Finally, the Church is one in doctrine on essential matters through the exercise of the infallibility of the successor of Peter, and of the bishops in communion with him.

Unity in Faith

This unity in doctrine is to be understood in two dimensions: throughout the world and throughout history. The Catholic Church holds the same doctrine today throughout the world because the faith of the universal Church is determined and defined by one head: the Vicar of Christ, the Pope.

Already at the end of the second century St. Irenaeus spoke of the unity of the faith of the Church throughout the world:

Having received this preaching and this faith, as I have said, the Church, although scattered in the whole world, carefully preserves it, as if living in one house. She believes these things [everywhere] alike, as if she had but one heart and one soul, and preaches them harmoniously, teaches them, and hands them down, as if she had but one mouth. For the languages of the world are different, but the meaning of the tradition is one and the same. Neither do the Churches that have been established in Germany believe otherwise, or hand down any other tradition, nor those among the Iberians, nor those among the Celts, nor in Egypt, nor in Libya, nor those established in the middle parts of the world. But as God's creature, the sun, is one and the same in the whole world, so also the preaching of the truth shines everywhere, and illumines all men who wish to come to the knowledge of truth. . . . For since the faith is one and the same, he who can say much about it does not add to it, nor does he who can say little diminish it.[4]

Later in the same work he writes: "The preaching of the Church is true and steadfast, in which one and the same way of salvation is shown throughout the whole world. For to her is entrusted the light of God.... For the Church preaches the truth everywhere, and she is the seven-branched candlestick which bears the light of Christ."[5]

St. Cyprian also gives beautiful witness to the unity of the Church in the middle of the third century:

---

[4] St. Irenaeus, *Against Heresies* 1.10.2, *ANF* 1:331.
[5] St. Irenaeus, *Against Heresies* 5.20, *ANF* 1:548.

So too the Church glowing with the Lord's light extends her rays over the whole world; but it is one and the same light which is spread everywhere, and the unity of her body suffers no division. She spreads her branches in generous growth over all the earth, she extends her abundant streams ever further; yet one is the head-spring, one the source, one the mother who is prolific in her offspring, generation after generation: of her womb we are born, of her milk we are fed, from her Spirit our souls draw their life-breath.[6]

The same, of course, can be said today. The Catholic faith is the same in Germany, China, Argentina, etc., because the Magisterium of the Church is universal and binds all faithful Catholics, no matter where. A powerful witness of this unity of faith is given in the World Youth Days, in which youth from all over the world experience their oneness in faith and communion with the successor of Peter.

At the beginning of the third century, St. Clement of Alexandria said:

Unity is a characteristic of the true, the really ancient Church, into which those that are righteous according to the divine purpose are enrolled. For God being one and the Lord being one, that also which is supremely honored is the object of praise because it stands alone, being a copy of the one First Principle. At any rate the one Church, which they strive to break up into many sects, is bound up with the principle of Unity. We say, then, that the ancient and Catholic Church stands alone in essence and idea and principle and pre-eminence. . . . And further, the pre-eminence of the Church, like the principle of its constitution, is in accordance with the Monad, surpassing all other things and having nothing like or equal to itself.[7]

The unity of the Catholic faith can also be affirmed in the temporal or historical sense. The Catholic Church holds the same doctrine today as it did throughout history in all essential points that have been infallibly defined. The Church teaches infallibly when the Pope, or an ecumenical council approved by the Pope, speaking as universal Pastor and Successor of the Apostles, defines that a doctrine concerning faith

---

[6] St. Cyprian, *On the Unity of the Church* 5, trans. Maurice Bévenot, in *De Lapsis and De Ecclesiae Catholicae Unitate* (Oxford: At the Clarendon Press, 1971), 67.

[7] Clement of Alexandria, *Stromateis* 7.17, trans. By J. B. Mayor, in *Alexandrian Christianity: Selected Translations of Clement and Origen*, ed. John Oulton and Henry Chadwick (Philadelphia: Westminster Press, 1954), 163.

and morals is to be firmly and definitively held by the universal Church.[8] Such definitive teachings are valid for all time and can never be overturned, thus ensuring unity of doctrine throughout history.

Without an infallible teaching office, it would be impossible in practice for the Church to maintain the unity of faith through time. We can see this in the doctrinal differences that we find in other religious bodies, especially in the Protestant world, but equally in Reform Judaism and in Islam. It follows that only a Church endowed with infallibility could possibly maintain its unity in doctrine over time. The Catholic claim to have an infallible teaching office, which is such a scandal to the secular world and to non-Catholics, is actually a great sign of the Church's divine origin.

The unity of the faith of the Church over time can be historically verified. If someone wishes to show that the Church has not maintained her unity in faith over the centuries, all they would have to do is show one doctrine concerning faith and morals that was definitively taught and then contradicted by a later teaching that was also presented as definitive and hence infallible. If the Church were to reverse an infallible teaching, then she could not be said to have maintained the same faith through time, and she would not be *one* in the full sense of the word.

Church Teaching on Contraception

A good example of unity in faith over time is given by the Church's constant teaching on the immorality of contraception, despite great pressures to change caused by the sexual revolution in Western society. In 1968, Pope Paul VI surprised the world by re-affirming this teaching in his encyclical *Humanae vitae*, despite expectations, fed by the media, that the Church would change her traditional teaching.

The Catholic doctrine on the illicitness of contraception goes back to Genesis 38:6–10,[9] in which God struck down Onan for spilling his seed on the ground. Onan's motivation in practicing contraception was

---

[8] See Vatican II, *Lumen gentium* 25; *CCC* 891: "The Roman Pontiff, head of the college of bishops, enjoys this infallibility in virtue of his office, when, as supreme pastor and teacher of all the faithful—who confirms his brethren in the faith—he proclaims by a definitive act a doctrine pertaining to faith or morals."

[9] Gen 38:6–10: "And Judah took a wife for Er his first-born, and her name was Tamar. But Er, Judah's first-born, was wicked in the sight of the Lord; and the Lord slew him. Then Judah said to Onan, 'Go in to your brother's wife, and perform the duty of a brother-in-law to her, and raise up offspring for your brother.' But Onan knew that the offspring would not be his; so when he went in to his brother's wife he spilled the semen on the ground, lest he should give offspring to his brother. And what he did was displeasing in the sight of the Lord, and he slew him also."

to avoid the Levirate duty of raising up offspring for his brother.[10] Nevertheless, it seems that the gravity of his act did not lie so much in his lack of charity for his brother's remembrance (for there was a legal provision for opting out of a Levirate marriage), as in his profanation of the conjugal act by contraception, which was said to be "displeasing in the sight of the Lord." The Talmud refers to contraception in general as the "deadly sin of Onan."[11]

From the first centuries of the Church,[12] contraception was condemned as gravely immoral. The first time a major Christian body dissented from the traditional teaching on contraception occurred in the Anglican Church's Lambeth Conference of 1930. In response, Pope Pius XI clearly and strongly reaffirmed the traditional position in his encyclical *Casti connubii*:

> Since, therefore, openly departing from the uninterrupted Christian tradition some recently have judged it possible solemnly to declare another doctrine regarding this question, the Catholic Church, to whom God has entrusted the defense of the integrity and purity of morals, standing erect in the midst of the moral ruin which surrounds her, in order that she may preserve the chastity of the nuptial union from being defiled by this foul stain, raises her voice in token of her *divine ambassadorship* and through Our mouth proclaims anew: any use whatsoever of matrimony exercised in such a way that the act is deliberately frustrated in its natural power to generate life is an offense against the law of God and of nature, and those who indulge in such are branded with the guilt of a grave sin.[13]

Pius XII saw the teaching of Pius XI in *Casti connubii* to be a solemn and definitive teaching. In his important Address to Italian Midwives of 1951, he stated:

---

[10] See Deut 25:5–6.

[11] See Tractate Niddah 13a, quoting rabbi Johanan ben Nappaha.

[12] See John T. Noonan, Jr., *Contraception: A History of Its Treatment by the Catholic Theologians and Canonists* (Cambridge, MA: Belknap Press of Harvard University Press, 1986). The Didache, from the late first century, probably alludes to contraception (under the term "magic" and/or "drugs") as a grave sin. See also John Hardon, S.J., "The Catholic Tradition on the Morality of Contraception," available online at www.therealpresence.org/archives/Abortion_Euthanasia/ Abortion_Euthanasia_004.htm. He writes: "These terms (*mageia*) and (*pharmaka*) were understood to cover the use of magical rites and/or medical potions for both contraception and abortion. Moreover, the context in the *Didache* refers to sex activity and the right to life."

[13] Pius XI, *Casti connubii* (1930), n. 56.

Our Predecessor, Pius XI, of happy memory, in his Encyclical *Casti Connubii*, of December 31, 1930, once again *solemnly proclaimed* the fundamental law of the conjugal act and conjugal relations. . . . This precept is in full force today, as it was in the past, and so it will be in the future also, and always, because it is not a simple human whim, but the expression of a natural and divine law.[14]

After the appearance of the birth control pill in the 1950's, John XXIII formed an advisory commission to study it, and this commission was broadened by Paul VI in preparation for the encyclical he was preparing on this issue.[15] The commission split into two quite opposed tendencies. Preparatory documents of the commission were leaked to the press in 1966 and were published by the National Catholic Reporter before the publication of the encyclical.[16]

The so-called "Minority Report" urged that the traditional teaching of the Church, as enunciated in *Casti connubii*, is an expression of the ordinary and universal Magisterium of the Church, which cannot lead the faithful astray in matters pertaining to eternal salvation.[17]

---

[14] Pius XII, Address to Italian Midwives, October 29, 1951 (my italics).

[15] See Paul VI, *Humanae vitae* 5: "The consciousness of the same responsibility induced Us to confirm and expand the commission set up by Our predecessor Pope John XXIII, of happy memory, in March, 1963. This commission included married couples as well as many experts in the various fields pertinent to these questions. Its task was to examine views and opinions concerning married life, and especially on the correct regulation of births; and it was also to provide the teaching authority of the Church with such evidence as would enable it to give an apt reply in this matter, which not only the faithful but also the rest of the world were waiting for."

[16] These documents are available in *The Birth Control Debate*, ed. Robert G. Hoyt (Kansas City, MO: National Catholic Reporter, 1968).

[17] See *The Birth Control Debate*, 37–38: "The Church cannot change her answer *because this answer is true*. Whatever may pertain to a more perfect formulation of the teaching or its possible genuine development, the teaching itself cannot not be substantially true. It is true because the Catholic Church, instituted by Christ to show men a secure way to eternal life, could not have so wrongly erred during all those centuries of its history. The Church cannot substantially err in teaching doctrine which is most serious in its import for faith and morals, through all centuries or even one century, if it has been constantly and forcefully proposed as necessarily to be followed in order to obtain eternal salvation. The Church could not have erred through so many centuries, even through one century, by imposing under serious obligation very grave burdens in the name of Jesus Christ, if Jesus Christ did not actually impose these burdens. The Catholic Church could not have furnished in the name of Jesus Christ to so many of the faithful everywhere in the world, through so many centuries, the occasion for formal sin and spiritual ruin, because of a false doctrine promulgated in the name of Jesus Christ. If the Church could err in such a way, the authority of the ordinary magisterium in moral matters

The "Majority Report" of the Commission, on the contrary, favored a change in the teaching of the Church, by proposing a new way of evaluating the morality of contraceptive acts and introducing a proportionalist analysis. They argued that the conjugal acts of married couples should be looked upon as a totality, and not singly. As long as the totality of the conjugal acts were not completely closed to life, they reasoned, the totality of those acts would not lose their moral dignity. Thus even if a couple contracepted 99% of the time, their conjugal life would not thereby be disordered, thanks to the 1% of time not contracepting.[18]

If Paul VI had followed the Majority Report, the mark of oneness of the faith of the Church through time would have been gravely compromised. One can argue, as did the theologians who wrote the Minority Report, that the teaching contained in *Humanae vitae* had already been infallibly taught by the Church in her *ordinary and universal Magisterium*.[19] When a particular doctrine is taught in a definitive and continuous way over time by the bishops of the world dispersed in their dioceses together with the Holy Father, then such a doctrine is held to be infallible.[20] In *Humanae vitae*, Paul VI emphasized various times that the teaching on the illicitness of contraception, which he decisively reaffirmed, was the "constant doctrine" of the Church, implying that it

---

would be thrown into question. The faithful could not put their trust in the magisterium's presentation of moral teaching, especially in sexual matters."

[18] In *Humanae vitae* 6, Paul VI states that he could not follow the conclusions of the Commission, both because they were irreconcilably divided among themselves, and because "certain criteria of solutions had emerged which departed from the moral teaching on marriage proposed with constant firmness by the teaching authority of the Church." Paul VI responded to the conclusions of the Majority Report in *Humanae vitae* 14: "Though it is true that sometimes it is lawful to tolerate a lesser moral evil in order to avoid a greater evil or in order to promote a greater good, it is never lawful, even for the gravest reasons, to do evil that good may come of it (see Rom 3:8)—in other words, to intend directly something which of its very nature contradicts the moral order, and which must therefore be judged unworthy of man, even though the intention is to protect or promote the welfare of an individual, of a family or of society in general. Consequently, it is a serious error to think that a whole married life of otherwise normal relations can justify sexual intercourse which is deliberately contraceptive and so intrinsically wrong."

[19] See Ermenegildo Lio, *Humanae vitae e infallibilità: Paolo VI, il Concilio e Giovanni Paolo II* (Città del Vaticano: Libreria editrice vaticana, 1986).

[20] See *Lumen gentium* 25: "They [the bishops] nevertheless proclaim Christ's doctrine infallibly whenever, even though dispersed through the world, but still maintaining the bond of communion among themselves and with the successor of Peter, and authentically teaching matters of faith and morals, they are in agreement on one position as definitively to be held."

already belonged to the ordinary and universal Magisterium of the Church.[21]

Humanae vitae is thus a beautiful testimony to the unity of faith in the Church over centuries, despite great opposition from the spirit of the world.[22] The Protestant world's change on this issue, as at the Lambeth Conference, on the other hand, is another clear sign of its lack of the mark of oneness.

Unity in Government

The second fundamental form of union in the Church is in government. Here too this oneness must be understood throughout history. The oneness of the Church in government means that the Church is one in the communion of bishops united with the successor of Peter, from the present back to her beginning at Pentecost. This communion of bishops with the successor of Peter is something visible and historically verifiable.

The Acts of the Apostles shows us a Church united around a visible principle of unity and authority: the college of Apostles with Peter at its head. Peter and the Apostles exercise authority over doctrine, discipline, and the sacramental life focusing on the "breaking of bread."[23]

As we have seen in chapter one, the letters of St. Ignatius of Antioch show us that the same hierarchical structure of the Church that we are familiar with today was already firmly established in the year 107 AD, less than a century after the crucifixion. St. Ignatius returns again and again in his letters to the theme of the unity of the Church, which is sacramentally founded on the Church's hierarchical structure, with one bishop in each diocese presiding over a college of presbyters and deacons dedicated to the works of charity. This is very valuable evidence that by the year 107 AD the hierarchical structure of the Church had exactly the same basic form that we know today.

---

[21] *Humanae vitae* 11: "The Church, nevertheless, in urging men to the observance of the precepts of the natural law, which it interprets by its *constant doctrine*, teaches that each and every marital act must of necessity retain its intrinsic relationship to the procreation of human life." (My italics.) Other passages that imply the definitive and constant nature of this teaching include *Humanae vitae* 4, 6, 10, 12, 20, 31. *Humanae vitae* 20 states that this teaching is "a promulgation of the divine law itself" and *HV* 31 speaks of "the unshakable teaching of the Church" (trans. Janet Smith, in *Humanae Vitae: A Generation Later* [Washington DC: Catholic Univ. of America Press, 1991], 288, 294).

[22] For an excellent discussion of *Humanae vitae*, see Janet Smith, *Humanae Vitae: A Generation Later*, and Janet Smith, ed., *Why Humanae Vitae Was Right: A Reader* (San Francisco: Ignatius Press, 1993).

[23] See Acts 2:42, 46.

In view of this 2,000-year stability in government and hierarchical structure, the First Vatican Council says, "Even the Church herself, because of her catholic unity and invincible stability, is a very great and perpetual motive of credibility and an incontestable witness of her own divine mission."[24] This unity in government will be the focus in the next chapter on the mark of apostolicity.

Unity in Sacraments

The unity of the Church, finally, is manifested in the unity of the sacraments, which have structured the Church in the same way from the beginning. The Church is what she is because of the sacraments. Indeed, the Church Fathers speak of the Church as being born from the pierced side of Christ on the Cross, from which poured water and blood. The water is a figure of Baptism, and the blood a figure of the Eucharist.

All seven sacraments by which the Church is formed, gathered, and sanctified were instituted directly by Christ and promulgated either by Christ in person or by the Apostles, as witnessed in Scripture. Baptism was explained to Nicodemus (Jn 3:1–6) and promulgated before Christ's Ascension in Matthew 28:19: "Go therefore and make disciples of all nations, baptizing them in the name of the Father and of the Son and of the Holy Spirit." Confirmation was first given on Pentecost, and we see it administered by the Apostles Peter and John in Acts 8:14–17 and by St. Paul in Acts 19:6. The Eucharist was explained in the synagogue of Capernaum after the miracle of the multiplication of the loaves and fish (Jn 6), and was formally instituted in the Last Supper. Penance was instituted on Easter Sunday, as we read in John 20:22–23: "He breathed on them, and said to them, 'Receive the Holy Spirit. If you forgive the sins of any, they are forgiven; if you retain the sins of any, they are retained.'"[25] The anointing of the sick, although it must have been instituted by Christ, is promulgated in James 5:14–16. Matrimony was raised to a sacrament by Christ, and we see it promulgated by St. Paul in Ephesians 5:31–32. Holy Orders, finally, was instituted during the Last Supper, when Jesus said, "Do this in memory of me." The entire life of the Church has been structured by the seven sacraments since Pentecost.

---

[24] Vatican I, Constitution *De fide catholica*, ch. 3, DS 3013 (D 1794).

[25] It is true that certain modes by which the sacrament has been administered have varied, for in the early Church there was a practice of giving severe public penance for very grave sins, which is no longer done. Nevertheless, the essence of the sacrament is the same throughout the centuries.

The Protestant World Lacks the Mark of Unity

Now let us look at non-Catholic Christian denominations, to see whether they have the mark of unity. The Protestant world, taken as a whole, manifestly lacks the mark of unity in all three aspects that we have been considering. There is no unity of government, for each sect governs itself. For the same reason there is no unity of sacramental or liturgical practice, nor of doctrine. Every Protestant denomination has a different conception of essential doctrine. Precisely for this reason, the Protestant world is composed of so many denominations or sects, numbering today some 10,000. This is an inevitable consequence of Luther's notion of private judgment, and the negation of papal authority to define doctrine.[26]

Even with regard to one particular article of Christian faith, such as the Eucharist, the number of significantly differing Protestant interpretations is enormous. Among the original leaders of the Protestant revolt, Luther, Zwingli, Calvin, the Anabaptists, Melanchthon, all had different interpretations of the four words of Christ: "This is my body." A sixteenth-century author wrote a book on these various rival Protestant interpretations, which he numbered already at some 200![27] Complaining of the deep dissensions among the early Protestants, Calvin wrote to Melanchthon:

> For you see how the eyes of many are turned upon us, so that the wicked take occasion from our dissensions to speak evil, and the weak are only perplexed by our unintelligible disputations. Nor, in truth, is it of little importance to prevent the suspicion of any difference having arisen between us from being handed down in any way to posterity; for it is worse than absurd that parties should

---

[26] The notion of private judgment of Scripture is implied in Luther's negation of the binding character of solemn magisterial teachings. Luther first took this step in a public dispute with the Catholic theologian Johann Eck in 1519. In this dispute, Luther was forced to affirm that ecumenical Councils could err and actually erred in the condemnation of John Huss (condemned by the Council of Constance in 1415). Eck responded that if ecumenical councils were subject to error, than there could no longer be any certainty on any point of faith.

[27] Christopher Rasperger, *Ducentæ verborum, 'Hoc est corpus meum' interpretationes* (Ingolstadt, 1577). The great French orator J.-B. Bossuet wrote a fascinating book entitled *History of the Variations of Protestant Churches* (Fraser, MI: American Council on Economics and Society, 1997), which seeks to show the great variations in matters of dogma among the Protestants in the course of the sixteenth century alone.

be found disagreeing on the very principles, after we have been compelled to divide ourselves from the rest of the world.[28]

Perhaps someone will say that the individual Protestant denominations have the mark of unity, even if the collection of Protestant denominations does not have it. An examination of each denomination disproves the claim. It is evident from a study of the history of Anglicanism, for example, that there has never been any true doctrinal unity in the Anglican Church. The same could be said for the other denominations and sects, such as the Mormons and the Jehovah's Witnesses. The doctrine of the Jehovah's Witnesses on the date of the end of the world has repeatedly changed, as their "prophecies" have failed to be realized. Charles Taze Russell first set the date at 1874, but after this failed to be realized, it was changed to 1914. Joseph Franklin Rutherford, Russell's successor, predicted that Abraham, Isaac, and Jacob would return physically to earth in 1925, and prepared a luxurious house for them, in which he lived in the meantime. The date for the end of the world was then set at 1975. When this third prophecy was not realized, a large number of members left the Witnesses. Of course, the Catholic doctrine on this particular point has not changed: no one knows the day and the hour when the Son of Man will come again.

However, even if individual Protestant denominations did have internal unity in doctrine, liturgy and government, the great problem would remain. How could they show that they and only they are the *one Church founded by Christ* in the year 30 AD? How can they show continuity—unity over time—with the Church described in the Acts of the Apostles and manifested in the writings of the Apostolic Fathers?

Let us look at the Orthodox world. Although it is far more united than the Protestant world, the Orthodox churches still lack unity, for there is no one head. Each patriarchate is considered to be auto-cephalous, a head unto itself.

The mark of unity inevitably goes together with communion with the Pope, for he is the rock on which Christian unity is founded. All Christians in communion with the Pope partake of that unity for which Christ prayed, and which the gates of hell will never destroy, according to His promise.

---

[28] John Calvin, Letter 305 to Melanchthon, of November 28, 1552, in *Letters of John Calvin*, vol. 2, ed. Jules Bonnet (New York: Burt Franklin, 1972) 376–77. (I have slightly modified the translation.) See also his letter to Melanchthon of January 21, 1545: "When I reflect on how much, at so unseasonable a time, these intestine quarrels divide and tear us asunder, I almost entirely lose courage" (ibid., 1:437).

Ecumenism

Does the existence of non-catholic Christian churches or ecclesial communities destroy the unity of the Church? It is important to observe that the sorrowful and tragic schisms and heresies in the Christian world do not diminish or destroy the mark of unity of the one true Church founded by Jesus Christ. Those who deliberately enter into formal heresy and schism, by that very act, separate themselves from the Body of Christ. The Body of Christ continues to be one body, but they are no longer members of it.

Those involved in the ecumenical movement sometimes think that the Church of Christ is lacking the mark of unity on account of the divisions that have been introduced among Christians and that it is necessary to *restore* the unity of the Church through ecumenical effort, as if it were lacking. However, the ecumenical movement does not have the goal of *creating Catholic union, as if currently it did not exist, but of bringing those who have strayed back into the unity of the one fold*, the Body of Christ, the Catholic Church. In other words, the goal of ecumenical effort and prayer for Christian unity is to *enlarge* Catholic unity by restoring separated members to full communion. For this reason, ecumenical effort must always be conceived as an effort of charity to help those who have tragically become separated to rejoin the one fold of Christ in the Catholic Church. This point is brought out forcefully by Pius XI in his encyclical on ecumenism, *Mortalium animos*:

> The union of Christians can only be promoted by promoting the return to the one true Church of Christ of those who are separated from it, for in the past they have unhappily left it. To the one true Church of Christ, we say, which is visible to all, and which is to remain, according to the will of its Author, exactly the same as He instituted it. During the lapse of centuries, the mystical Spouse of Christ has never been contaminated, nor can she ever in the future be contaminated, as Cyprian bears witness: "The Bride of Christ cannot be made false to her Spouse: she is incorrupt and modest. She knows but one dwelling, she guards the sanctity of the nuptial chamber chastely and modestly." The same holy Martyr with good reason marveled exceedingly that anyone could believe that "this unity in the Church which arises from a divine foundation, and which is knit together by heavenly sacraments, could be rent and torn asunder by the force of contrary wills." For since the mystical body of Christ, in the same manner as His physical body, is one, compacted and fitly joined together, it would be foolish and out of place to say that the mystical body is made up of members which are disunited and scattered abroad: whosoever therefore is not

united with the body is no member of it, neither is he in communion with Christ its head.[29]

The four marks of the Church—one, holy, Catholic, and apostolic—are properties of the true Church which can never be lacking to her, any more than the ability to laugh can be lacking to human nature. The true Church founded by Christ as a visible body in the world can never fail to be *one*. It can never be divided. This may sound paradoxical, but it is Catholic dogma. A schism or heresy does not actually divide the Mystical Body of Christ (although it may try to), because the Church is indefectibly one.[30] The declaration *Dominus Jesus* of 2000 affirms this explicitly: "The oneness of the Church founded by Christ must be firmly believed as a truth of the Catholic faith."[31] And, as we have seen, the Credo of the People of God (1968) states that the Church "is indefectibly one in faith, worship, and the bond of hierarchical communion." Two thousand years of history bear out this claim.

---

[29] Pius XI, *Mortalium animos* (1928), n. 10.

[30] Although schisms and heresies do not destroy the interior unity of the Catholic Church, they undoubtedly are a tremendous obstacle to the manifestation of that unity to the world.

[31] Congregation for the Doctrine of the Faith, declaration *Dominus Jesus* 16.

CHAPTER 6

The Church Is Apostolic

Christ Built His Church on the Apostles

Part of the scandal of the Catholic Church to Protestants and unbelievers in general is the mystery that the "Kingdom of God" is built on the foundation of sometimes very imperfect human beings: the Apostles and their successors. People often think that a spiritual kingdom ought to be completely spiritual, without any visible *institutional* structures like the episcopal college based on apostolic succession, and the papacy, based on succession from Peter. This scandal was at the heart of the Protestant revolt. How could God build His kingdom using institutional structures manned by sinners like Pope Alexander the Sixth and corrupt bishops? But yet Christ chose Judas to be one of the Apostles!

Throughout salvation history, it is clear that God is pleased to use the weak things of this world to confound the proud. He used the Apostles for this reason, who at first were quite imperfect, to show us that all the glory is His, and He continues to use men like them to govern His Church according to the same model that He established during His public ministry.

The fact that Christ built His Church on the Apostles is a beautiful example of the principle of mediation and the sacramental principle. God wills to make use of mediators in His governance and salvation of mankind. He made use of Moses in giving the Law to Israel and of Aaron and his descendants to be High Priests. Above all, God made use of the humanity of Christ as the Mediator between God and man, and He likewise makes use of Peter and the other Apostles as mediators with respect to the Mediator. The Apostles sacramentally represent Christ and share in His mediation. Christ said to the Apostles on Easter Sunday, "As the Father has sent me, even so I send you" (Jn 20:21). And in His priestly prayer after the Last Supper He prayed: "As thou didst send me into the world, so I have sent them into the world" (Jn 17:18).

In His government of the world, God could conceivably direct everything Himself immediately, without giving any share of direction or kingship to any creature. We might think that such a way of governing would be more appropriate for the majesty of God and the manifestation of His glory. This would be the Protestant tendency, which seeks, at least in theory, to dispense with human mediation.

However, this is not the way that God has ordered His creation. His glory is shown not by reserving everything to Himself, but by giving a participation of His kingship to creatures in a hierarchical way. He has given to mankind in general a kingship over the rest of material creation, as seen in first chapters of Genesis. He set man in the garden to tend and cultivate it, and He gave man the order to dominate the earth. In the words of Psalm 8:4–7:

> What is man that thou art mindful of him, and the son of man that thou dost care for him? Yet thou hast made him little less than God, and dost crown him with glory and honor. Thou hast given him dominion over the works of thy hands; thou hast put all things under his feet, all sheep and oxen, and also the beasts of the field.

The angelic creation is also hierarchical. It can be seen in Scripture that there is a hierarchy of angelic beings, and it is reasonable to think that the higher ones illuminate the lower ones. Pseudo-Dionysius profoundly developed this principle of mediation among the angelic hierarchies:

> The first intelligences [angels] perfect, illuminate, and purify those of inferior status in such a fashion that the latter, having been lifted up through them to the universal and transcendent source, thereby acquire their due share of the purification, illumination, and perfection of the One who is the source of all perfection. The divine source of all order has established the all-embracing principle that beings of the second rank receive enlightenment from the Godhead through the beings of the first rank.[1]

Similarly, within human society, a share of God's authority and kingship is given to parents within the family, and to governors over nations and societies. Without hierarchy and headship of some type, every human society would dissolve into anarchy. The same is true of intermediate societies formed by association. Every business requires a leader, and every athletic team needs a captain.

Even the human body is hierarchical, in that the head must lead the other members, all of which complement one another, even though some are more noble than others. Now if this is true in the human body and in human societies, it is no less fitting that there be hierarchy in the supernatural order in the Church.

---

[1] Pseudo-Dionysius, *The Celestial Hierarchy* 8.2, in *Pseudo-Dionysius: The Complete Works*, trans. Colm Luibheid (New York: Paulist Press, 1987), 168.

The worship of Israel was hierarchically ordered in three grades—the high priest, the priests, and the Levites—which prefigure the division of Holy Orders in the Church into bishops, priests, and deacons. The Levites, like deacons in the Catholic Church, aided the priests, who were under the supreme authority of the High Priest.

The book of Numbers 16 describes a revolt against the priestly hierarchy established by God in the Law of Moses, led by Korah, Dathan, and Abiram, who, although they were not priests, claimed equality in priestly power with Aaron and his descendants, saying that the entire community had been consecrated by the Lord, and not just Aaron and his children. God defended the Aaronic priesthood by having the ground open, swallowing up Korah, Dathan, Abiram, and their followers.[2]

The Hierarchical Principle

The hierarchical principle is the idea that God's creation involves complementarity in distinction, in which each level receives a certain share in God's kingship, to be used for the common good. No creature is self-sufficient, but each is called to serve the others, according to his particular state.

St. Paul develops this idea in his doctrine of the Body of Christ, which is composed of many members. Among these members there is also the head. The head is Christ, but He rules His Church through visible mediators, who share in a particular sacramental way in His kingship, through the sacrament of Holy Orders. After His Ascension, Christ is the invisible head of the Church, but His Body must also have a visible head, which is Peter and his successors, and the successors of the Apostles. Through the power of Orders, those who receive it are enabled to act *in persona Christi*, in the very person of Christ. They do this when they consecrate the Eucharist, absolve sins in the sacrament of Penance, or ordain men to the priesthood. The recipients of Holy Orders, especially in the highest grade of the episcopate, also participate in God's kingship through receiving the power of jurisdiction in the Church: the power to teach and govern the People of God.

The Apostles and their successors are mediators in two dimensions.[3] They mediate vertically, acting as God's vicar and oracle in their infallible teaching, and offering up the supplications of the Church in the liturgy to the Father. However, they also mediate horizontally through time. Each generation of the successors of the Apostles passes

---

[2] Num 16:31–35.

[3] See Charles Cardinal Journet, *Theology of the Church* (San Francisco: Ignatius Press, 2004), 155–56.

on to the following generation what they have received from their predecessors, which they ultimately received from Christ. This horizontal transmitting of the apostolic office from generation to generation is called apostolic succession. The true Church of Christ is the one which contains, and in fact is built on, this succession. Without this succession, what Jesus accomplished in forming the Apostles would have been lost after their death. Leo XIII explains:

> It was consequently provided by God that the Magisterium instituted by Jesus Christ should not end with the life of the Apostles, but that it should be perpetuated. We see it in truth propagated, and, as it were, delivered from hand to hand. For the Apostles consecrated bishops and each one appointed those who were to succeed them immediately "in the ministry of the word." Nay more: they likewise required their successors to choose fitting men, to endow them with like authority, and to confide to them the office and mission of teaching. "Thou, therefore, my son, be strong in the grace which is in Christ Jesus: and the things which you have heard of me by many witnesses, the same command to faithful men, who shall be fit to teach others also" (2 Tim 2:1–2). Wherefore, as Christ was sent by God and the Apostles by Christ, so the Bishops and those who succeeded them were sent by the Apostles.[4]

The apostolic succession is parallel to that earlier succession by which the descendants of Aaron transmitted the high priesthood from generation to generation.

Apostolic Succession

Apostolicity is one of the four marks of the Church. As such, it is part of the essence of the Church and is a clear visible sign of the true Church. It is of the essence of the Church to be *apostolic*, built on the Apostles and their successors, just as Biblical Israel was built on Moses and Aaron, and their successors.

Why must this be so? This is because the very essence of the Church is to be a continuation of Christ's humanity such that He can reach every human being on the planet through history. Christ's physical body has ascended into heaven, and so He cannot touch us directly in that visible humanity that He assumed in the moment of the Annunciation. Thus Christ instituted a sacramental plan of salvation in which His humanity is continued in time and space sacramentally. This happens above all in the Eucharist and in the sacrament of Penance.

---

[4] Leo XIII, encyclical *Satis cognitum* (1896), n. 8.

However, it also happens in an equally important way through the sacrament of Holy Orders, the fullness of which is the episcopacy. The recipients of the fullness of this sacrament are the successors of the Apostles.

For this reason He chose Apostles during His public ministry to be the sacramental continuation of His humanity and His heralds. Even Protestants recognize this, although they limit it to the apostolic age. However, the need for a sacramental ministry of headship was not limited to the time of Christ's public ministry and the first decades of the Church. Christ always needs visible and authorized apostles to continue His mission in a visible and sacramental way. The Church is to be structured on the apostolic succession until the end of time. The reason for this is simple: the Church that Christ formed before His Ascension was to last for all time, and the Church that Christ formed was apostolic, entirely centered on the authoritative witness of the Twelve that He chose to be the pillars and foundation of the Church.

In Ephesians 2:19–20, St. Paul says: "You are . . . members of the household of God, built upon the foundation of the Apostles and prophets, Christ Jesus Himself being the cornerstone." In Revelation 21:10–14, John is shown a vision of the New Jerusalem descending from heaven, the "Bride of the Lamb," which is the Church. The walls of this holy City are built on twelve foundations, on which are written "the twelve names of the twelve Apostles of the Lamb." The very structure and architecture of the Church is based on the apostolic office, which must always remain vital and continuous in the Church.

In his Letter to the Corinthians (96 AD), Pope Clement I (ordained by St. Peter and third in succession from him as bishop of Rome) stressed the doctrine of apostolic succession:

> So then Christ is from God, and the apostles are from Christ. Both, therefore, came of the will of God in good order. . . . So, preaching both in the country and in the towns, they [the apostles] appointed their first fruits, when they had tested them by the Spirit, to be bishops and deacons for the future believers. And this was no new thing they did. . . . Our apostles likewise knew, through our Lord Jesus Christ, that there would be strife over the bishop's office. For this reason, therefore, having received complete foreknowledge, they appointed the officials mentioned earlier and afterwards they gave the offices a permanent character;

that is, if they should die, other approved men should succeed to their ministry.[5]

A hundred years later, St. Irenaeus wrote:

> True knowledge is the doctrine of the apostles, and the ancient constitution of the Church throughout all the world, and the distinctive manifestation of the body of Christ according to the *successions of the bishops*, by which they have handed down that Church which exists in every place, and has come even to us.[6]

Apostolic succession, in consequence, is also a clear sign or mark of the true Church and has something of a miraculous nature in its constancy and continuation over time. The Church founded by Christ is visibly apostolic, and it must continue to be so until the end of time. Therefore, if a Christian denomination cannot demonstrate apostolic succession, including Petrine succession, it cannot be the true Church.

The Relation of the Apostles to Peter

The Apostles were called and constituted by Christ to be the foundation of the Church. They were all given a unique and unrepeatable charism to be the foundation of the Church after Christ's Ascension. This charism consisted in being absolutely authoritative and infallible witnesses of Christ's humanity, His death and Resurrection, His teaching, His interpretation of the Old Testament Scriptures, His sacraments, and the lineaments of His Church. Each Apostle had a total authority in this regard.

Nevertheless, the apostolic witness was instituted to found *one* Church. Thus the other Apostles were constituted under Peter; they too were part of the flock that Christ entrusted to Peter when He said three times: "Feed my sheep" (Jn 21:15–17). *All* of Christ's sheep were entrusted to Peter, even the other Apostles.

All of the Apostles were endowed with infallibility in matters of faith and morals, but nevertheless, nothing was given to them collectively that was not given to Peter individually.[7] The apostolic

---

[5] Clement I, *Letter to the Corinthians* 42, 44, in *The Apostolic Fathers: Greek Texts and English Translations*, ed. Michael W. Holmes, 3rd ed. (Grand Rapids, MI: Baker Academic, 2007), 101–103.

[6] Irenaeus, *Against Heresies* 4.33.8, *ANF* 1:508.

[7] See St. Leo the Great, Sermon 4.2 (quoted by Leo XIII in *Satis cognitum* 14): "So that whereas Peter alone received many things, He [Christ] conferred nothing on any of the rest without Peter participating in it."

authority was infallible, but was under the supreme tutelage of Peter and could never be separated from him or put in conflict with him.[8]

When the Apostles are listed in the Gospels, Peter is always put in the first place. For example, Matthew (10:2) says: "First, Simon, who is called Peter."[9] Peter speaks on behalf of the Twelve (Lk 12:41); together with James and John, he is witness to the Transfiguration and the agony of Jesus in Gethsemane; he is cited as the first witness to the Resurrection (Lk 24:34; 1 Cor 15:5). In the Book of Acts, it is Peter who appoints Matthias (Acts 1:15–26) and who speaks to the crowds after Pentecost (Acts 2); it is Peter who performs the first healing in Church history (Acts 3:1–16); he addresses the Sanhedrin (Acts 4:5–22); he has authority to discipline (Acts 5:1–12); he endorses the spread of the Gospel to Samaria and to the Gentiles (Acts 10, 11:1–18); and he sums up the teaching of the Council of Jerusalem (Acts 15:6–11).[10]

Another important text concerning the primacy of Peter is Luke 22:32. During the Last Supper, Jesus foretells Peter's imminent betrayal and conversion: "Simon, Simon, behold, Satan demanded to have you, that he might sift you like wheat, but I have prayed for you that your faith may not fail; and when you have turned again, strengthen your brethren." Now when Christ prays for something, it could not fail to be answered. Christ did not pray that Peter not fall into sin, but that his faith not fail, and that he be able to strengthen his brethren in the faith, who are the other Apostles and disciples.

Leo XIII says: "He willed then that he whom He had designated as the foundation of the Church should be the defense of its faith."[11] And St. Ambrose said in the fourth century: "Could not Christ who confided to him the Kingdom by His own authority have strengthened the faith

---

[8] Cardinal Journet, *Theology of the Church*, 129, explains this well: "They [the Apostles] have presided at her birth, as it were, and have left their mark on her forever. Such privileges were found in an equal degree in each of the apostles. As they were granted, however, for the sake of founding the one Church, governed by one visible head, these privileges tended by their own force to move the apostles—in that which concerns the government of the universal Church—toward a dependence on the supreme transapostolic power confided to Peter by the Savior. Hence, the apostles themselves were ranked among the sheep of Christ, having Peter as their visible pastor. And when Peter died, they remained, with respect to the government of the Church, submitted to the supreme regular power of governing the Church, which Peter transmitted to his successors."

[9] See also Mk 3:16; Lk 6:14; Acts 1:13.

[10] See *Ignatius Catholic Study Bible: The New Testament* (San Francisco: Ignatius Press, 2010), 211. The Acts of the Apostles does not mention St. Peter again after the Council of Jerusalem, perhaps because given his importance, and after repeated threats on his life, St. Luke could not safely reveal that he was residing in Rome.

[11] Leo XIII, *Satis cognitum* 12.

of one whom He designated a rock to show the foundation of the Church?"[12]

The Church has always understood this prayer—that Peter's faith not fail—to extend to all his successors. For Christ's concern was not with the apostolic Church alone, but with the Church of all ages. What good would it have done, if Peter's faith had not failed, but that of his successors had: Linus, Cletus, Clement, etc., up to Benedict XVI?

The Petrine office is essentially that of conserving the faith, confirming the brethren in the faith and in the bond of charity, and of feeding *all* the sheep of Christ. As Cardinal Prefect of the Congregation for the Doctrine of the Faith, Joseph Ratzinger wrote:

> From the beginning and with increasing clarity, the Church has understood that, just as there is a succession of the Apostles in the ministry of Bishops, so too the ministry of unity entrusted to Peter belongs to the permanent structure of Christ's Church and that this succession is established in the see of his martyrdom.[13]

Since Peter and his successors serve as the ministry of unity in the Church, it is said that "Where Peter is, there you have the Church. Where the Church is, there you find not death but life eternal."[14]

Catholic Understanding of the Primacy of Peter

Protestants often think of the Catholic claim of the primacy of Peter as an arrogant attempt to put a human authority above the Word of God, which would thus be a radical corruption of the Gospel. However, in the Catholic understanding of the primacy, its meaning is entirely at the service of the Gospel. The task of the apostolic witness of the universal episcopacy and the Petrine witness of the bishop of Rome is to maintain the deposit of faith intact through all centuries, so that all the faithful may be free with the freedom won for us by Christ.

Cardinal Ratzinger explained this beautifully in the previously mentioned document of 1998:

---

[12] St. Ambrose of Milan, *De fide* 4.5.56, in *Corpus Scriptorum Ecclesiasticorum Latinorum*, vol. 78 (Vindobonae: Hoelder-Pichler-Tempsky, 1962), 176.

[13] Congregation for the Doctrine of the Faith, *The Primacy of the Successor of Peter in the Mystery of the Church* 3, October 30, 1998, published in *L'Osservatore Romano* (Weekly Edition in English), November 18, 1998, pp. 5–6.

[14] St. Ambrose of Milan, *Enarrationes in Psalmos* 40.30, in *Commentary of Saint Ambrose on Twelve Psalms*, trans. Íde M. Ní Riain, (Dublin: Halcyon Press, 2000), 197. The original Latin is: "*Ubi Petrus, ibi ergo Ecclesia, ubi Ecclesia, ibi nulla mors, sed vita aeterna.*"

The Roman Pontiff—like all the faithful—is subject to the Word of God, to the Catholic faith, and is the guarantor of the Church's obedience; in this sense he is *servus servorum Dei*. He does not make arbitrary decisions, but is spokesman for the will of the Lord, who speaks to man in the Scriptures lived and interpreted by Tradition; in other words, the *episkope* of the primacy has limits set by divine law and by the Church's divine, inviolable constitution found in Revelation. The Successor of Peter is the rock which guarantees a rigorous fidelity to the Word of God against arbitrariness and conformism: hence the martyrological nature of his primacy.[15]

Patristic Witness to Apostolic Succession and the Primacy of Peter

The early Fathers of the Church were very aware of the reality of apostolic succession and its importance. Perhaps the first significant witness outside the New Testament is given by a letter of Pope St. Clement, the third successor to St. Peter, to the Corinthians, dated c. 96 AD. This work was so highly esteemed in the early Church that it was read in the liturgical assembly in some places, as if it were a part of the canon of Scripture. The occasion for the letter was a schism in the Church in Corinth. It seems that the authority of the ordained bishops (*episkopoi*) and presbyters was being challenged by some claiming a more charismatic authority, based not on the sacrament of Orders and apostolic succession, but on charismatic gifts and a higher knowledge (*gnosis*). Perhaps the schism was the work of incipient Gnosticism, which was the first major heresy to trouble the Church.

It is highly significant that the bishop of Rome intervened to settle the conflict with a mixture of authority and theological persuasion, focusing on examples from the Old Testament. The bishop of Rome clearly saw the welfare of all the churches to be his responsibility, especially in an issue so central to the divine constitution of the Church: the hierarchical principle of ecclesiastical authority, given through the sacrament of Orders. The Apostle John was still alive when this letter was written, but it is not John who writes to the Corinthians, but Peter's successor Clement.

We have seen how St. Ignatius of Antioch stressed apostolic succession over and over again in his letters written on his journey to martyrdom in the Coliseum. In the beginning of his letter to the Romans, St. Ignatius seems to allude to a primacy of the see of Rome, although it is somewhat obscure and disputed. He addresses the church

---

[15] Congregation for the Doctrine of the Faith, *The Primacy of the Successor of Peter in the Mystery of the Church* 7.

in Rome with a very formal and elaborate praise, as "the church . . . which also *presides* in the place of the district of the Romans, worthy of God, worthy of honor, worthy of blessing, worthy of praise, worthy of success, worthy of sanctification, and *presiding over love*, observing the law of Christ."[16]

The expression, "presiding over love" (*agape*), could also be rendered, "presiding over the communion [of the Church]," in that the communion and unity of the Church is the proper fruit and expression of charity. The grammatical structure favors this interpretation, for one presides properly over a community, which here would be the universal church itself,[17] formed by the love of Christ, poured forth in our hearts through the Holy Spirit.[18] Furthermore, in other places St. Ignatius uses the term "*agape*" to designate the communion of the church in various cities.[19] In the Letter to the Romans 4 he mentions that he does not give them orders "like Peter and Paul," thus alluding to the pre-eminent apostolic authority of the see of Rome.

Another great witness to the apostolic nature of the Church is St. Irenaeus, from the end of the second century. He stresses the apostolic succession and the unity of the faith and the Tradition throughout the universal (Catholic) Church in his battle against the Gnostic heretics of his day, who claimed to have a secret apostolic authority but completely lacked any visible connection with the Apostles.

---

[16] St. Ignatius, Letter to the Romans, salutation, trans. Michael Holmes, *The Apostolic Fathers*, 225. See the comments on this text by Benedict XVI in his General Audience of March 14, 2007: "Ignatius was the first person in Christian literature to attribute to the Church the adjective 'catholic' or 'universal': 'Wherever Jesus Christ is,' he said, 'there is the Catholic Church' (*Smyrnaeans*, 8: 2). And precisely in the service of unity to the Catholic Church, the Christian community of Rome exercised a sort of primacy of love: 'The Church which presides in the place of the region of the Romans, and which is worthy of God, worthy of honour, worthy of the highest happiness... and which presides over love, is named from Christ, and from the Father...' (*Romans*, Prologue). As can be seen, Ignatius is truly the 'Doctor of Unity': unity of God and unity of Christ (despite the various heresies gaining ground which separated the human and the divine in Christ), unity of the Church, unity of the faithful in 'faith and love, to which nothing is to be preferred' (*Smyrnaeans*, 6:1)."

[17] See G. Bareille, "Ignace d'Antioche (saint)," in *Dictionnaire de theologie catholique*, vol. 7/1 (Paris: Librairie Letouzey et Ané, 1927), 709.

[18] See Rom 5:5. *Agape* also has a clear Eucharistic reference in the letters of St. Ignatius, for the unity of charity is sacramentally communicated to the Church through the Eucharist.

[19] See St. Ignatius, Letter to the Trallians 13.1: "The church [*agape*] of the Smyrneans and Ephesians greets you"; Letter to the Romans 9.3; Letter to the Philadelphians 11.2; Letter to the Smyrnaeans 12.1.

The Gnostics professed a host of esoteric doctrines, differing in every sect (of which there were many), which they claimed were passed down secretly from Christ and the Apostles within their sect. To counter this absurd claim, St. Irenaeus stressed the public teaching of the Church through the bishops who have succeeded the Apostles. The true faith is that which comes from the Apostles, has been taught always and everywhere in the Catholic Church,[20] and is taught now by the successors of the Apostles in communion with the successor of Peter.

The Gnostic heresiarchs, on the contrary, could show no continuity for their doctrine, either in time or geographically. They lacked the marks of unity, Catholicity, and apostolic origin. St. Irenaeus reproached them: "For there were no Valentinians before Valentinus, or Marcionites before Marcion."[21] We can say the same in modern times: there were no Lutherans or Calvinists before Luther and Calvin.

In order to ascertain the true faith and preserve oneself from the heresies of the Gnostics, it is necessary to remain with the apostolic Tradition that has been preserved in the Church through the apostolic succession. Thus the true faith can be found in all doctrine taught by the successors of the Apostles in common. However, St. Irenaeus singles out the Church in Rome as being pre-eminent in the preservation of the faith, with which every other Church must agree:

> It is within the power of all, therefore, in every Church, who may wish to see the truth, to contemplate clearly the tradition of the apostles manifested throughout the whole world; and we are in a position to reckon up those who were by the apostles instituted bishops in the Churches, and [to demonstrate] the succession of these men to our own times. . . .
>
> Since, however, it would be very tedious, in such a volume as this, to reckon up the successions of all the Churches, we do put to confusion all those who, in whatever manner . . . assemble in unauthorized meetings, by indicating that tradition derived from the apostles, of the very great, the very ancient, and universally known Church founded and organized at *Rome* by the two most glorious apostles, Peter and Paul; as also [by pointing out] the faith

---

[20] See Vincent of Lerins, who gave the classical expression of this doctrine: "In the Catholic Church itself, all possible care must be taken, that we hold that faith which has been believed everywhere, always, and by all. For that is truly and in the strictest sense 'Catholic' which, as the name itself and the reason of the thing declare, comprehends all universally. This rule we shall observe if we follow universality, antiquity, consent" (*Commonitory*, ch. 2, *PL* 50:639; *Nicene and Post-Nicene Fathers*, 11:132).

[21] St. Irenaeus, *Against Heresies*, 3.4.3, trans. Cyril Richardson, in *Early Christian Fathers* (New York: Macmillan, 1970), 375.

preached to men, which comes down to our time by means of the successions of the bishops. For it is a *matter of necessity that every Church should agree with this Church, on account of its pre-eminent authority.*[22]

St. Irenaeus goes on to list the succession of twelve bishops of Rome up until his time:

The blessed apostles, then, having founded and built up the Church, committed into the hands of Linus the office of the episcopate. Of this Linus, Paul makes mention in the Epistles to Timothy. To him succeeded Anacletus; and after him, in the third place from the apostles, Clement was allotted the bishopric. This man, as he had seen the blessed apostles, and had been conversant with them, might be said to have the preaching of the apostles still echoing [in his ears], and their traditions before his eyes. Nor was he alone [in this], for there were many still remaining who had received instructions from the apostles. In the time of this Clement, no small dissension having occurred among the brethren at Corinth, the Church in Rome dispatched a most powerful letter to the Corinthians, exhorting them to peace, renewing their faith, and declaring the tradition which it had lately received from the apostles. . . . To this Clement there succeeded Evaristus. Alexander followed Evaristus; then, sixth from the apostles, Sixtus was appointed; after him, Telephorus, who was gloriously martyred; then Hyginus; after him, Pius; then after him, Anicetus. Sorer having succeeded Anicetus, Eleutherius does now, in the twelfth place from the apostles, hold the inheritance of the episcopate. *In this order, and by this succession, the ecclesiastical tradition from the apostles, and the preaching of the truth, have come down to us.* And this is most abundant proof that there is one and the same vivifying faith, which has been preserved in the Church from the apostles until now, and handed down in truth.[23]

About the same time as St. Irenaeus, Tertullian refuted the heretical sects of his time by saying:

Let them produce the original records of their churches; let them unfold the roll of their bishops, running down in due succession from the beginning in such a manner that that first bishop of theirs shall be able to show for his ordainer and predecessor one of the apostles or of apostolic men who were in communion with the apostles. For this is the manner in which the apostolic churches

---

[22] St. Irenaeus, *Against Heresies* 3.3.1–2, *ANF* 1:415.
[23] Ibid., 3.3.3, *ANF* 1:416.

transmit their registers: as the church of Smyrna, which records that Polycarp was placed therein by John; as also the church of Rome, which makes Clement to have been ordained in like manner by Peter.[24]

St. Cyprian, who died a martyr in 258, wrote a tract *On the Unity of the Church* in 251, in which he simply supports the primacy of the successor of Peter from the Gospels:

> But if anyone considers those things carefully, he will need no long discourse or arguments. The proof is simple and convincing, being summed up in a matter of fact. The Lord says to Peter: "I say to thee, that thou art Peter, and upon this rock I will build my Church. . . ." And he says to him again after the resurrection: "Feed my sheep" (Jn 21:17). It is on him that He builds the Church, and to him that He entrusts the sheep to feed. And although He assigns a like power to all the Apostles, yet He founded a single Chair, thus establishing by His own authority the source and hallmark of the [Church's] oneness. No doubt the others were all that Peter was, but a primacy is given to Peter, and it is made clear that there is but one Church and one Chair. So too, even if they are all shepherds, we are shown but one flock which is to be fed by all the Apostles in common accord. If a man does not hold fast to this oneness of Peter, does he imagine that he still holds the faith? If he deserts the Chair of Peter upon whom the Church was built, has he still confidence that he is in the Church? The authority of the bishops forms a unity, of which each holds his part in its totality.[25]

St. Cyprian also refers to the Roman Church "as to the Chair of Peter and to the principal Church whence sacerdotal unity has sprung."[26] On this basis, St. Cyprian goes on to formulate a very important principle: if someone separates himself from the apostolic

---

[24] Tertullian, *On Prescription against Heretics* 32, *ANF* 3:258.

[25] St. Cyprian, *On the Unity of the Church* 4, trans. Maurice Bévenot, *De Lapsis and De Ecclesiae Catholicae Unitate* (Oxford: At the Clarendon Press, 1971), 61–63. This important text exists in two versions. The other version, called the *textus receptus*, reads as follows: "it is on one man that He builds the Church and although He assigns a like power to all the Apostles after His resurrection, saying: "As the Father hath sent me, I also send you. . ." (Jn 20:21–23). Yet, in order that the oneness might be unmistakable, He established by His own authority a source for that oneness having its origin in one man alone. No doubt the other Apostles were all that Peter was, endowed with equal dignity and power, but the start comes from him alone, in order to show that the Church of Christ is unique" (ibid., 63).

[26] St. Cyprian, Epistle 59 to Cornelius, n. 14, in *Letters*, trans. Rose Donna (Washington DC: Catholic Univ. of America Press, 1964), 186.

Church in communion with Peter, then he cannot inherit the promises of the Church:

> Whoever breaks with the Church and enters on an adulterous union, cuts himself off from the promises made to the Church; and he who turns his back on the Church of Christ will not come to the rewards of Christ: he is an alien, a worldling, an enemy. *You cannot have God for your Father if you no longer have the Church for your mother.* If there was any escape for one who outside the ark of Noah, there will be as much for one who is found to be outside the Church.[27]

Towards the end of the fourth century St. Jerome wrote to Pope Damasus as follows: "My words are spoken to the successor of the Fisherman, to the disciple of the Cross. . . . I communicate with none save your Blessedness, that is with the chair of Peter. For this I know is the rock on which the Church is built."[28] Union with the See of Peter is to him always the public criterion of a Catholic: "He who clings to the chair of Peter is accepted by me."[29]

In the same way, St. Augustine writes that "the primacy of the Apostolic chair always flourished" in the Church of Rome[30]; and he says: "You are not to be looked upon as holding the true Catholic faith if you do not teach that the faith of Rome is to be held."[31] In the Pelagian controversy, Pelagius was condemned in a North African synod, which was sent to Rome for confirmation. When the confirmation arrived, St. Augustine famously said that Rome has spoken, and thus the case is closed (*Roma locuta est, causa finita est*). Actually, the full text is as follows: "You see, there have already been two councils about this matter, and their decisions sent to the Apostolic See; from there rescripts have been sent back here. The case is finished; if only the error were finished too, sometime!"[32]

In the mid-fifth century, the greatest protector of the faith of the Church concerning the great Christological and Trinitarian controversies was Pope St. Leo the Great. With regard to the primacy, he says:

---

27. St. Cyprian, *On the Unity of the Church* 6, trans. Bévenot, 67.

28 St. Jerome, Letter 15 to Pope Damasus, n. 2, trans. W. H. Fremantle, NPNF series 2, 6:18.

29 St. Jerome, Letter 16 to Pope Damasus, n. 2, NPNF series 2, 6:20.

30 St. Augustine, Letter 43.7, in *St. Augustine: Letters*, vol. 1, trans. Wilfrid Parsons (New York: Fathers of the Church, Inc., 1951), 187.

31 St. Augustine, Sermon 120.13, cited in Leo XIII, *Satis cognitum* 13.

32 St. Augustine, Sermon 131.10, in *Sermons*, vol. 4, trans. Edmund Hill (Brooklyn: New City Press, 1992) 322.

Yet out of the whole world Peter alone has been chosen to be put in charge of the universal convocation of peoples as well as of every apostle and all the Fathers of the Church. Although there are many priests and many shepherds among the people of God, it is Peter who properly rules each one of those whom Christ also rules principally.[33]

A century and a half later, St. Gregory the Great, writing to the Emperor Maurice Augustus, says:

It is clear, therefore, to all who know the gospel, that the Lord's voice committed the care of the whole Church to the apostle Saint Peter, the prince of all the apostles. Because it was to him that it was said: "Peter, do you love me? Feed my sheep." . . . Behold, he accepts the keys of the kingdom of Heaven, to him the power of binding and of loosing is attributed, to him the care of the whole Church.

It is evident to all who know the gospel that the charge of the whole Church was committed to St. Peter, the Apostle and Prince of all the Apostles, by the word of the Lord. . . . Behold! he has received the keys of the heavenly kingdom; the power of binding and loosing is conferred upon him. The care of the whole government of the Church is confided to him.[34]

Nor should it be thought that the primacy of Peter and his successors was recognized only by the Western Latin portion of the Church. The Eastern Church had repeatedly recognized the primacy of Peter over the universal Church in the most important matters.[35] The See of Peter was the final court of appeal in questions of faith and ecclesiastical government. Warren Carroll writes:

Papal primacy as a general proposition had been recognized in the Eastern Church *from the beginning of the Christian era*, with the letter of Pope Clement I to the Greek church in Corinth in 95 AD. . . . Because of slow communication and transportation, Papal primacy was not exercised nearly as often in the East as in the West in

---

[33] St. Leo the Great, Sermon 4.2, in *St. Leo the Great: Sermons*, trans. Jane Freeland and Agnes Conway, The Fathers of the Church 93 (Washington DC: Catholic Univ. of America Press, 1996), 26.

[34] St. Gregory the Great, Letter 37 of book 5 to Maurice Augustus of June 595, in *The Letters of Gregory the Great*, trans. John Martyn, vol. 2 (Toronto: Pontifical Institute of Mediaeval Studies, 2004), 352.

[35] The first example is given by the Letter of Pope Clement I to the Corinthians. Another example, discussed below, is the Council of Chalcedon of 451.

specific acts, such as confirming or deposing bishops. But it had been not only acknowledged but trumpeted, made the basis of appeal after appeal for help, by the iconodule[36] bishops and monks throughout the iconoclastic controversy.[37]

Popes Compared with the Patriarchs of the Other Apostolic Sees

Christ promised to pray for Peter's faith, so that he could confirm the brethren. He did not extend this prayer to the other bishops in the Catholic world—successors of the other Apostles—and thus they do not enjoy the infallible promise of protection against formally teaching heresy. It is instructive to compare the Popes of Rome with the patriarchs of the other apostolic sees: Alexandria, Antioch, and Constantinople, with regard to heresy.

Alexandria was regarded as the second see in the Catholic world, being founded by St. Mark, the spiritual son of Peter. The patriarchs of Alexandria were strong in the fourth and early fifth centuries, and were a credit to their rank of honor. St. Athanasius was the great patriarch who did more than anyone else to protect the Church from Arianism, the heresy denying the divinity of Christ. St. Cyril of Alexandria in 430 also was the providential defender against the heresy of Nestorianism, which denied the hypostatic union in Christ, promoted by the patriarch of Constantinople. However, in the very next generation, Cyril's successor Dioscorus ended up very aggressively promoting the heresy of Monophysitism, begun by a monk of Constantinople named Eutyches, teaching that there is only the divine nature in Christ, thus effectively denying His full humanity. A general council was called in Ephesus in 449, in which Dioscorus had the support of the imperial Court. Cardinal Newman describes the council:

> The proceedings which followed were of so violent a character, that the Council has gone down to posterity under the name of the Latrocinium or "Gang of Robbers." Eutyches was honorably acquitted, and his doctrine received; but the assembled Fathers showed some backwardness to depose St. Flavian. Dioscorus had been attended by a multitude of monks, furious zealots for the Monophysite doctrine from Syria and Egypt, and by an armed force. These broke into the Church at his call; Flavian was thrown down and trampled on, and received injuries of which he died the

---

[36] That is, those who defended the use of images of Christ and the saints against the iconoclasts.

[37] Warren Carroll, *The Building of Christendom* (Front Royal, VA: Christendom College Press, 1987), 352 (italics original).

third day after. The Pope's legates escaped as they could; and the Bishops were compelled to sign a blank paper, which was afterwards filled up with the condemnation of Flavian. These outrages however, were subsequent to the Synodical acceptance of the Creed of Eutyches. . . . The proceedings ended by Dioscorus excommunicating the Pope, and the Emperor issuing an edict in approval of the decision of the Council.[38]

Cardinal Newman then describes the danger threatening the faith of the Church which came from this "Robber Council" (*latrocinium*):

If the East could determine a matter of faith independently of the West, certainly the Monophysite heresy was established as apostolic truth in all its provinces from Macedonia to Egypt.

There has been a time in the history of Christianity, when it had been Athanasius against the world, and the world against Athanasius. The need and straitness of the Church had been great, and one man was raised up for her deliverance. In this second necessity, who was the destined champion of her who cannot fail? When did he come, and what was his name? He came with an augury of victory upon him, which even Athanasius could not show; it was Leo, Bishop of Rome.[39]

At this juncture another council was called in 451 in Chalcedon, attended by 630 bishops (including only 4 from the West: two Africans and two Roman legates). The Roman legates demanded the right to open the council as representing Rome, "which is the head of all the Churches." Dioscorus was charged for having "presumed to hold a Council without the authority of the Apostolic See, which had never been done nor was lawful to do,"[40] and for not having the Letter of the Pope read to the Council (the famous Tome of St. Leo).

After the Tome of Leo was read during the Council of Chalcedon, the assembled bishops cried out: "This is the faith of the Fathers; this is the faith of the Apostles. So we all believe, thus the orthodox believe. Anathema to him who does not thus believe. Peter has spoken thus through Leo. So taught the Apostles."[41]

Dioscorus was condemned with these words:

The most holy and blessed Leo, archbishop of the great and elder Rome, through us, and through this present most holy synod

---

[38] John Henry Newman, *An Essay on the Development of Christian Doctrine* (Notre Dame, IN: Univ. of Notre Dame Press, 1989), 300.

[39] Ibid., 306–7.

[40] Ibid., 308.

[41] Acts of the Council of Chalcedon, session 2, in *NPNF* second series, 14:259.

together with the thrice blessed and all-glorious Peter the Apostle, who is the rock and foundation of the Catholic Church, and the foundation of the orthodox faith, hath stripped him of the episcopate, and hath alienated from him all hieratic worthiness.[42]

Warren Carroll remarks that "Pope Leo had little to fear from Attila the Hun, but much to fear from Dioscorus. For it was with those who denied the fullness of Christ's salvific human nature that the ultimate battle of this age was fought."[43] Although the Catholic Church was protected from heresy through the Council of Chalcedon, the see of Alexandria was not. After the heresiarch Dioscorus, they had a string of other Monophysite patriarchs[44] out of communion with Rome.

What about the third most important see of Christianity, that of Antioch? Did it fare better? In the third century, a patriarch of Antioch, Paul of Samosata, denied the divinity of Christ, holding Him to be a mere man, adopted by God as His Son. In the fourth century, there were eight Arian patriarchs of Antioch, denying the divinity of Christ. In the fifth through seventh centuries, they had three heretical Monophysite bishops and a Monothelite, denying His full humanity.

Constantinople fared no better than Alexandria and Antioch. It had four Arian bishops in the fourth century, followed by the heresiarch Nestorius in the fifth. In the sixth century there were two Monophysite bishops, and three Monothelites in the seventh. There followed a string of iconoclast bishops, who prohibited the use of images in Christian worship.

Of the 544 years (323–867) from the founding of the see of Constantinople to the schism of Photius in the ninth century, it was separated from communion with Rome over 200 years on account of these various heresies.[45] Even the Orthodox Church today recognizes

---

[42] Council of Chalcedon, session 3, *NPNF* second series, 14:259–60.

[43] W. Carroll, *The Building of Christendom*, 109.

[44] John II (497), John III (505), Dioscorus II (515), Timothy IV (519), Theodosius I (536).

[45] See Adrian Fortescue, "The Eastern Schism," *The Catholic Encyclopedia*, vol. 13 (New York: Robert Appleton Company, 1912), online at http://www.newadvent.org/cathen/13535a.htm: "From the beginning of the See of Constantinople to the great schism in 867 the list of these temporary breaches of communion is a formidable one. There were fifty-five years of schism (343–98) during the Arian troubles, eleven because of St. John Chrysostom's deposition (404–15), thirty-five years of the Acacian schism (484–519), forty-one years of Monothelite schism (640–81), sixty-one years because of Iconoclasm. So of these 544 years (323–867) no less than 203 were spent by Constantinople in a state of schism. We notice too that in every one of these quarrels Constantinople was on the wrong side; by the consent of the Orthodox, too, Rome in all stood out for right. And already we see that the

that it was on the wrong side in all those breaches of communion. The principal reason for Constantinople's frequent fall into heresy was clearly the pressure of secular political interests: the frequent *de facto* control of the Church by the emperor for his political interests (known as *Caesaropapism*). Now if the patriarchs were in the wrong in separation from Rome for two hundred years before the final schism of the eleventh century, why should one think that they are in the right in their current state of schism?

In all this time, the Holy See alone never fell into heresy.

---

influence of the emperor (who naturally always supported his court patriarch) in most cases dragged a great number of other Eastern bishops into the same schism."

CHAPTER 7

Apostolic Tradition and the "Oral Torah"

The mark of apostolicity of the Church refers both to the sacramental succession of bishops from the Apostles and the continual passing on of the apostolic doctrine in the life of the Church. The Church is apostolic in both ways—through conserving apostolic succession and through conserving the apostolic Tradition. The apostolic succession serves the preservation and transmission of the apostolic Tradition.

Sacred Tradition

God's Revelation comes to us through two channels: Tradition and Scripture. Tradition is the revealed doctrine on faith and morals, given by God to the custody of the Church, which was not directly written down in Holy Scripture, but which the Apostles transmitted orally in their preaching and life, and which is continuously transmitted from generation to generation in the entire life of the Church through the action of the Holy Spirit. The word "tradition" comes from the Latin word *tradere*, which means to "pass on." Tradition is a sacred heritage passed on from generation to generation.

The existence of Tradition can be seen in the missionary mandate given by Christ to the Apostles before He ascended into heaven. In Mark 16:15, Jesus commanded the Apostles: "Go into all the world and preach the gospel to the whole creation." He did not tell them to *write* the Gospel, but to preach it, which means to transmit orally the teaching they received. Likewise, in the missionary mandate in Matthew 28:18–20, Jesus gave the commission to His Apostles to *"make disciples* of all nations, baptizing them in the name of the Father and of the Son and of the Holy Spirit, *teaching* them to observe all that I have commanded you; and lo, I am with you always, to the close of the age." By teaching the nations all that Jesus taught them, the Apostles transmitted the salvific Tradition to the Church and, in a special way, to their successors, the bishops, who passed it on to their successors, and so on to the present day. This transmission will continue until the end of the world because of Jesus' promise that He will remain with them until the end of time. Thus the Tradition that is imparted by the Apostles and their successors is a *living Tradition*, bringing each new generation of disciples into vital contact with Christ and His Gospel.

In Acts 1:8, Jesus' last reported words to the Apostles enjoin the same mission: "You shall receive power when the Holy Spirit has come upon you; and *you shall be my witnesses in Jerusalem and in all Judea and Samaria and to the end of the earth.*" The witness of the Apostles and their successors in their preaching and governance of the Church is the principal way in which the apostolic Tradition is transmitted to all generations and places, imparting vital contact with Jesus Christ, source of grace and truth. This witness is made possible, as Jesus makes clear, through the full outpouring of the power of the Holy Spirit on Pentecost. It follows that the Holy Spirit must be the main protagonist in the passing on of Tradition. Reception of the outpouring of the gifts of the Spirit makes one an effective transmitter of Tradition.

This text of Acts (1:8) also shows us the itinerary of the passing on of Tradition. It began in Jerusalem and Judea and then passed to Samaria (Acts 8) and gradually to the rest of the world through the aid of the synagogues and God-fearing Gentiles in the diaspora. We might think of Tradition as a fountain of life-giving waters that comes from a high place—Jerusalem—and progressively forms streams and rivers that water the valleys of the earth.

The prophets speak of the transmission of the apostolic Tradition in various Messianic prophecies. In Isaiah 2:2–4, the prophet pictures Tradition as going out from Zion:

> It shall come to pass in the latter days that the mountain of the house of the Lord shall be established as the highest of the mountains, and shall be raised above the hills; and all the nations shall flow to it, and many peoples shall come, and say: "Come, let us go up to the mountain of the Lord, to the house of the God of Jacob; that he may teach us his ways and that we may walk in his paths." For out of Zion shall go forth the law, and the word of the Lord from Jerusalem.

Another magnificent prophetic image of apostolic Tradition is given in Ezekiel 47 through the image of a spring of water coming out from the east gate of the Temple and giving life to the desert of Judah and making the waters of the Dead Sea fresh and full of life.

Since Tradition is the transmission of the very life of Christ and the Church, animated by the Holy Spirit, the transmission of Tradition through the generations serves to "gather" the new Israel to the one pastor of the flock—Jesus the Messiah—according to the prophecy of

Ezekiel 34:23, in which God promises to "set up over them one shepherd, my servant David, and he shall feed them."[1]

It should never be forgotten that the first recipients of the apostolic Tradition were the Israelites. Only by first gathering a faithful remnant[2] of the lost sheep of Israel could the apostolic message then go out to the nations, so as to incorporate them as well into the new Israel of the Messianic age, which is the fulfillment of the prophecies of the Messianic Kingdom. "For out of Zion shall go forth the law, and the word of the Lord from Jerusalem" (Is 2:3). The Church, in its founding at Pentecost, was entirely Jewish, drawn entirely from Israel. Jesus Himself says that He was sent to gather the lost sheep of Israel. And the choosing of the Twelve Apostles was clearly meant to be a reconstituting of Israel, according to the Biblical prophecies about the Messianic age.

Benedict XVI spoke profoundly about this in his Wednesday Audiences on the Apostles:

> In this regard, it must be said that the message of Jesus is completely misunderstood if it is separated from the context of the faith and hope of the Chosen People: like John the Baptist, his direct Precursor, *Jesus above all addresses Israel in order to "gather" it together in the eschatological time that arrived with him.*[3]

> To whom would the Apostles be sent? In the Gospel Jesus seemed to limit his mission to Israel alone: "I was sent only to the lost sheep of the house of Israel." In a similar way he seemed to restrict the mission entrusted to the Twelve (Mt 10:5ff). . . . A certain rationally inspired modern criticism saw these words as showing a lack of universal awareness by the Nazarene. Actually, they should be understood in the light of his special relationship with Israel, the community of the Covenant, in continuity with the history of salvation. According to the Messianic expectation, the divine promises directly addressed to Israel would reach fulfillment when God himself had gathered his people through his Chosen One as a shepherd gathers his flock: "I will save my flock, they shall no longer be a prey. . . . I will set up over them one shepherd, my servant David, and he shall feed them. . ." (Ezek 34:22–24).

> Jesus is the eschatological shepherd who gathers the lost sheep of the house of Israel and goes in search of them because he knows and loves them. Through this "gathering together," the Kingdom of God is proclaimed to all peoples: "I will set my glory among the nations; and all the nations shall see my judgment. . ."

---

[1] See also Ezek 36:24.

[2] See Rom 9:27 and 11:5.

[3] Benedict XVI, Audience of March 15, 2006 (my italics).

(Ezek 39:21). And Jesus followed precisely this prophetic indication. His first step was to "gather together" the people of Israel, so that all the people called to gather in communion with the Lord might see and believe.

Thus the Twelve, taken on to share in the same mission as Jesus, cooperate with the Pastor of the last times, also seeking out the lost sheep of the house of Israel, that is, addressing the people of the promise whose reunion is the sign of salvation for all peoples, the beginning of the universalization of the Covenant. Far from belying the universal openness of the Nazarene's Messianic action, the initial restriction to Israel of his mission and of the Twelve thus becomes an even more effective prophetic sign.[4]

Christ laid the foundation for the "gathering" of Israel through His Incarnation, preaching, and Paschal mystery. The Apostles were inserted into His mission and were "sent"—which is the meaning of the word "apostle"— through the power of the Spirit to continue to "gather" Israel through the transmission of the apostolic Tradition. In the same way, as we shall see, the Apostles appointed successors to continue to fulfill this mission until the end of time.

As they gathered the new Israel, Gentiles were also gathered into the Church through the power of the Spirit. The grace given to the Gentiles to enter into the inheritance of Messianic Israel is beautifully expressed by St. Paul in Ephesians 2:19–22:

So then you are no longer strangers and sojourners, but you are fellow citizens with the saints and members of the household of God, built upon the foundation of the apostles and prophets, Christ Jesus himself being the cornerstone, in whom the whole structure is joined together and grows into a holy temple in the Lord; in whom you also are built into it for a dwelling place of God in the Spirit.

In the Acts of the Apostles and the Letters of St. Paul we see the prophetic image of the Word of the Lord that goes out from Zion to all nations progressively realized through the preaching of the Apostles. St. Paul solemnly gives witness of Tradition in 1 Corinthians 15:3–4: "I delivered to you as of first importance what I also received, that Christ died for our sins in accordance with the scriptures, that he was buried, that he was raised on the third day."

Furthermore, St. Paul says that his oral preaching is the Word of God. In 1 Thessalonians 2:13, he writes: "And we also thank God constantly for this, that when you received the word of God which you

---

[4] Benedict XVI, Audience of March 22, 2006.

heard from us, you accepted it not as the word of men, but as what it really is, the word of God, which is at work in you believers." And in 2 Thessalonians 2:15 he puts his oral preaching on the same level as his canonical letters: "Therefore, brethren, stand fast and hold to the *traditions* which you were taught by us, either by word of mouth or by letter." Earlier in the same chapter (2 Thess 2:5), speaking of the signs of the Second Coming of Christ, the Apostle had said: "Do you not remember that when I was still with you I told you this?"

In the Second Letter to Timothy, St. Paul speaks of his oral teaching as a sacred deposit that Timothy is to guard faithfully and pass on to others: "Hence I remind you to rekindle the gift of God that is within you through the laying on of my hands. . . . Follow the pattern of the sound words which you have heard from me . . . ; guard the truth that has been entrusted to you by the Holy Spirit who dwells within us."[5] And again: "What you have heard from me before many witnesses entrust to faithful men who will be able to teach others also."[6] It can be seen that for St. Paul, the Holy Spirit is the true source of the effective transmission of the apostolic Tradition. Furthermore, this transmission is not to end with Paul and the other Apostles, but is entrusted by Paul to Timothy and Titus, who are charged to entrust the transmission of the sacred deposit to their successors in turn.[7]

Another fundamental text which speaks of Tradition is Romans 10:14–17:

> But how are men to call upon him in whom they have not believed? And how are they to believe in him of whom they have never heard? And how are they to hear without a preacher? And how can men preach unless they are sent? As it is written, "How beautiful are the feet of those who preach good news!" But they have not all obeyed the gospel; for Isaiah says, "Lord, who has believed what he has heard from us?" So faith comes from what is heard, and what is heard comes by the preaching of Christ.

The Gospel is transmitted to all nations and generations through *preaching*, which is the oral transmission of the apostolic Tradition.

One of the most tragic innovations of Protestantism was the negation of the existence of Tradition as a source of Revelation (together with the negation of the infallibility of the Magisterium),

---

[5] 2 Tim 1:6, 13–14.

[6] 2 Tim 2:2.

[7] It can also be seen in these texts that the action of the Holy Spirit in the transmission of the deposit is intimately connected with the sacrament of Holy Orders, alluded to by Paul in the reference to the laying on of his hands.

leaving Scripture as the only norm of faith and morals. This position is summarized in the phrase: *sola Scriptura*. The tragedy of it is that it implies that the Holy Spirit had abandoned the Church in such a way that the truths of the apostolic preaching were no longer thought to be living in the Church at the time of the Reformation and for a millennium before, despite the promise of our Redeemer to be with His Church in all generations, even to the end of time.

The existence of Tradition was solemnly defined as a dogma of faith in the Council of Trent, against the position of Luther:

> The holy, ecumenical and general Council of Trent . . . clearly perceives that these truths and instruction [of the Gospel] are contained in the written books and in the *unwritten traditions*, which, received by the Apostles from the mouth of Christ Himself, or from the Apostles themselves, the Holy Spirit dictating, have come down to us, transmitted as it were from hand to hand. Following, then, the examples of the orthodox Fathers, it receives and venerates with piety and reverence all the books both of the Old and New Testaments, since one God is the author of both; *also the traditions, whether they relate to faith or to morals, as having been dictated either orally by Christ or by the Holy Spirit, and preserved in the Catholic Church in unbroken succession.*[8]

The Function of Tradition

Sacred Tradition is necessary for the Church in all times for many reasons. Protestants tend to admit its necessity only in the beginning of the Church before the formation of the New Testament.

First of all, Scripture without Tradition is a dead letter which has no key of interpretation. *Through the life-giving action of the Holy Spirit, Tradition conserves the true sense of Revelation and of Holy Scripture. Without Tradition, it would be impossible to defend the faith against heretics who cite Scripture against its true meaning.* The Holy Fathers easily detected the presence of heresy because it clashed with their sense of the living Tradition. The fragmentation of the Protestants into 28,000 branches is a demonstration of what would happen to the Church if she were stripped of her Tradition.

The necessity of an authoritative Tradition for the interpretation of Scripture can be seen in Christ's parables. Questioned by the disciples, He Himself had to interpret the parables for them. Similarly, He interpreted the Scriptures that referred to His Paschal mystery on Easter Sunday and "opened their minds to understand the scriptures" (Lk

---

[8] Council of Trent, session 4, DS 1501 (D 783) (my italics).

24:45). Tradition involves the living transmission of that understanding to all generations.

Secondly, Tradition is more ample than Holy Scripture and contains truths that are not *explicitly* contained in the Bible. For example, St. John concludes his Gospel (21:25) with this affirmation: "But there are also many other things which Jesus did; were every one of them to be written, I suppose that the world itself could not contain the books that would be written." Evidently, St. John knew much more of the doctrine of Christ than he wrote in the fourth Gospel, and therefore it is certain that he taught many truths orally that were never written down in the Bible. And on account of the reverence in which the Apostles were held, these truths were faithfully guarded and transmitted by the successors of the Apostles, the first bishops.

For example, St. Irenaeus, eminent Father of the Church and Bishop of Lyons at the end of the second century and beginning of the third, told of how in his early youth he had heard many things—and remembered them with great clarity—from the holy martyr St. Polycarp, his master, who died in 169 AD after having been a bishop for perhaps some sixty or seventy years.[9] St. Polycarp, in his turn, as a very young man had been a disciple of St. John the Evangelist at the end of the first century, as well as a disciple of St. Ignatius of Antioch, who was a direct disciple of St. Peter and St. John.

The fact that the apostolic Tradition is more ample than the explicit contents of Sacred Scripture has important practical consequences. Not all revealed truths are found explicitly in the Bible, and therefore the Church can define dogmas of faith on the basis of her Tradition alone. For example, the Assumption of Our Lady is not narrated in Scripture, but was defined as dogma on the basis of the living Tradition. Similarly, the fittingness of the discipline of clerical celibacy (or more precisely, perfect continence for bishops, priests, and deacons) was understood by

---

[9] See Eusebius, *History of the Church* 5.20.6, p. 227: "When I was still a boy I saw you in Lower Asia in Polycarp's company. . . . I have a clearer recollection of events at that time than of recent happenings—what we learn in childhood develops along with the mind and becomes a part of it—so that I can describe the place where blessed Polycarp sat and talked, his goings out and comings in, the character of his life, his personal appearance, his addresses to crowded congregations. I remember how he spoke of his intercourse with John and with the others who had seen the Lord; how he repeated their words from memory; and how the things that he had heard them say about the Lord, His miracles and His teaching, things that he had heard direct from the eye-witnesses of the Word of Life, were proclaimed by Polycarp in complete harmony with Scripture. To these things I listened eagerly at that time, by the mercy of God shown to me, not committing them to writing but learning them by heart. By God's grace, I constantly and conscientiously ruminate on them."

the Fathers to be an apostolic Tradition, even though it is not directly contained in Scripture.[10] Another example is the canon of Scripture. No text of Scripture teaches which are the true books of the Bible. *We know the canon of Scripture from Tradition alone.*

This means that all Protestants, while rejecting the authority of Tradition, have nevertheless received their Bible from the Church (although they eliminated a few books).[11] However, even when a truth of faith is contained directly in Scripture, Tradition is always necessary as a witness of the correct interpretation. Thus truths can be defined solely on the basis of Tradition (although rarely), but never solely on the basis of Scripture.

Tradition and Traditions

It is important to recognize that not everything taught by the Fathers of the Church is part of Tradition in the proper sense of the word. Any individual Father could make mistakes in particular matters. However, if the Fathers speak with a common and definitive voice concerning matters of faith and morals, there we should recognize the presence of Tradition. Numerical unanimity is not necessary and would be impossible to find or verify. The key criterion is moral unanimity, which means a general *consensus* on matters of faith and morals to be held by all the faithful.

Tradition with a capital "T" refers to the deposit of Revelation that has been entrusted to the Church. It is the apostolic Tradition. However, there are also venerable ecclesiastical traditions which do not necessarily form part of the deposit of Revelation, even though they have great importance in the life of the Church. The difference is that the ecclesiastical traditions are not a matter of doctrine. They are disciplinary, and therefore they can change to a certain degree. Examples are the practice of fasting from meat on Fridays and in Lent, praying facing towards the east, women's head coverings in church, and the like. The apostolic Tradition, on the other hand, cannot change, although it gradually grows by becoming more explicit, as we shall see.

---

[10] See Stefan Heid, *Celibacy in the Early Church* (San Francisco: Ignatius Press, 2000); Christian Cochini, S.J., *Apostolic Origins of Priestly Celibacy* (San Francisco: Ignatius Press, 1990); Alfons Maria Cardinal Stickler, *The Case for Clerical Celibacy* (San Francisco: Ignatius Press, 1995).

[11] Protestants rejected Tobit, Judith, Wisdom, Sirach, Baruch, 1 and 2 Maccabees, and parts of Esther and Daniel, despite the fact that these books had been accepted and used by the Church from the earliest centuries. The Council of Trent formally defined the Catholic canon of Scripture, in which these books are included.

Ecclesiastical traditions generally have a doctrinal root which certainly belongs to the apostolic Tradition.[12] Fasting and other penitential practices, for example, are based on the doctrinal truth that we must do penance of some sort for our sins and in remembrance of the Passion of Christ. Liturgical traditions are based on the doctrinal truths concerning the sacraments and salvation history. Thus, although subject to reform, ecclesiastical traditions merit great respect. It is a sign of a lack of ecclesial spirit to denigrate the venerable traditions of the Church, whether liturgical or ascetical.

Vatican II on Tradition, Scripture, and the Magisterium

In the Second Vatican Council, the Dogmatic Constitution on Divine Revelation, *Dei Verbum* 7–10, discusses the transmission of Revelation in Tradition and Scripture, and its preservation through the Church's Magisterium. Although Tradition and Scripture differ in the way they hand on Revelation, these two means of transmitting Revelation flow from one original source—the words of Christ and the prophets—and work together in intimate union, forming one unified "sacred deposit" of faith.[13] Tradition came first in time, for the Apostles preached orally before the books of the New Testament were written down, just as Moses and the prophets preached before some of their words were written down in inspired form.

Furthermore, Tradition enabled the Apostles and their successors, through all ages of the Church, to "preserve this word of God faithfully, explain it, and make it more widely known" (*DV* 9). It will continue to perform this necessary function until the end of time. Tradition is always necessary in the Church, for Scripture does not ensure its own proper interpretation, nor does it necessarily contain all that God revealed. Even after the establishment of the New Testament and its canon, we still need Tradition to ensure that the message of Christ's Gospel remains genuine.

---

[12] See Yves Congar, *The Meaning of Tradition*, trans. A. N. Woodrow (San Francisco: Ignatius Press, 2004), 44: "There exist . . . numerous traditions that are ecclesiastical by origin, having been laid down by the Church during her historical existence: institutions, rites, customs, discipline. Sometimes these are the historical form, or modification, perhaps, of a reality that is apostolic or even divine in origin. For example, the obligation of hearing Mass on Sunday or of the annual Easter Communion is an ecclesiastical modification of a divine or apostolic reality. The papacy, in the form fixed by centuries of history, is a historical form of a divine institution (that of Peter as supreme pastor and head of the apostolic college), itself already modified by an apostolic initiative (the fact that Peter had his 'see' at Rome)."

[13] See *DV* 10.

Dei Verbum seeks to present Scripture and Tradition in greater unity than had been the case before. John Paul II, in an address of February 27, 2000, said:

> The Dogmatic Constitution *Dei Verbum* put the Word of God at the heart of the Church's life with renewed awareness. This centrality stems from a more vivid perception of the unity of Sacred Scripture and Sacred Tradition. The Word of God, which is kept alive by the faith of the holy people of believers under the guidance of the Magisterium, also asks each of us to accept our own responsibility for preserving intact the process of transmission.

Dei Verbum 9 states:

> Hence there exists a close connection and communication between Sacred Tradition and Sacred Scripture. For both of them, flowing from the same divine wellspring, in a certain way merge into a unity and tend toward the same end. For Sacred Scripture is the Word of God inasmuch as it is consigned to writing under the inspiration of the divine Spirit, while *Sacred Tradition takes the Word of God entrusted by Christ the Lord and the Holy Spirit to the Apostles, and hands it on to their successors in its full purity, so that led by the light of the Spirit of truth, they may in proclaiming it preserve this word of God faithfully, explain it, and make it more widely known.* Consequently it is not from Sacred Scripture alone that the Church draws her certainty about everything which has been revealed. Therefore both Sacred Tradition and Sacred Scripture are to be accepted and venerated with the same sense of loyalty and reverence.

In *Dei Verbum* 8, the content of Tradition is indicated, which is very broad, including the entire life of the Church: "Now what was handed on by the Apostles includes everything which contributes toward the holiness of life and increase in faith of the People of God; and so the Church, in her teaching, life, and worship, perpetuates and hands on to all generations *all that she herself is, all that she believes.*"

Development of Tradition

Dei Verbum 8 also treats the very important subject of the development of Tradition in the Church, which grows through a gradual increase in the understanding of God's Revelation:

> This Tradition which comes from the Apostles develops in the Church with the help of the Holy Spirit. For there is a growth in the understanding of the realities and the words which have been

handed down. This happens through the contemplation and study made by believers, who treasure these things in their hearts (see Luke 2:19, 51), through a penetrating understanding of the spiritual realities which they experience, and through the preaching of those who have received through episcopal succession the sure gift of truth. For as the centuries succeed one another, the Church constantly moves forward toward the fullness of divine truth until the words of God reach their complete fulfillment in her.

The continual enrichment of Tradition in the life of the Church is a very important doctrine, with great practical consequences. Every age in the life of the Church has something to contribute to the gradual enrichment of the Church's faith. In every period, certain revealed truths are grasped more profoundly and more explicitly. It follows from this that we cannot view any major period in the life of the Church as barren or unfruitful, as if Christ and His Spirit had failed to be present in the life of the Church at that time.

A very common Protestant attitude is to think that the Church had basically fallen astray from the time of Constantine, more or less, until the advent of Martin Luther. Such an idea is absolutely impossible, for Christ promised to be present always in His Church and to send His Spirit to lead her into all truth.

Sometimes certain Catholics fall into a similar error, denigrating large epochs in the history of the Church such as the Middle Ages, Scholasticism, the period from Trent to Vatican II, or the period since Vatican II. Such views are incompatible with the development of Tradition in the life of the Church as affirmed in this text from *Dei Verbum* 8.

In order to help Protestants and others to rediscover the beauty of Tradition, *Dei Verbum* 8 mentions some great examples of the witness of Tradition from patristic times:

> The *words of the holy Fathers witness to the presence of this living Tradition*, whose wealth is poured into the practice and life of the believing and praying Church. Through the same Tradition the Church's *full canon* of the sacred books is known, and the sacred writings themselves are more profoundly understood and unceasingly made active in her; and thus God, who spoke of old, *uninterruptedly converses* with the bride of His beloved Son; and the *Holy Spirit*, through whom the living voice of the Gospel resounds in the Church, and through her, in the world, leads unto all truth those who believe and makes the word of Christ dwell abundantly in them (see Col 3:16).

One interesting example of the importance of Tradition in the life of the Church mentioned in this text concerns the recognition of the inspired books of the Bible. The canon of Scripture is obviously not contained in Scripture itself, and is known by the Church only through Tradition.[14] From the second to the fourth centuries, some local churches had certain doubts about which books were included in the canon of inspired Scripture. These doubts were gradually dissipated until by the end of the fourth century, the true canon of Scripture was defined in councils in North Africa and approved by the Roman Pontiff. This same canon was later infallibly defined in the Council of Trent.

Tradition in Israel: The Oral Torah

The notion of Tradition, of course, is not an invention of the Church or of Jesus, but was present in Israel from the beginning of her existence. God's Revelation was given to Israel not only in the written form of Scripture, but also in oral form to be passed on from generation to generation. As for the Church, Israel knew the canon of her sacred books from oral Tradition.

The notion of oral Tradition in Judaism is expressed in the words of the Mishnah: "Moses received Torah at Sinai and handed it on to Joshua, Joshua to elders, elders to prophets, and prophets handed it on to the men of the Great Assembly."[15] The "Great Assembly" refers to the sages of the time of Ezra and Nehemiah, who were the link between the last prophets after the Exile (Haggai, Zachariah, and Malachi) and the rabbis of the following generations.

The Old Testament itself shows us that Israel's knowledge of revealed truth was in constant development. This can be seen in the gradual growth of knowledge about the Last Things: the Resurrection, heaven and hell, the necessity of prayers for the faithful departed, and so forth, as witnessed, for example, in the books of Maccabees, in which the mother and her seven martyred sons give witness to their faith that God will gloriously raise their mutilated bodies.

Despite the infidelity of individual men, Revelation was maintained, passed on, and developed according to God's plan. This was accomplished by the mutual witness of the written and the oral Torah, for the written Torah is explained and understood by the light of the oral Tradition.

---

[14] Obviously, the Protestant claim that Scripture alone is sufficient founders on this point, for Scripture alone does not indicate the very canon of Scripture.

[15] Mishnah-tractate Avot 1:1.

Apostolic Tradition and the Oral Torah

What is the connection between the oral Torah and the apostolic Tradition of the Church?

First of all, the apostolic Tradition includes the oral Torah, insofar as the oral Torah was an integral part of God's continuing Revelation to Israel. This Revelation culminated with the Incarnation, teaching, death, and Resurrection of the Messiah. The apostolic Tradition is thus the complete deposit of which the oral Torah was only a part. The deposit of faith that Jesus passed on to His Church through the Apostles included all the Revelation made to Israel, understood as leading up to and preparing for the mystery of the Messiah and the Messianic Kingdom (Christ and the Church). That Revelation was illuminated and transfigured by the light of the fullness of Christ and the New Covenant sealed in His Blood.

In consequence, much of the oral Torah of Israel, as put down later in the Talmud, is not directly pertinent to the Church because it deals primarily with the ceremonial law and judicial precepts of the Mosaic Law, which are no longer binding in the Church, for the Church has a new ceremonial law centering on the seven sacraments of the New Covenant.[16]

The Oral Torah in Rabbinical Judaism

Although at work since the calling of Abraham and the revelation on Sinai, the oral Torah took on a new prominence in the life of Israel after the destruction of Jerusalem and the Temple at the hands of the Roman legions under the general Titus in 70 AD and the ensuing 2,000-year exile from the land of Israel, after the catastrophe of the Second Jewish War.[17] Since all sacrifice had to be offered in the one Temple, the destruction of the Temple of Jerusalem meant the end of the sacrificial system. With the loss of the offering of sacrifice, the Old Testament priesthood lost its principal function and its reason for existing. As a result, the axis of Jewish life became the synagogue rather than the Temple; and it centered on the rabbis who interpreted the Mosaic Law rather than on the priests and Levites, who could no longer offer sacrifice. In this context of upheaval and tragedy, it became gradually imperative to write down the oral Torah so as to preserve it for the

---

[16] As seen above on page 43, the medieval theologians distinguished three kinds of precepts in the Mosaic Law (whether written or oral): the moral law, the ceremonial law, and judicial precepts. Christ fulfilled the entire Law, but only the precepts of the moral law continue as such in the Church.

[17] The Jews mourn that destruction in an annual fast, *Tisha B'Av* (ninth day of the Jewish month of Av).

following generations. This was the time in which the Mishnah and the Talmud were written.

Interestingly, the formative period of the Church corresponded chronologically with the formative period of rabbinical Judaism, for the oral Torah was written down by the sages of Israel during the first through the seventh centuries.

Rabbinical Judaism as it has existed for the past fifteen hundred years cannot be understood without understanding the role of the "oral Torah" in shaping Jewish life and the Jewish world-view. What is the oral Torah? Rabbi Jacob Neusner gives a good explanation:

> Judaism has always maintained that God revealed a dual Torah to Moses at Sinai: One Torah was to be transmitted to the people of Israel through the medium of writing; the other was to be handed down orally, memorized by successive sages. These words of God were specifically formulated to be memorized. . . . The written Torah and the oral Torah together constitute a single whole Torah—the full and exhaustive statement of God's will for Israel and humanity. . . .
>
> The writing down of the oral Torah began with the Mishnah, a philosophical law code, at ca. 200 C.E. It concluded with the closure of the Talmud of Babylonia, a sustained exposition of both the Mishnah and Scripture, at ca. 600 C.E. . . . Sayings in these documents derive from sages who flourished from somewhat before the first century C.E. to the conclusion of the Talmud of Babylonia, hence over a period of more than six hundred years.[18]
>
> Authoritative writings that say a single harmonious truth constitute not a library, but a canon. The canon of Judaism, made up of the authoritative books, so constitutes not merely a collection of writings but a coherent and harmonious statement, that is, torah, or instruction. . . .
>
> At stake in this book is the integrity of Judaism. Why? The Judaic religion stands or falls on the claim of the unity and cogency of the one whole Torah, oral and written, of Sinai. If I make my point stick, then I provide the key to living and believing as an informed Jew. If I do not, then I contribute merely a useful source of information about some books. So much more matters, in the pages that follow, than mere questions of detail. Specifically, details flow together into a single, whole, and cogent proposition.[19]

---

[18] Jacob Neusner, *The Oral Torah: The Sacred Books of Judaism: An Introduction* (San Francisco: Harper & Row, 1986), vii.

[19] Neusner, *The Oral Torah*, ix.

The unity of the written and oral Torah is crucial for understanding the nature of the Church. She is founded on the Word of God known through Scripture and apostolic Tradition, transmitted in written and oral form. This twofold mode of transmission has been God's plan from the beginning.

Revelation came to Israel through this twofold channel. It continues to come to Israel and the Church in this twofold channel today and will continue in this way until the end of time. The two channels—oral and written—of the one Revelation of God form a unitary whole and enable the Church to remain in the whole truth.

It follows that the investigation of the history of the early centuries of the Church is not merely an investigation of details of history. Rather it is an investigation into the early sources of the current of Tradition that was transmitted from Christ to the Apostles, and from them to their successors, down to our day. In this chain of witnesses, the early Fathers have a special place.

The same was true in the formation of rabbinical Judaism. The Fathers—rabbis from the first to the seventh centuries AD—formulated in writing the substance of the oral Torah. This written corpus is referred to as the Mishnah and the Talmud. Together with the written Scriptures, the Mishnah and Talmud form the basis of Jewish life.

As Neusner states, *"The Judaic religion stands or falls on the claim of the unity and cogency of the one whole Torah, oral and written, of Sinai."* In the same way, Christianity depends on the claim of the unity and cogency of the one whole Torah, oral and written, begun on Sinai and consummated in the teaching and Paschal mystery of Jesus the Messiah and transmitted to his Apostles and their successors. This is why it is crucial to study the early Fathers of the Church, together with the Scriptures.

Benedict XVI on Tradition

Benedict XVI has given a beautiful catechesis on the nature of apostolic Tradition in his Wednesday Audiences of April 26 and May 3, 2006, as an introduction to the series of catecheses on the Apostles and Fathers of the Church.

He emphasizes that Tradition is the transmission of the Church's life to all succeeding generations. It is not simply the passing on of formulas committed to memory by the Apostles. Rather, it is transmission of the spirit of *life in Christ*, made possible by the communication of the Holy Spirit. Tradition cannot be understood apart from the Holy Spirit, who spoke through the prophets, and through whom all Revelation is communicated and kept alive in the Church. Benedict writes:

The Church's apostolic Tradition consists in this transmission of the goods of salvation which, through the power of the Spirit, makes the Christian community the permanent actualization of the original communion. It is called "original" because it was born of the witness of the Apostles and of the community of the disciples at the time of the origins. It was passed on under the guidance of the Holy Spirit in the New Testament writings and in the sacramental life, in the life of the faith, and the Church continuously refers to it—to this Tradition, which is the whole, ever up-to-date reality of Jesus' gift—as her foundation and her law, through the uninterrupted succession of the apostolic ministry. . . .

Tradition is the communion of the faithful around their legitimate Pastors down through history, a communion that the Holy Spirit nurtures, assuring the connection between the experience of the apostolic faith, lived in the original community of the disciples, and the actual experience of Christ in his Church.

In other words, Tradition is the practical continuity of the Church, the holy Temple of God the Father, built on the foundation of the Apostles and held together by the cornerstone, Christ, through the life-giving action of the Spirit: "So then you are no longer strangers and sojourners, but you are fellow citizens with the saints and members of the household of God, built upon the foundation of the apostles and prophets, Christ Jesus himself being the cornerstone, in whom the whole structure is joined together and grows into a holy temple in the Lord; in whom you also are built into it for a dwelling place of God in the Spirit" (Eph 2:19–22).

Thanks to Tradition, guaranteed by the ministry of the Apostles and by their successors, the water of life that flowed from Christ's side and his saving blood reach the women and men of all times. Thus, Tradition is the permanent presence of the Saviour who comes to meet us, to redeem us and to sanctify us in the Spirit, through the ministry of his Church, to the glory of the Father.

Concluding and summing up, we can therefore say that Tradition is not the transmission of things or words, a collection of dead things. Tradition is the living river that links us to the origins, the living river in which the origins are ever present, the great river that leads us to the gates of eternity. And since this is so, in this living river the words of the Lord . . . are ceaselessly brought about: "I am with you always, to the close of the age" (Mt 28:20).[20]

---

[20] Benedict XVI, General Audience, April 26, 2006.

Apostolic tradition is something essential to the Church of Christ; the true Church of Christ is that in which apostolic Tradition is continually transmitted and revered as the life-giving river by which each generation receives the deposit of faith in its fullness.

CHAPTER 8

The Sanctity of the Church

In What Sense Is the Church Holy?

We profess in the Creed that the Church is "holy," and furthermore, we hold that this is one of the essential distinguishing marks of the Church, by which her true identity as a supernatural society founded by God is manifested in the world.

Holiness is the Church's very reason for being. Christ founded the Church to communicate His sanctity to men. The Church exists to be a mother of supernatural life, a channel of grace, and a means of sanctity, sanctifying individuals and society itself.

However, the sanctity of the true Church is a more difficult mark to explain in apologetics. There are two reasons for this difficulty. First of all, sanctity is something interior which cannot be quantified, nor empirically demonstrated. Secondly, the sanctity of the Church does not exclude the presence of sin and sinners in her midst. For members of the true Church do not always live in accordance with the sanctity of Christ and the grace of the Holy Spirit which vivifies the Church. As we know, members of the Church can be abominable sinners.

In the Church, there are *living members*, who are in a state of sanctifying grace, and *dead members*, who are in a state of mortal sin, despite their baptism and their outward profession of the Catholic faith. The dead members no longer possess the grace of the Mystical Body, and thus can be said to be cut off from her life.

The sanctity of the Church is manifested only by the living members, and especially by those who not only live in a state of grace, but who excel in holiness. Such holy members have never been lacking in the history of the Church, as can be seen in the beatification and canonization of the saints. Therefore, the sanctity of the Catholic Church, insofar as it is a sign of credibility or divine credential, can be seen above all in these holy people. For this reason, it is very important for Catholics to nourish their spiritual lives by familiarity with the lives of the saints.

Despite the difficulty of using this mark in apologetics, the mark of sanctity of the Catholic Church is very important in the process of conversion, for this is generally what attracts people to the Church.

However, since this mark of the sanctity of the Church is obscured by the sins of the visible members of the Church, it is important to clarify some fundamental questions at the outset. First of all, is the Church immaculate, or is she stained through the sin of her members? Second, if we answer that the Church is immaculate, in what sense is this true? Third, in what ways is the sanctity of the Church manifested externally, such that it can serve as a true sign or mark of the true religion?

Biblical Testimony (Ephesians 5:25–27)

Let us begin with the first question: is the Church immaculate, or is she stained through the sins of her members? The answer of Scripture is clear: the Church is immaculate and not stained. The clearest testimony on this score is the classic text of Ephesians 5:25–27, which concerns matrimony as a sacrament of Christ's union with the Church:

> Husbands, love your wives, as Christ loved the Church and gave himself up for her, that he might sanctify her, having cleansed her by the washing of water with the word, that he might present the Church to himself in splendor, without spot or wrinkle or any such thing, that she might be holy and without blemish.

The Church is immaculate because Christ has cleansed her, above all through His sacraments. In this text St. Paul is speaking especially of the sacrament of Baptism from which the living members of the Church are born, by which she is cleansed *"by the washing of water with the word,"* so as to be made fit to be Christ's bride. All of us are called to be made holy through the sacraments and our correspondence to grace so as to be worthy recipients of the privilege of being made members of Christ's bride, and thus brought into a spousal relation with God.

The Sins of the Members of the Church Do Not Truly Stain the Church

It is common to say that the Church is "stained" by the grave sins of her members, as in the cases of pedophilia or other abominable crimes. However, it is important to recognize that this is only a metaphorical and inexact way of speaking. The Church is certainly stained by such sins *in the eyes of the world.* However, theologically speaking, she is not properly stained by such sins, because such acts are not *hers*, any more than an act of heresy would be. All grave sins involve a severing of the sinning member from the life of the Church, so that it is not the Church that is stained by the grave sin, but the sinner alone, who has thereby separated himself from the life-giving vine.[1] The *members* of Christ's Body are stained by sin, but not the Church herself. Pius XII shows us how we should speak of this: "Let everyone then abhor sin, which defiles the mystical *members* of our Redeemer."[2]

It is true that a member of the Church who commits a mortal sin other than heresy or schism is still a visible member of the Church. Nevertheless, he is a dead member whose acts are not vivified by the soul of the Church, but stand in opposition to it.

The only way a member of the Church can commit a grave sin is by receding from the Church's life and the Church's life-giving moral doctrine. The only way that he can return to the life-giving trunk to become a living member is by having his grave sins obliterated through contrition and the sacrament of Penance, at which time he is no longer a grave sinner but a repentant one.

This doctrine has been authoritatively proclaimed in the Credo of the People of God, promulgated by Paul VI in 1968:

> She [the Church] is therefore holy, though she has sinners in her bosom, because she herself has no other life but that of grace: it is by living by her life that her members are sanctified; it is by removing themselves from her life that they fall into sins and disorders that prevent the radiation of her sanctity. This is why she suffers and does penance for these offenses, of which she has the power to heal her children through the blood of Christ and the gift of the Holy Spirit.[3]

Thus it can be seen that grave sin is incompatible with the life of the Church. Every sin is opposed to the Church's life, her influence of grace, the example of her Founder, and her moral teaching. Nevertheless, it cannot touch the life of the Church so as to contaminate it directly.

What about venial sin? Although it does not exclude those who commit it from the life of grace, it does diminish the splendor of that grace and limit its sanctifying action. Thus it too is opposed to the true life of the Church, which is grace.

Channels of Grace

The Church is holy above all in that she is endowed with seven stable channels of grace, which are the seven sacraments. These channels efficaciously and unfailingly give grace unless an obstacle is posed to

---

[1] See Jn 15:1–6.
[2] See Pius XII, *Mystici Corporis* 24.
[3] See *CCC* 827, which cites Paul VI, Credo of the People of God 19.

their efficacy, such as lack of faith in those above the age of reason, lack of repentance, or a contrary will.

The Church is holy first of all through Baptism, by which she is endowed with the means of granting a person a new birth into the life of grace, cancelling all the stains of sin incurred in his past life. The Church, therefore, is holy in that she is spiritually fecund: she has been endowed with the supernatural ability to engender into the supernatural life of grace all who enter her life-giving waters with the right disposition.

Second, she is holy in strengthening that supernatural life through the sacrament of Confirmation, in which a fuller outpouring of the gifts of the Holy Spirit is given to advance the recipient in spiritual maturity. This makes one capable of fighting the good fight of the faith, thus becoming a soldier of Christ (*miles Christi*).

Third, she is holy in giving a spiritual nourishment that is no less efficacious for the spiritual life than healthy food is for the physical life. The Eucharist, worthily received, communicates a greater union with Christ through an increase of charity. The extent of the increase depends on the fervor of one's disposition. Furthermore, this sacrament sanctifies the Church by making Christ substantially present on every altar, so that He may reside in every tabernacle. The Eucharist also makes the Church holy in that it makes her capable of offering an immaculate and infinitely pleasing sacrifice to God the Father: the very sacrifice of Calvary, made present on our altars in every valid Mass.

Fourth, the Church is holy through having received a sacrament by which to restore the supernatural life when it is unfortunately lost through grave sin: the sacrament of Penance. Fifth, the Anointing of the Sick gives added grace in times of grave physical illness. Sixth, the sacrament of Matrimony sanctifies the fundamental building block of society, the family, and gives the spouses a series of sacramental graces to sanctify their marriage, educate their children in the grace of God, and to be a sign in the world of Christ's love for His Church and of her love for Him.

Finally, the sacrament of Holy Orders sanctifies the Church by enabling the recipients of the sacrament to act in the very person of Christ, the Head of the Church, in the consecration of the Eucharist, and in absolution of sin. Holy Orders also provides a sacramental foundation for the exercise of authority in the Church for teaching and governing. That authority is not a mere exercise of human power, but a sacramental sharing in the power of Christ for the building up of His Body. The recipients of Holy Orders, like those who receive the sacrament of Matrimony, are also given a series of sacramental graces to make them worthy ministers of the multiform grace of Christ.

The Church herself, by being endowed with this sevenfold life-giving power, can also be spoken of as a "universal sacrament of salvation." The life-giving grace and sanctification she imparts is itself the seed of future glory. Her unity with God and man on earth is itself the seed of the ultimate union of mankind with God in the Church triumphant. *Lumen gentium* 1 states: "The Church is in Christ like a sacrament or . . . a sign and instrument both of a very closely knit union with God and of the unity of the whole human race." *Lumen gentium* 48 returns to this same idea: "Rising from the dead, he sent his life-giving Spirit upon his disciples and through him has established his body, which is the Church, as the universal sacrament of salvation."

The Second Vatican Council did not mean to say that the Church is the eighth sacrament, but rather that the Church herself, which was born from the seven sacraments, is an efficacious sign of union with God and all men, and is a source of salvation, precisely because she carries the seven life-giving sacraments in her bosom as her dowry. Just as Eve was called the "mother of the living" (Gen 3:20), so the Church is the new Eve, the mother of those living in the order of grace.

Finally, the Church is holy also because of her communion with the saints in heaven. Those who have already gained the vision of God are still members of the Church, now triumphant, and their bond to us on earth is not weakened, but strengthened.[4] Thus *Lumen gentium* 49 states:

> The union of the wayfarers with the brethren who have gone to sleep in the peace of Christ is not in the least weakened or interrupted, but on the contrary . . . is strengthened by communication of spiritual goods. For by reason of the fact that those in heaven are more closely united with Christ, they establish the whole Church more firmly in holiness, lend nobility to the worship which the Church offers to God here on earth and in many ways contribute to its greater edification. . . . Thus by their brotherly interest our weakness is greatly strengthened.

Works of Mercy in the Church

Charity expressed in the seven corporal and the seven spiritual works of mercy has always been one of the outstanding signs of the holiness of the Church. Although it is of course true that other organizations also offer works of philanthropy, the Church, over the past 2,000 years, has always been most outstanding in this area.

We see this in the Church already on the morrow of Pentecost, as it is depicted magnificently in Acts 2:42: "And all who believed were

---

[4] The Church is a complex whole composed of three states: the Church militant, the Church suffering, and the Church triumphant.

together and had all things in common; and they sold their possessions and goods and distributed them to all, as any had need."

Again in Acts 4:32–35, we are told:

> Now the company of those who believed were of one heart and soul, and no one said that any of the things which he possessed was his own, but they had everything in common. . . . There was not a needy person among them, for as many as were possessors of lands or houses sold them, and brought the proceeds of what was sold and laid it at the apostles' feet; and distribution was made to each as any had need.

In the third century, Tertullian was able to say: "But it is mainly the deeds of a love so noble that lead many to put a brand upon us. See, they say, how they love one another (for they themselves are animated by mutual hatred); how they are ready even to die for one another."[5] Thus even the pagans were compelled to admit that the Christians were exemplary in works of fraternal charity.

The anonymous second-century Letter to Diognetus makes a similar claim:

> Like others, they marry and have children, but they do not expose them. They share their meals, but not their wives. They live in the flesh, but they are not governed by the desires of the flesh. They pass their days upon earth, but they are citizens of Heaven. Obedient to the laws, they yet live on a level that transcends the law. Christians love all men, but all men persecute them.[6]

During the Middle Ages, the Church was exceedingly magnanimous in offering the works of mercy. The Benedictine monasteries, for example, became an international chain of hospitality for pilgrims and travelers, as well as serving as free schools and hospitals for the sick. Europe once could boast over 30,000 such monasteries. One historian writes:

> Following the fall of the Roman Empire, monasteries gradually became the providers of organized medical care not available elsewhere in Europe for several centuries. Given their organization and location, these institutions were virtual oases of order, piety, and stability in which healing could flourish. To provide these caregiving practices, monasteries also became sites of medical

---

[5] Tertullian, *Apology* 39, in *ANF* 3:46 (translation slightly modified), *PL* 1:471. Benedict XVI cites this in *Deus caritas est* 22. See also 23–24.

[6] Letter to Diognetus 5, in *The Apostolic Fathers*, 703.

learning between the fifth and tenth centuries, the classic period of so-called monastic medicine.[7]

The works of mercy by societies of religious life through the ages are uncountable. In our own time, the charitable works of Blessed Teresa of Calcutta are a beacon to the world.

The Holiness of the Church's Doctrine

Human reason is also capable of seeing that the Catholic Church is holy in her doctrine. This is true above all with regard to the moral teaching of the Church, her doctrine on the dignity of man, and her teaching on the family. Such doctrine can serve as a powerful motive of credibility for upright souls.[8] Paradoxically, it is precisely this aspect of the teaching of the Church that is most often attacked. The same was true in the first centuries of the Church, as we see in the Letter to Diognetus of the second or third century, which states:

> The body hates the soul and wars against it, not because of any injury the soul has done it, but because of the restriction the soul places on its pleasures. Similarly, the world hates the Christians, not because they have done it any wrong, but because they are opposed to its enjoyments. . . . It is by the soul, enclosed within the body, that the body is held together, and similarly, it is by the Christians, detained in the world as in a prison, that the world is held together.[9]

One of the clearest manifestations of the holiness of the doctrine of the Church can be seen in the teaching on marriage and the family. The Catholic Church firmly maintains everything necessary for the defense of the sanctity and well-being of the family, which is the bedrock of society and the cradle in which every human being comes into the world and first learns how to love and respect God, his fellow human beings, and the truth. Any weakening of the family is a great loss to the sanctity of any society.

Today the teaching of the Church on marriage is a solemn proclamation of the sacred character of human life in the face of a culture of death. The Church so often seems to be practically alone in defending the sanctity of marriage in its fullness: its indissolubility, its monogamous character between one man and one woman, and the

---

[7] Guenter Risse, *Mending Bodies, Saving Souls: A History of Hospitals* (New York: Oxford Univ. Press, 1999), 95.

[8] For an explanation of the motives of credibility, see the second volume in this series, *The Mystery of Israel and the Church: Things New and Old*, chapter 1.

[9] Letter to Diognetus 6, in *The Apostolic Fathers*, 705.

inseparability of the procreative and unitive dimensions of the conjugal act.

Mary, Mother of the Church

The holiness of the Church is perfectly realized in Mary Immaculate, who is the Mother of the Church, her perfect exemplar, and the model of her sanctity. Mary perfectly realized the finality of the Church in her own person. For this reason, the Second Vatican Council decided to put its teaching on Mary as the conclusion of the Dogmatic Constitution on the Church, *Lumen gentium*. If we want to understand the Church, we must look at Our Lady.

This also shows a very important corollary: where Marian devotion grows, love of the Church will generally grow; and where Marian devotion languishes, love of the Church will languish, and we can expect to see dissension. A classical example of this occurred in the Protestant Reformation.

In the Fathers of the Church, Mary and the Church are constantly seen together. As Mary is immaculate, so the Church is immaculate, without spot or wrinkle. As Mary is Virgin Mother, so the Church is virgin mother of the Body of Christ. As the Virgin Mary was fruitful beyond all conception, giving birth to the Word Incarnate, so the Church gives birth to Christ's Mystical Catholic Body. The Church is the most fruitful of mothers, giving birth to each of us through the water of Baptism, giving birth to the Body of Christ in all nations.

Furthermore, as Mary is ever virgin in fidelity to God, so the Church is ever virgin in fidelity to Christ. St. Paul says to the Church in Corinth that he has espoused her as a chaste virgin to Christ (2 Cor 11:2): "I feel a divine jealousy for you, for I betrothed you to Christ to present you as a pure bride to her one husband." Nevertheless, he fears that some of the members of the Church in Corinth may fall short of their sublime calling: "But I am afraid that as the serpent deceived Eve by his cunning, your thoughts will be led astray from a sincere and pure devotion to Christ" (2 Cor 11:3). Similarly, the prophet Hosea speaks of the future Church, where God says (Hos 2:19–20): "I will betroth you to me for ever; I will betroth you to me in righteousness and in justice, in steadfast love, and in mercy. I will betroth you to me in faithfulness; and you shall know the Lord." The Old Testament frequently likens religious infidelity to harlotry and fidelity in religious faith to chaste virginity.

To speak of the Church as *ever virgin* is another way of expressing the infallibility of the Church, which cannot ever stray from the true faith, although her erring members can. Nevertheless, in doing so they move away from her, until, through formal heresy, they leave her bosom.

St. Cyprian expresses this with great power:

The spouse of Christ cannot be defiled, she is inviolate and chaste; she knows one home alone, in all modesty she keeps faithfully to one chamber. It is she who preserves us for God, she who seals for the kingdom the sons whom she has borne. Whoever breaks with the Church and enters on an adulterous union, cuts himself off from the promises made to the Church. . . . You cannot have God for your Father if you no longer have the Church for your mother.[10]

St. Augustine writes:

He [Mary's Son] has made His Church like to His mother, he has given her to us as a mother, He has kept her for Himself as a virgin. . . . The Church, like Mary, is a virgin ever spotless and a mother ever fruitful. What He bestowed on Mary in the flesh, He has bestowed on the Church in the spirit. But Mary gave birth to the One, and the Church gives birth to the many, who through the One are gathered together in one.[11]

Lumen gentium 53 sets forth Mary's relationship with the Blessed Trinity, with ourselves, and with the Church:

Redeemed by reason of the merits of her Son and united to Him by a close and indissoluble tie, she is endowed with the high office and dignity of being the Mother of the Son of God, by which account she is also the beloved daughter of the Father and the temple of the Holy Spirit. Because of this gift of sublime grace she far surpasses all creatures, both in heaven and on earth. At the same time, however, because she belongs to the offspring of Adam she is one with all those who are to be saved. She is "the mother of the members of Christ . . . having cooperated by charity that faithful might be born in the Church, who are members of that Head."[12] Wherefore she is hailed as a pre-eminent and singular member of the Church, and as its type and excellent exemplar in faith and charity. The Catholic Church, taught by the Holy Spirit, honors her with filial affection and piety as a most beloved mother.

The divine maternity of Mary is imitated by the Church, who is also virgin and mother, our mother in the supernatural life inaugurated by Baptism. The Church gave birth to us and continues to nourish us

---

[10] St. Cyprian, *On the Unity of the Church* 6, trans. Bévenot, 67.
[11] St. Augustine, Sermon 195.2, PL 38:1018.
[12] St. Augustine, *Holy Virginity* 6: PL 40:399.

throughout our lives through her preaching, her sacraments, and her entire life. The Church has a profound Marian dimension, which expresses her deepest essence. It is no accident that *Lumen gentium* concludes with the Marian dimension of the Church:

> The Church indeed, contemplating her hidden sanctity, imitating her charity and faithfully fulfilling the Father's will, by receiving the word of God in faith becomes herself a mother. By her preaching she brings forth to a new and immortal life the sons who are born to her in baptism, conceived of the Holy Spirit and born of God. She herself is a virgin, who keeps the faith given to her by her Spouse whole and entire. Imitating the mother of her Lord, and by the power of the Holy Spirit, she keeps with virginal purity an entire faith, a firm hope and a sincere charity.
>
> But while in the most holy Virgin the Church has already reached that perfection whereby she is without spot or wrinkle, the followers of Christ still strive to increase in holiness by conquering sin. And so they turn their eyes to Mary who shines forth to the whole community of the elect as the model of virtues. . . . The Virgin in her own life lived an example of that maternal love, by which it behooves that all should be animated who cooperate in the apostolic mission of the Church for the regeneration of men.[13]

Mary is the Mother of the Church, the perfect model of the Church, and the exemplar of the sanctity to which all of her members are called.

Are There Elements of Sanctity Outside the Church?

Can there be elements of Christian sanctity outside the Catholic Church? Indeed there can, but they come from the Word Incarnate and His Church, and rightly belong to her as their rightful source and nurturer.

Lumen gentium 8 takes up this question in a discussion of whether the Church founded by Christ as "one, holy, catholic, and apostolic" is to be identified with the Catholic Church as she exists today and throughout the ages.[14] Is the Mystical Body "which coalesces from a divine and a human element" identical with the Catholic Church? *Lumen gentium* 8 responds:

> This is the one Church of Christ which in the Creed is professed as one, holy, catholic and apostolic, which our Saviour, after His Resurrection, commissioned Peter to shepherd, and him and the other apostles to extend and direct with authority, which He

---

[13] *Lumen gentium* 64–65.

[14] This question was addressed earlier by Pius XII in two encyclicals: *Mystici Corporis* (1943) and *Humani generis* (1950).

erected for all ages as "the pillar and mainstay of the truth." This Church constituted and organized in the world as a society, subsists in the Catholic Church, which is governed by the successor of Peter and by the Bishops in communion with him, although many elements of sanctification and of truth are found outside of its visible structure. These elements, as gifts belonging to the Church of Christ, are forces impelling toward catholic unity.

There has been much discussion of the exact meaning of the expression "*subsists in* the Catholic Church." In the original draft of the text, instead of "subsists," it said "*is.*" "The Church of Christ that we confess in the Creed . . . is the Catholic Church."

Is the change of wording significant? I would argue that the significance of the change is not very great, but is intended to add greater precision. In philosophical terminology, the word "subsist" means to have being in oneself. It means to exist in a substantial rather than an accidental mode. Thus the meaning is that the Church instituted by Christ has its *substantial being* in the Catholic Church alone, although many elements of the Church are found also outside the borders of the Catholic Church in a separated and unnatural state.[15] For example, the Eastern Orthodox churches still have the apostolic succession, together with the seven sacraments, the complete Bible, and the apostolic Tradition as witnessed in the Fathers, Councils, saints, and ecclesiastical writers of the first millennium. Obviously, they have many elements of sanctification which impel toward unity! Although the Protestant denominations have fewer, they still have very important elements. First of all, they have the Scriptures, although they are missing seven books of the Old Testament. Secondly, they preserve a significant part of the apostolic Tradition, despite their explicit rejection of its binding value. Finally, they have the sacrament of Baptism.

Another meaning of the word "subsist" is to *continue in being*, to *retain its being* despite attacks and obstacles. Thus the meaning is that the Church instituted by Christ, the Church of Pentecost, continues to be present in the world with all its essential elements in the Roman Catholic Church alone, despite all the attacks and betrayals of centuries.[16] This continuity is guaranteed by the apostolic and Petrine succession.

---

[15] The Acts of the Council indicate that this is the reason for the change from "is" to "subsist." The conciliar Fathers were officially informed that it was changed so as to harmonize better with the following sentence which tells us that outside her visible structure there only exist "*elements*" of that same Church which tend and lead toward the Catholic Church.

[16] See Congregation for the Doctrine of the Faith, *Responses to Some Questions Regarding Certain Aspects of the Doctrine on the Church*, June 29, 2007, Response to question 2: "In number 8 of the Dogmatic Constitution *Lumen gentium* 'subsistence'

This dual aspect of the word *subsistit* is confirmed by the important Declaration of the Congregation for the Doctrine of the Faith of 2000, *Dominus Jesus*, which says:

> The Catholic faithful *are required to profess* that there is an historical continuity—rooted in the apostolic succession—between the Church founded by Christ and the Catholic Church. . . . With the expression *subsistit in*, the Second Vatican Council sought to harmonize two doctrinal statements: on the one hand, that the Church of Christ, despite the divisions which exist among Christians, continues to exist fully only in the Catholic Church, and on the other hand, that "outside of her structure, many elements can be found of sanctification and truth," that is, in those Churches and ecclesial communities which are not yet in full communion with the Catholic Church.[17] But with respect to these, it needs to be stated that "they derive their efficacy from the very fullness of grace and truth entrusted to the Catholic Church."[18]

The Declaration *Dominus Jesus* makes this clarification because many theologians have sought to argue for a kind of "ecclesiological relativism" on the basis of *Lumen gentium* 8, as if it meant that the Church instituted by Christ subsists in the Catholic Church, but also in

---

means this perduring, historical continuity and the permanence of all the elements instituted by Christ in the Catholic Church."

[17] *Dominus Jesus* has the following footnote: "The interpretation of those who would derive from the formula *subsistit in* the thesis that the one Church of Christ could subsist also in non-Catholic Churches and ecclesial communities is therefore contrary to the authentic meaning of *Lumen gentium*. The Council instead chose the word *subsistit* precisely to clarify that there exists only one 'subsistence' of the true Church, while outside her visible structure there only exist *elementa Ecclesiae*, which—being elements of that same Church—tend and lead toward the Catholic Church" (Congregation for the Doctrine of the Faith, *Notification on the Book "Church: Charism and Power" by Father Leonardo Boff: AAS* 77 [1985], 756–762)."

[18] *Dominus Jesus* 16. Cardinal Ratzinger also spoke of the meaning of *subsistit* in a discourse given in a conference (held on Feb. 25–27, 2000) on the implementation of Vatican II, "L'ecciesiologia della costituzione *Lumen gentium*," in Rino Fisichella, ed., *Il Concilio Vaticano II: Recezione e attualità alla luce del Giubileo* (Cinisello Balsamo [Milan]: San Paulo, 2000), 78: "The Second Vatican Council, with the formula of the *subsistit*—in accordance with Catholic tradition—thus intended to teach the exact opposite of 'ecclesiological relativism': the Church of Jesus Christ truly exists. He himself willed her, and, beginning at Pentecost, the Holy Spirit continuously creates her in spite of every human failing and sustains her in her essential identity. The institutional element is not an unavoidable but theologically irrelevant or even harmful externalization, but belongs, in its essential nucleus, to the concreteness of the Incarnation."

other Christian denominations, although perhaps to a lesser degree.[19] Such an interpretation is clearly contrary to the text of *Lumen gentium* and the intention of the Church's Magisterium.[20]

The Congregation for the Doctrine of the Faith has recently returned to this question in an important, although very short, document of 2007, *Responses to Some Questions Regarding Certain Aspects of the Doctrine on the Church*. The second question asks about the meaning of the word "subsists" in *Lumen gentium* 8. The document responds that "the word 'subsists' can only be attributed to the Catholic Church alone precisely because it refers to the mark of unity that we profess in the symbols of the faith (I believe . . . in the 'one' Church); and this 'one' Church subsists in the Catholic Church."

Furthermore, the correct interpretation of this conciliar text can only be found by putting it in a harmonious relationship of development with the preceding Magisterium, which is the first rule of interpretation of magisterial acts. In 1943, Pius XII affirmed in *Mystici Corporis* that Christians not in communion with Rome were not members of the Mystical Body of Christ,[21] although some theologians were asserting the contrary. This condemnation was then repeated in even stronger terms in 1950 in *Humani generis*, where the following position is condemned: "Some say they are not bound by the doctrine, explained in Our Encyclical Letter of a few years ago, and based on the Sources of Revelation, which teaches that the Mystical Body of Christ and the Roman Catholic Church are *one and the same thing*."[22] The text of *Lumen*

---

[19] See, for example, Leonardo Boff, *Church, Charism and Power: Liberation Theology and the Institutional Church* (New York: Crossroad, 1985).

[20] See an interview with Cardinal Ratzinger published in the *Frankfurter Allgemeine Zeitung* on 22 September 2000: "I was there at the Second Vatican Council when the term 'subsistit' was chosen and I can say I know it well. . . . The 'subsistit' means precisely this: the Lord guarantees the Church's existence despite all our errors and sins, which certainly are also clearly found in her. With 'subsistit,' the intention was to say that, although the Lord keeps his promise, there is also an ecclesial reality outside the Catholic community, and it is precisely this contradiction which is the strongest incentive to pursue unity. If the Council had merely wished to say that the Church of Jesus Christ is also in the Catholic Church, it would have said something banal. The Council would have clearly contradicted the entire history of the Church's faith, which no Council Father had in mind."

[21] Pius XII, *Mystici Corporis* 22: "Actually only those are to be included as members of the Church who have been baptized and profess the true faith, and who have not been so unfortunate as to separate themselves from the unity of the Body, or been excluded by legitimate authority for grave faults committed. . . . It follows that those who are divided in faith or government cannot be living in the unity of such a Body, nor can they be living the life of its one Divine Spirit."

[22] My italics. Notice that Pius XII says that this teaching, contained in *Mystici Corporis*, is "based on the Sources of Revelation": Tradition and Scripture. This

gentium 8, properly interpreted, is a harmonious development of the teaching of Pius XII, for it states the same essential truth enunciated by Pius XII, but formulated in a more nuanced and precise way. The Church founded by Christ *retains its substantial being* in the Catholic Church, "although many elements of sanctification and of truth are found outside of its visible structure."

Salvation Outside the Church?

The fact that there are elements of sanctification outside the visible Church leads us to the difficult question concerning salvation for those who are not visible members of the Church. *Lumen gentium* treats this theme in article 14:

> Basing itself upon Sacred Scripture and Tradition, it [the Second Vatican Council] teaches that the Church, now sojourning on earth as an exile, is *necessary for salvation*. Christ, present to us in His Body, which is the Church, is the one Mediator and the unique way of salvation. In explicit terms He Himself affirmed the necessity of faith and baptism and thereby affirmed also the necessity of the Church, for through baptism as through a door men enter the Church. *Whosoever, therefore, knowing that the Catholic Church was made necessary by Christ, would refuse to enter or to remain in it, could not be saved.*

All men are called to the Church, and all salvation comes through the Church from the redemptive sacrifice of Christ, made present in the Church in the Eucharist, which renews on our altars that sacrifice from which all grace flows.

Although the Church is necessary for salvation, unbelievers are not aware of this, sometimes through no fault of their own. There can still be salvation for those who remain outside the Catholic Church due to invincible ignorance (ignorance through no fault of their own), but not for those who are aware of the obligation but still refuse to enter, through causes such as prejudice, negligence, or fear of worldly disadvantage or suffering. Similarly, one cannot be considered to have

---

means that it is revealed by God (although not formally defined), and it would seem that it cannot be denied without danger of heresy, as excellent theologians have argued. See J. Vodopivec, "Ecclesia Catholica Romana Corpus Christi Mysticum," in *Euntes Docete* (1951), *In Litteras Encyclicas «Humani Generis» Pii PP. XII Commentarium* (Rome: Editiones Urbanianae, 1951), who cites the authoritative opinion of Fr. S. Tromp, who, incidentally, appears to be the theological expert who suggested the term "subsistit" in the theological commission responsible for drafting *Lumen gentium* 8.

invincible or inculpable ignorance if one's ignorance is caused by a lack of searching for the truth about God. *Lumen gentium* 16 states:

> Those also can attain to salvation who through no fault of their own do not know the Gospel of Christ or His Church, yet sincerely seek God and moved by grace strive by their deeds to do His will as it is known to them through the dictates of conscience. Nor does Divine Providence deny the helps necessary for salvation to those who, without blame on their part, have not yet arrived at an explicit knowledge of God and with His grace strive to live a good life.

The number of people who are saved in this way is "known only to God."[23]

God grants sufficient grace to all men to begin and to sustain the process of conversion and sanctification, but not all choose to cooperate with the sufficient grace that they receive. It is important, however, to note the conditions that are necessary for someone to be saved outside the visible body of the Church. There must be invincible ignorance, which excludes religious indifferentism or grave negligence; there must be the sincere desire to do the will of God as known by conscience; there must be supernatural acts of faith, hope, and charity; and there must be perfect contrition for grave sins.

In 1949, the Holy Office (predecessor of the Congregation for the Doctrine of the Faith) wrote an important letter to Archbishop Cushing of Boston on this issue of salvation outside the Church. A priest of that diocese, Fr. Leonard Feeney, held an overly severe view on salvation outside the Church. The Holy Office affirmed the possibility of salvation for those outside the Church through invincible ignorance, who had a true and efficacious desire to follow God's will for their salvation. Such a desire would implicitly include a desire to enter the Church, if one knew it was the ark of salvation. However, the letter adds: "It must not be imagined that any desire whatsoever of entering the Church is sufficient for a person to be saved. It is necessary that the desire by which one is related to the Church be informed with perfect charity. And an implicit desire cannot have its effect unless one has

---

[23] Paul VI, *Credo of the People of God* (1968). See also Pius XII, *Mystici Corporis* (1943), DS 3821, in which he exhorts those "who do not belong to the visible bond of the Catholic Church" to "strive to take themselves from that state in which they cannot be sure of their own eternal salvation; for even though they are ordered to the mystical body of the Redeemer by a certain desire and wish of which they are not aware [implicit in the general wish to do what God wills], yet they lack so many and so great heavenly gifts and helps which can be enjoyed only in the Catholic Church."

supernatural faith."[24] The document here quotes Hebrews 11:6: "Without faith it is impossible to please him. For whoever would draw near to God must believe that he exists and that he rewards those who seek him."

The Church and Evangelization

The fact that salvation is possible for some who are not within the visible fold of the Church does not in any way lessen the Church's missionary mandate to preach the Gospel to every creature (see Mk 16:15). The missionary mandate comes from Christ Himself as His last testament to His disciples before His Ascension into heaven (Mt 28:19–20): "Go therefore and make disciples of all nations, baptizing them in the name of the Father and of the Son and of the Holy Spirit, teaching them to observe all that I have commanded you."

Vatican II, in the *Decree on the Mission Activity of the Church*, therefore says: "Although in ways known to himself God can lead those who, through no fault of their own, are ignorant of the Gospel, to that faith without which it is impossible to please him, the Church still has the obligation and also the sacred right to evangelize all men."[25]

Not only does the Church have the sacred right to evangelize, but also every man has the sacred right to hear the Good News of the Gospel, simply because Christ shed His sacred Blood for all men who would ever be born. Every soul was purchased at a great price, and thus all men have a sacred right to know the extent of God's love for them and to be incorporated into the Mystical Body of the Savior who died for them. All men have the right to be evangelized, because God created them so that they might become living members of Christ's Body the Church, at least in heaven, and, insofar as possible, here on earth.

Vatican II said that "the pilgrim Church is missionary by her very nature, since it is from the mission of the Son and the mission of the Holy Spirit that she draws her origin."[26] As the Son was sent forth by the Father in the Incarnation, and the Holy Spirit was sent at Pentecost by the Father and the Son, so the Church is sent into the world by the Son through the power of the Spirit. As Christ and the Spirit were sent into the world, so the Church is sent into the world to bring the presence of Christ and the power of the Spirit to every human being. After the Last Supper, Jesus prayed to His Father (Jn 17:18): "As thou didst send me into the world, so I have sent them into the world."

---

[24] The Holy Office, letter of August 8, 1949 to Archbishop Richard Cushing of Boston.

[25] Vatican II, *Ad gentes* 7.

[26] Vatican II, *Ad gentes* 2.

Furthermore, the missionary nature of the Church implies continuous expansion of her radius of activity, as we see in Jesus' parting words to the disciples in Acts 1:8: "You shall receive power when the Holy Spirit has come upon you; and you shall be my witnesses in Jerusalem and in all Judea and Samaria and to the end of the earth." John Paul II stressed the urgent need for the continual expansion of missionary activity in his encyclical on the permanent validity of the Church's missionary mandate, *Redemptoris missio* of 1990:

> The mission of Christ the Redeemer, which is entrusted to the Church, is still very far from completion. As the second millennium after Christ's coming draws to an end, an overall view of the human race shows that this mission is still only beginning and that we must commit ourselves wholeheartedly to its service. It is the Spirit who impels us to proclaim the great works of God: "For if I preach the Gospel, that gives me no ground for boasting. For necessity is laid upon me. Woe to me if I do not preach the Gospel!" (1 Cor 9: 16) In the name of the whole Church, I sense an urgent duty to repeat this cry of St. Paul. From the beginning of my Pontificate I have chosen to travel to the ends of the earth in order to show this missionary concern. My direct contact with peoples who do not know Christ has convinced me even more of the *urgency of missionary activity*. . . . The missionary thrust therefore belongs to the very nature of the Christian life.[27]

All Catholics are called to participate in this mission, each in his own place and vocation in the Mystical Body. The key to our effectiveness will be the love that we bear for Holy Mother Church and the degree of our incorporation into her life through growth in sanctity. Let us ask God for an ever greater love for our Mother the Church and an ever greater appreciation for the magnitude of the gift that we have received in being made members of the Mystical Body of the Word Incarnate.

---

[27] John Paul II, encyclical *Redemptoris missio* 1 (1990).

CHAPTER 9

Universal Call to Holiness in Israel and the Church

One of the most fundamental aspects of the Second Vatican Council was its emphasis on the universal call to holiness. This call to holiness lies at the heart of what it means to be the People of God, called to participate in God's own sanctity and inner life. Every human being is called to strive for holiness—which is a participation in God's own purity and love.

What Is Holiness?

In the cultures of the world, something is said to be sacred or holy insofar as it is consecrated to God and set aside for divine worship, and separated from what is of the earth or worldly. Thus the notion of sacred is contrasted with that of profane or secular. Every natural religion makes use of the distinction between the sacred and the profane. The sacred refers to places of divine worship, times of such worship, vessels consecrated to worship, vestments for worship, and persons dedicated to worship and prayer, such as priests, and frequently also contemplatives, such as the vestal virgins. Things that are consecrated to divine worship are removed from ordinary human usage.

In the Jewish and Christian context, the common meaning of sacred is not destroyed but elevated and perfected. Supernatural religion has sacred things set aside for divine worship, like natural religion, but which are far more sacred because of God's intervention: the liturgy established by God in the Mosaic Law, and the seven sacraments of the Church established by Christ.

Here, however, we are concerned with the notion of "sacred" or "holy" as applied to persons in general, regardless of their state of life. In what sense can we speak of persons being holy? Applying the common notion, a person would be holy insofar as he or she is truly consecrated to God, dedicated to God and His glory as his or her overriding end. This is realized essentially through the virtue of *charity* (*agapè*), by which we love God above all things and adhere to Him as our Father and as the Spouse of our souls.

God Himself is infinitely holy because He has only one end: the infinite glory of the divine Goodness and Love, which is the common good of all beings and of the whole universe. He is untouched by any particular interest that could cause Him to deviate from absolute and eternal adherence to the Total Good (which is Himself). God is totally simple; He is pure and total Love.

The holiness of God refers to His transcendent purity. As St. Paul says (1 Tim 6:16), the King of kings and Lord of lords "dwells in unapproachable light, whom no man has ever seen or can see," unless God Himself brings us to share in His light in the beatific vision.[1] Hence the angels sing: "Holy, holy, holy is the Lord of hosts; the whole earth is full of His glory" (Is 6:3). Not surprisingly, both the synagogue and the Church give this verse a prominent place in the liturgy, as we join our voices to the celestial liturgy of the angelic choir.

Men and angels are holy insofar as they imitate and participate in this total adherence to the divine Love. This involves purity of heart freed from attachment to other ends, and firmness of adherence to God through faith, hope, and charity.[2] This, therefore, is the goal of the spiritual life.

Blessed Marmion explains this well:

> The divine holiness, then, comes down to the very perfect love and the sovereignly immutable fidelity with which God loves Himself infinitely. . . . From this it follows that the divine holiness serves as first foundation, as universal example and as unique source of

---

[1] See Ps 36:9: "For with thee is the fountain of life; in thy light do we see light."

[2] St. Thomas explains sanctity with reference to the two notions of purity and firmness, in the *Summa of Theology* II-II, q. 81, a. 8: "The word 'sanctity' seems to have two meanings. In one way it denotes purity; and this corresponds with its etymology in Greek, for *hagios* means 'unsoiled.' In another way it denotes firmness. . . . In either case the signification requires sanctity to be ascribed to those things that are applied to the Divine worship; so that not only men, but also the temple, vessels and such like things are said to be sanctified through being applied to the worship of God. *For purity is necessary in order that the mind be applied to God*, since the human mind is soiled by contact with inferior things, even as all things depreciate by admixture with baser things, for instance, silver by being mixed with lead. Now in order for the mind to be united to the Supreme Being it must be *withdrawn from inferior things*: and hence it is that without purity the mind cannot be applied to God. Wherefore it is written (Heb 12:14): 'Follow peace with all men, and holiness, without which no man shall see God.' Again, *firmness is required for the mind to be applied to God*, for it is applied to Him as its last end and first beginning, and such things must needs be most immovable. Hence the Apostle said (Rom 8:38–39): 'I am sure that neither death, nor life . . . shall separate me from the love of God.' Accordingly, it is *by sanctity that the human mind applies itself and its acts to God*."

every created holiness. . . . Therefore the more there is in us of dependence of love in regard to God, of conformity of our free will to our primordial end which is the manifestation of the Divine glory, the more we adhere to God (something which can only be achieved through detachment from everything that is not God), the more, finally, that this dependence, this conformity, this adhesion, this detachment is firm and stable—the higher will be our holiness.[3]

The Call to Holiness in the Law of Moses

At the heart of God's Revelation to Israel and the Church is the universal call to holiness.

The Mosaic covenant sanctified Israel by giving her a participation in the holiness of God Himself. This participation involved the holiness of the moral law given in the Ten Commandments, the holiness of worship in the liturgy of Israel, and the judicial precepts by which the Ten Commandments were safeguarded within the judicial system of ancient Israel. Thus the Mosaic Law—the Torah—included these three aspects: the moral law, the ceremonial (or liturgical) law, and the judicial precepts. All three aspects were means by which God sanctified Israel, making them His People. Obedience to the Torah constitutes Israel's part in the covenant by which they become the People of God.

In Exodus 19:5–6, before revealing the Ten Commandments, God said to Israel: "Now therefore, if you will obey my voice and keep my covenant, you shall be my own possession among all peoples; for all the earth is mine, and you shall be to me a kingdom of priests and a *holy nation*." It can be seen that holiness in Israel has a communal or "ecclesial" aspect. All of Israel is called to share in God's holiness, by becoming a "kingdom of priests and a holy nation."

The Ten Commandments are introduced by emphasizing that God called Israel into relation with Him (and thus to holiness), by bringing them out of Egypt (Ex 20:2): "I am the Lord your God, who brought you out of the land of Egypt, out of the house of bondage."

The more particular judicial precepts are also proclaimed as a call to participate in the holiness of God. The call to holiness is translated into specific commandments in the service of fraternal charity, as can be seen in Leviticus 19:1–18. This fundamental text begins with the requirement of holiness—"You shall be holy; for I the Lord your God am holy" (Lev 19:1)—and ends with fraternal love: "You shall not take vengeance or

---

[3] Bl. Columba Marmion, *Christ the Life of the Soul*, trans. Alan Bancroft (Bethesda, MD: Zaccheus Press, 2005), 15–16.

bear any grudge against the sons of your own people, but you shall love your neighbor as yourself: I am the Lord" (Lev 19:18).

By keeping the covenant, Israel both sanctified herself and sanctified God's name, manifesting His glory. In Leviticus 22:32, God says: "And ye shall not profane my holy name; but I will be hallowed among the children of Israel." God's name is to be sanctified not only in prayer and worship, but also in work, family life, and social relations. God's name is sanctified in these aspects of life when one lives them in accordance with God's will. By sanctifying God's name in work, family life, and social life, one's own life becomes sanctified, together with that of the community. Sanctity thus always has a social aspect in Jewish thought, as it does in the Church.

The Call to Holiness in the Sermon on the Mount

In the Sermon on the Mount, Jesus reformulates the fundamental principles of the moral law, making clear that the center of His preaching lies in the call to holiness. He begins with the beatitudes, which give a summary of holiness, focusing on the internal dispositions of the heart in which sanctity lies: poverty of spirit, meekness, mourning over sin, hunger and thirst for justice, mercy, purity of heart, peacemaking, and the courage to undergo persecution for Christ's sake. The beatitudes provide a picture of Jesus' own interior life, and thus they are a model of the sanctity to which disciples of Christ are called.

The sanctity of His followers is to be such that they are to be the salt of the earth and the light of the world. It is a sanctity that fulfills the Law and the prophets, but which is to go beyond the sanctity of the pious Israelite, exemplified by the scribes and Pharisees: "For I tell you, unless your righteousness exceeds that of the scribes and Pharisees, you will never enter the kingdom of heaven" (Mt 5:20).[4] Jesus concludes the section on the moral law by telling His disciples of all ages: "You, therefore, must be perfect, as your heavenly Father is perfect" (Mt 5:48).

Jesus calls us to make a supreme effort to attain sanctity. He does not promise that it will be easy. On the contrary, He says that no one can be His disciple without denying himself, taking up his cross, and following after His example.[5] Praising John the Baptist's fidelity unto martyrdom, He says: "From the days of John the Baptist until now the kingdom of heaven has suffered violence, and men of violence take it by force" (Mt 11:12). The "men of violence" are the saints who wage

---

[4] This greater righteousness is made possible through the grace of the Eucharist and the other sacraments, received with the right disposition.

[5] Lk 14:27: "Whoever does not bear his own cross and come after me, cannot be my disciple." See Mt 16:24.

spiritual combat against sin, the temptations of the devil and of the flesh, human respect, and the worldly values transmitted by the media of every age.[6]

Jesus compares sanctity to a narrow gate: "Enter by the narrow gate; for the gate is wide and the way is easy, that leads to destruction, and those who enter by it are many. For the gate is narrow and the way is hard, that leads to life, and those who find it are few" (Mt 7:13–14). Ultimately, the narrow gate is the example of the holiness of Jesus' own life, by which He lived charity "to the end" (Jn 13:1).

The Call to Holiness in the Letters of St. Paul

St. Paul likewise exhorts the first Christians to holiness in every letter that he wrote. As in the Old Testament, the holiness to which the new Israel is called is based on God's saving work. With the Incarnation of Christ, God has assumed human life and utterly sanctified it. Sanctification therefore will involve taking up the life of Christ and thus participating in His holiness.

In Ephesians 1:4, St. Paul says that we have been "chosen in Christ before the foundation of the world, that we should be holy and blameless before him." In 1 Thessalonians 4:3, St. Paul says: "For this is the will of God, your sanctification."

In Philippians 2:6–8, he stresses the humility involved in the Christian call to sanctity, and its basis in the example of Christ, who "did not count equality with God a thing to be grasped, but emptied himself, taking the form of a servant, being born in the likeness of men. And being found in human form he humbled himself and became obedient unto death, even death on a cross." Christian sanctity, therefore, is to conform oneself to the very humility of Christ.

In Romans 13:14, St. Paul exhorts Christians to "put on the Lord Jesus Christ, and make no provision for the flesh, to gratify its desires." It was this verse, by the way, through which St. Augustine's final conversion was accomplished. When he heard a boy say "take and read," he took it as a divine command, opened the Letters of St. Paul, and came upon this verse.

Earlier, in Romans 12:1–2, St. Paul says that Christians are to offer their very bodies and daily life "as a living sacrifice, holy and acceptable to God, which is your spiritual worship. Do not be conformed to this

---

[6] See, for example, St. Jerome's commentary on this verse in his *Commentary on Matthew*, trans. Thomas Scheck (Washington DC: Catholic Univ. of America Press, 2008), 132: "For there is great violence involved when we who have been born on the earth seek to possess a heavenly home through virtue, which we have not retained through nature."

world but be transformed by the renewal of your mind, that you may prove what is the will of God, what is good and acceptable and perfect."

The Universal Call to Holiness in the Early Church

A beautiful testimony to this interior transformation of the Christian can be found in an anonymous letter from the second century AD, the age of the martyrs, called the Letter to Diognetus. The unknown author's characterization of Christians puts us to shame, and shows us what we are called to be. He writes:

> For Christians are not distinguished from the rest of humanity by country, language, or custom. For nowhere do they live in cities of their own, nor do they speak some unusual dialect, nor do they practice an eccentric way of life. This teaching of theirs has not been discovered by the thought and reflection of ingenious people, nor do they promote any human doctrine, as some do. But while they live in both Greek and barbarian cities, as each one's lot was cast, and follow the local customs in dress and food and other aspects of life, at the same time they demonstrate the remarkable and admittedly unusual character of their own citizenship. They live in their own countries, but only as nonresidents; they participate in everything as citizens, and endure everything as foreigners. Every foreign country is their fatherland, and every fatherland is foreign. They marry like everyone else, and have children, but they do not expose their offspring. They share their food but not their wives. They are in the flesh, but they do not live according to the flesh. They live on earth, but their citizenship is in heaven. They obey the established laws; indeed in their private lives they transcend the laws. They love everyone, and by everyone they are persecuted. They are unknown, yet they are condemned; they are put to death, yet they are brought to life. They are poor, yet they make many rich; they are in need of everything, yet they abound in everything. They are dishonored, yet they are glorified in their dishonor; they are slandered, yet they are vindicated. They are cursed, yet they bless; they are insulted, yet they offer respect. When they do good, they are punished as evildoers; when they are punished, they rejoice as though brought to life. By the Jews they are assaulted as foreigners, and by the Greeks they are persecuted, yet those who hate them are unable to give a reason for their hostility.
>
> In a word, what the soul is to the body, Christians are to the world. The soul is dispersed through all the members of the body, and Christians throughout the cities of the world. The soul dwells in the body, but is not of the body; likewise Christians dwell in the world, but are not of the world. The soul, which is invisible, is

confined in the body, which is visible; in the same way, Christians are recognized as being in the world, and yet their religion remains invisible. The flesh hates the soul and wages war against it, even though it has suffered no wrong, because it is hindered from indulging in its pleasures; so also the world hates the Christians, even though it has suffered no wrong, because they set themselves against its pleasures.[7]

Recognizing that we are made for heaven means that we cannot put our final end in the things of this world. We live in the world, have families, go to school, work at all kinds of jobs, suffer misfortunes. However, being Christian means that our lives are transformed from the inside and gain a new dimension not shared by our neighbors: the life of faith, hope, and charity. That life ought to be the soul of the social environment in which we find ourselves, as we see in the Letter to Diognetus. That life ought to make us live on this earth as those who know that they are just passing through on the way to something infinitely more satisfying. Our Lord tells us that where our treasure is, there our heart will be. The point is that our heart ought to be with Christ in heaven.

Vatican II and the Universal Call to Holiness

Each one of us is called to an imitation of Christ in our own human reality in which we have been called, and which Christ has redeemed. And the imitation of Christ is nothing more or less than striving for holiness and the perfection of charity, upon which "depends all the law and the prophets" (Mt 22:40). It follows that since Christ became man for all, that all men and women are called to holiness. In fact, we can say that the solemn proclamation of the universal call to holiness is the heart of the Second Vatican Council, for it is the very finality of Christ's mission and that of the Church. It is the Church's response to the question of *humanism*—the true perfection of man. True humanism is seeking for sanctity.

Paul VI made clear the centrality of this doctrine to the Second Vatican Council: "This strong invitation to holiness could be regarded as the most characteristic element in the whole magisterium of the Council, and so to say, its ultimate purpose."[8]

John Paul II repeatedly reaffirmed this point:

The Vatican Council has significantly spoken on the universal call to holiness. It is possible to say that this call to holiness is precisely

---

[7] Letter to Diognetus 5–6, in *The Apostolic Fathers*, 701–5.
[8] Paul VI, motu proprio *Sanctitatis clarior* (March 19, 1969): *AAS* 61 (1969), 149.

the basic charge entrusted to all the sons and daughters of the Church by a Council which intended to bring a renewal of Christian life based on the Gospel.[9]

As we have seen, holiness is one of the four indefectible marks of the Church, for she was washed by the Blood of her divine Spouse and made pure.[10] This holiness of our Mother the Church should shine in her children, who are the members of Christ's Body. Thus all are called to holiness, for in the Church all receive superabundant means to achieve it, especially through the sacramental life of the Church.[11]

Although very many Catholics are evidently not holy, it is not the fault of holy Mother Church, but of the fact that many live the life of the Church superficially or not at all. Nevertheless, all are called to sanctity, which means to live the life of Christ in the Church. As Jesus says: "Many are called but few are chosen" (Mt 22:14).

The Council states this call in *Lumen gentium* 40: "Thus it is evident to everyone, that *all the faithful of Christ of whatever rank or status, are called to the fullness of the Christian life and to the perfection of charity*; by this holiness as such a more human manner of living is promoted in this earthly society." Each of the faithful must strive for sanctity according to his state of life, duties of state, and particular condition.

Notice that the Council speaks of sanctity as the "perfection of charity." Sanctity does not consist simply in following the Law, in ceremonial practices, in knowledge of theology, in ecclesiastical office, or even in giving all our substance to the poor, as St. Paul reminds us in 1 Corinthians 13:3: "If I give away all I have, and if I deliver my body to be burned, but have not charity, I gain nothing." And what is charity?

By charity, we mean the supernatural virtue of love expressed in the double commandment: love of God above all things and love of our neighbor for God's sake. St. Thomas Aquinas defines charity as a

---

[9] John Paul II, apostolic exhortation *Christifideles laici* 16.

[10] See Eph 5:25–27: "Christ loved the Church and gave himself up for her, that he might sanctify her, *having cleansed her by the washing of water with the word*, that he might present the Church to himself *in splendor, without spot or wrinkle or any such thing, that she might be holy and without blemish*."

[11] See Vatican II, *Lumen gentium* 39: "The Church, whose mystery is being set forth by this Sacred Synod, is believed to be indefectibly holy. Indeed Christ, the Son of God, who with the Father and the Spirit is praised as 'uniquely holy,' loved the Church as His bride, delivering Himself up for her. He did this that He might sanctify her. He united her to Himself as His own body and brought it to perfection by the gift of the Holy Spirit for God's glory. Therefore in the Church, everyone whether belonging to the hierarchy, or being cared for by it, is called to holiness, according to the saying of the Apostle: 'For this is the will of God, your sanctification.'"

particular kind of love: love of friendship with God and love of benevolence for all His sons and daughters.

Holiness and the Sanctification of Work and Daily Life

Since we are called to be holy in our own state of life and circumstances, it is clear that sanctification must come about through fidelity to God in the little things of every day and in our daily work and family life. This truth is clearly taught both in Judaism and Catholicism.

In the Jewish context, Jacob Neusner writes:

> The sages see Israel as a sacred society, "a kingdom of priests and a holy people," and, within that context, quite logically, they view work not as a mere secular necessity but as a sacred activity. Thus they situate their definition of work within their larger statement of what it means to form holy Israel, God's first love on earth. Work is not merely something we are supposed to do in the interests of the community, so that the tasks of the world will be carried out and each of us will earn a living. Of greatest importance is that the Hebrew word for work is *abodah*, the same word used for "divine service," "liturgy," or the labor of the priests in the Temple in making offerings to God.[12]

Ultimately, the sanctification of work is rooted in the fact that God "worked" in creation; we are called to the imitation of God by participating in His kingly task of governing creation. Rabbi Neusner says: "Just as it is a religious duty to rest on the Sabbath, so it is a religious duty to work during the week. . . . In Judaism, we must work so that there can be the Sabbath."[13]

The sanctification of daily work is also taught in the New Testament.[14] Above all, however, it is taught by the example of Jesus who labored for most of His earthly life in the carpenter's workshop in Nazareth.[15]

---

[12] Jacob Neusner, "Work in Formative Judaism," in *The Encyclopedia of Judaism*, vol. 3, ed. Jacob Neusner, Alan J. Avery-Peck, and William Scott Green (New York: Continuum, 1999), 1502–3.

[13] Ibid., 1503.

[14] See 2 Thess 3:6–13.

[15] See Paul VI, Address of January 5, 1964, given in Nazareth: "The lesson of domestic life: may Nazareth teach us the meaning of family life, its harmony of love, its simplicity and austere beauty, its sacred and inviolable character; may it teach us how sweet and irreplaceable is its training, how fundamental and incomparable its role on the social plane. The lesson of work: O Nazareth, home of 'the carpenter's son,' we want here to understand and to praise the austere and redeeming law of human labor, here to restore the consciousness of the dignity of

The Second Vatican Council calls attention to this in *Gaudium et spes* 22: "For by His Incarnation the Son of God has united Himself in some fashion with every man. He *worked with human hands*, He thought with a human mind, acted by human choice and loved with a human heart."

Although the divine Word united Himself only to one human nature, nevertheless every human life and every human reality is immeasurably ennobled by the Incarnation. For He redeemed and ennobled every human reality that He assumed: being carried in the womb, birth, infancy, childhood, family life, play, learning, obedience, adolescence, work, supporting others and receiving from others, eating and sleeping, teaching, prayer, divine worship, all human passions and emotions, joy and sorrow, humor, wonder, exhaustion, waiting, patience, temptation, extreme humiliation, calumny, betrayal, unbearable suffering, and death. All of these human realities have now been given a redemptive and a divine aspect. They all hold a divine treasure for us, if we know how to see Christ in them. This has tremendous implications for our own lives. In virtue of the Incarnation, no human reality can be considered merely mundane, banal, or without importance or transcendent significance, for Christ has taken it up. The Incarnation has implanted a divine dimension into the smallest and most modest of human realities, including all human work.

Lumen gentium 41 speaks of the sanctification of work in terms of the imitation of Christ:

> Those who engage in labor—and frequently it is of a heavy nature—should better themselves by their human labors. They should be of aid to their fellow citizens. They should raise all of society, and even creation itself, to a better mode of existence. Indeed, they should imitate by their lively charity, in their joyous hope and by their voluntary sharing of each others' burdens, the very Christ who plied His hands with carpenter's tools and Who in union with His Father, is continually working for the salvation of all men. In this, then, their daily work they should climb to the heights of holiness and apostolic activity.

In a similar way, married life is also a state that can be sanctified in the imitation of Christ who loved the Church and gave Himself for her. *Lumen gentium* 41 states:

---

labor, here to recall that work cannot be an end in itself, and that it is free and ennobling in proportion to the values—beyond the economic ones—which motivate it. We would like here to salute all the workers of the world, and to point out to them their great Model, their Divine Brother, the Champion of all their rights, Christ the Lord!"

Furthermore, married couples and Christian parents should follow their own proper path (to holiness) by faithful love. They should sustain one another in grace throughout the entire length of their lives. They should imbue their offspring, lovingly welcomed as God's gift, with Christian doctrine and the evangelical virtues. In this manner, they offer all men the example of unwearying and generous love; in this way they build up the brotherhood of charity; in so doing, they stand as the witnesses and cooperators in the fruitfulness of Holy Mother Church; by such lives, they are a sign and a participation in that very love, with which Christ loved His Bride and for which He delivered Himself up for her. A like example, but one given in a different way, is that offered by widows and single people, who are able to make great contributions toward holiness and apostolic endeavor in the Church.

Holiness and Our State in Life

St. Francis de Sales, back in the early seventeenth century, spoke of the universal call to holiness at the beginning of his classic book on the spiritual life: *Introduction to the Devout Life*. For St. Francis de Sales, the word "devotion" essentially means what we understand by sanctity: the perfection of charity—charity that is fervent and eager. His key point is that this perfection must be realized by each one of us, in accordance with our human realities, and in our own state of life with all its prosaic circumstances:

> At the creation God commanded the plants to bear fruit each according to its kind and he likewise commands Christians, the living branches of the vine, to bear fruit by practising devotion according to their state in life.
>
> The practice of devotion must differ for the gentleman and the artisan, the servant and the prince, for widow, young girl or wife. Further, it must be accommodated to their particular strength, circumstances and duties.
>
> Is the solitary life of a Carthusian suited to a bishop? Should those who are married practice the poverty of a Capuchin? If workmen spent as much time in church as religious, if religious were exposed to the same pastoral calls as a bishop, such devotion would be ridiculous and cause intolerable disorder. Such faults are, however, very common; and the world, which cannot or will not distinguish between true devotion and the indiscretions of the self-styled devout, blames and criticizes devotion itself as responsible for those disorders.

True devotion, Philothea, never causes harm, but rather perfects everything we do; a devotion which conflicts with anyone's state of life is undoubtedly false. . . . [True devotion] makes the care of a family peaceful, the love of a husband and wife more sincere, the service of one's king more faithful, and every task more pleasant and a joy.

It is not only erroneous, but a heresy, to hold that life in the army, the workshop, the court, or the home is incompatible with true devotion. . . . Under the old law, the lives of Abraham, Isaac, Jacob, David, Job, Tobias, Sara, Rebecca and Judith are a proof of this. Under the new law, St. Joseph, Lydia and St. Crispin were perfectly devout in the workshop; St. Anne, St. Martha, St. Monica, Aquila, Priscilla in their homes; Cornelius, St. Sebastian, St. Maurice in the army; Constantine, Helen, St. Louis, Blessed Amadeus and St. Edward in the courts. . . . No, Philothea, wherever we find ourselves we not only may, but should, seek perfection.[16]

God has an eternal plan for each person and for his concrete vocation and mission in the Church. Sanctity can be understood as our ever fuller correspondence with God's eternal plan or idea for our perfection.

Plato spoke of the divine Ideas as the blueprint for creation. The Fathers of the Church, such as St. Augustine, adopted Plato's doctrine of the divine Ideas, seeing them as ideas in the divine mind that serve as the exemplar causes of creation, as a blueprint is the model of a building to be built. God has an idea for every being that He has created and will create, as an exemplar or plan for that thing. The multiplicity of God's ideas does not detract from His simplicity, for God understands all things through His own essence, which is one, and through His one perfect Word, which is the Son of God.

God's idea for each person involves a particular imitation of Christ, the universal Exemplar, in the particular circumstances in which he has been placed. God has an idea of the sanctity to which each person is called and also an idea of our free resistance to His grace and how we fall short of the ideal to which we are called and could really achieve if we were to collaborate more fully with His grace. He has an idea of the glory that we can give Him in all of our acts if we cooperate with grace. Our task is to realize God's idea of sanctity intended for each one of us from before the foundation of the world.

God's idea for each of us is a dynamic reality: something called to develop and come to ever greater conformity with the divine exemplar

---

[16] St. Francis de Sales, *Introduction to the Devout Life*, part 1, ch. 3, trans. Michael Day (Westminster, MD: Newman Press, 1956), 13–15.

who is Christ. Finding our identity implies gradually discovering and realizing the particular imitation of Christ to which God is calling us.

Surprisingly, experience shows that the saints, who are those who most imitate Christ in their lives, are the most "original" of men. We do not cease to become unique and original individuals by striving to imitate Christ, because each one is called, according to God's eternal idea of us, to imitate Christ in a *most particular way*. God's idea of us involves bringing out a *particular aspect of Christ's infinite sanctity*. God's idea of me will be incomparably more original, unique, and rich than any other model that I could propose for myself. If I do not seek God's idea for me, I will end up being a mere copy of the aspirations of the "world."

How do we know God's *particular* idea for us, so that we can realize it in practice? God wills us to ask for this in prayer. We must pray to know, first, who He is calling us to be, and, secondly, to have the strength and determination to put it into practice. The best way to give glory to God is by striving to realize His eternal plan for us in Christ. Sin, on the contrary, defaces the divine idea to which we are called to conform ourselves.

In our dealings with our neighbor, we should remember that God has an idea of sanctity for our spouse, children, parents, colleagues, etc., that we are called to help bring into being. The secret to giving spiritual counsel is seeking to foster God's plan for the person and not imposing our own preferences and plans.

Sanctity and the Glory of God

If the goal of the Christian life is sanctity, can we also say that our goal is the glorification of God and His holy name (*kiddush ha-shem*)?[17] If so, how are they related?

God's glory and our perfection (or sanctity) go hand in hand, for our perfection and happiness consist in giving glory to God in all our acts, and every true perfection of the creature inevitably gives glory to God as its Source.

It is important, however, that we observe the right order between the two. We are to seek sanctity not for our own sake, but ultimately for God's sake: for the sake of the glory of His name from whom every good thing comes. Sanctity consists essentially in charity, by which we love God above all things as Friend and Father. Charity, therefore, makes us love charity itself for God's sake, just like everything else. To love everything for God's sake is to seek to give glory to God in

---

[17] See "Kiddush ha-Shem" in *The Jewish Encyclopedia*, vol. 7 (New York: Ktav Publ. House, 1964), 484–85.

everything. Sanctity thus is the love of God which seeks to give glory to the Beloved in every way. To love God above all things is to seek God's own end in all things, and this is the glory of God: the manifestation of His Goodness.

A soul seeking sanctity must therefore place the glory of God as the ultimate goal of its striving. It is no accident that Jesus puts this as the first petition in the Lord's Prayer: "Hallowed be thy name." Hallowing God's name means giving glory to God. St. John of the Cross, on the summit of the mount of perfection, inscribes these words: "Here on this mount dwell only the honor and glory of God."[18] St. Paul instructs the early Christians of Corinth to give glory to God in all things (1 Cor 10:31): "So, whether you eat or drink, or whatever you do, do all to the glory of God." St. Ignatius of Loyola made this into his constant motto: "Ad majorem Dei gloriam," which means "for the greater glory of God."

Means to Grow in Holiness

Since all of us are called to seek holiness as our most fundamental vocation, it is very important for us to know some general practical means by which sanctity can be attained.

God Himself provides us with an abundant means of sanctification: the trials, difficulties, and crosses of our lives, which, if we accept them with fidelity, perseverance, and love, become the providential means for maturing in charity.

On our part, sanctity can only be attained through the persevering practice of daily prayer, by which we raise our minds to speak to God as to our Father, our most intimate friend, and the Spouse of our souls. St. Teresa of Avila gives a beautiful definition of mental prayer in her autobiography: "For mental prayer in my opinion is nothing else than an intimate sharing between friends: it means *taking time frequently to be alone with him who we know loves us.*"[19] Daily mental prayer helps us to recognize God's presence in our lives throughout the day, in all its trials.

In order to help make time for daily prayer, it is very useful to establish a regular plan of life, by which we resolve to pray for a certain time every day, frequent the sacraments, do spiritual reading, and engage in works of charity or apostolate. Spiritual reading involves setting some

---

[18] See St. John of the Cross, drawing of Mount Carmel, in *The Collected Works of Saint John of the Cross*, trans. Kieran Kavanaugh and Otilio Rodriguez (Washington DC: ICS Publications, 1991), 111.

[19] St. Teresa of Avila, *Life* 8.5, in *The Collected Works of St. Teresa of Avila*, vol. 1, trans. Kieran Kavanaugh and Otilio Rodriguez (Washington DC: ICS Publications, 1987), 96.

time aside every day to read Scripture, the lives of the saints, and other classics of spiritual theology.

Although we are only required to go to confession once a year, frequent confession is a great means of sanctification. Obviously, we should go to confession as soon as we can after falling into mortal sin. However, it is not necessary to have mortal sins in order to derive great fruit from the sacrament of Penance. Frequent confession of the venial sins that particularly afflict us is a great means of rooting out such sins from our lives. Every valid confession not only forgives our sins, but also gives us a sacramental grace to strengthen us in resisting such sins in the future, so that charity can govern our lives more fully.

Frequent confession presupposes that we make a frequent or daily examination of conscience. This in itself is a great means of growing in sensitivity and formation of conscience and contrition for sins. Furthermore, frequent confession will make frequent communion far more fruitful.

The Eucharist and the Universal Call to Holiness

The greatest means of growing in holiness is frequent and fervent reception of the Eucharist. The universal call to holiness is itself intimately linked with the Eucharist, in which we receive Christ, who is holiness itself.

In the Eucharist, Christ wished to institute a sacrament that would nourish His life in us, the divine life, consisting in holiness, grace, and charity. This nourishment is represented through the species of bread and wine under which Christ is made present as our spiritual sustenance. Thus the sacrament produces the spiritual nourishment that it symbolically represents by feeding us with grace, and strengthening our intimate union with Christ, whom we literally take into ourselves.[20]

However, as St. Augustine relates in his *Confessions*, he heard the voice of Christ as it were saying to him: "You shall not change Me into yourself as bodily food, but into Me you shall be changed."[21] We change our physical food into our own substance, whereas the Eucharist transforms us spiritually into the image of Christ, if we receive Holy Communion with the proper dispositions. The Eucharist therefore

---

[20] See the *Decretum pro Armenis* of the Council of Florence (1439), DS 1322 (D 698): "Every effect which bodily food and bodily drink have for the corporeal life, by preserving, increasing, restoring, and refreshing, is produced by this Sacrament for the spiritual life."

[21] St. Augustine, *Confessions* 7.10.16, in *The Confessions of St. Augustine*, trans. F. J. Sheed, 145.

deepens and perfects our incorporation into the Body of Christ by infusing charity into our hearts.

At the same time, as a necessary consequence, it also works to deepen our communion with one in another in the Mystical Body, and thus it is the sacrament of ecclesiastical unity.[22] St. Paul states this in 1 Corinthians 10:17: "For we, being many, are one bread, one body, all that partake of one bread." The Eucharist binds us into one Body by strengthening our unity with Christ and with one another.

In summary, the sacramental sign of bread and wine symbolizes (1) spiritual nourishment, (2) union with Christ, and (3) union of the faithful with one another in the consolidation of the Body of Christ. The sacrament is efficacious in producing what it symbolizes when we receive it with the proper dispositions.

In addition to producing these effects, the Eucharist offers a sacramental representation of Christ's sacrificial act of pouring out His Blood for us. This occurs in the separate consecration of the Body and Blood under the species of bread and wine, mystically representing the real separation of His Body and Blood in His death on the Cross. This significance is clearly shown in the words of the consecration: "This cup which is poured out for you is the new covenant in my blood" (Lk 22:20).[23]

The Eucharist, therefore, should nourish us in the holiness of sacrificial love—for God and neighbor. The fundamental purpose of the Incarnation—the sanctification of man—is thus most perfectly accomplished through the Eucharist, which feeds us in grace by giving us sacramentally the very Author of all grace, Christ Himself. The Eucharist is a fountain of grace for all those who are correctly disposed to receive it (that is, for all those who already are constituted in grace through Baptism and Penance). It is that fountain of living water that Christ promised to the Samaritan woman at the well (Jn 4:14). The Eucharist is the divine means to realize and perfect the divine interchange by which He who took on our humanity gives to us a mysterious share in His divinity and in His divine Life.

This principal end of the Eucharist is admirably expressed in the prayers of the Offertory of the Mass in the extraordinary form of the Latin rite: "O God, who hast wonderfully framed man's exalted nature, and still more wonderfully restored it: *grant us*, by the mystic signification of this commingling of water and wine, *to become partakers of His Godhead*

---

[22] Hence St. Thomas Aquinas refers to the Eucharist as the "Sacrament of Church unity" (*ST* III, q. 82, a. 2, ad 3).

[23] See also Mt 26:28: "This is my blood of the covenant, which is poured out for many for the forgiveness of sins."

who vouchsafed to become partaker of our manhood, Jesus Christ."[24] In the offertory prayers, we ask God to grant the proper effects of the Eucharist, which is nothing less than that we may "become partakers of His Godhead."

St. Leo the Great gave classic expression to this divinization of the Christian: "Christian, recognize your dignity, and now that you share in God's own nature, do not return by sin to your former base condition. Remember who is your Head and of whose Body you are a member."[25]

The Eucharist is not the only channel by which God gives us sanctifying grace and charity. The life of grace begins with Baptism, through which we are first incorporated into Christ's Mystical Body. Sanctifying grace is then increased through our good works and prayers performed in a state of grace, as well as the worthy reception of the other sacraments. However, the Eucharist is the *principal channel* for the increase and nourishing of supernatural charity, for it was instituted precisely for this end. It is the *sacrament of love* and sanctification or "divinization," and the sacrament of ecclesial charity and communion.

---

[24] This ancient and exquisite prayer goes back in its present form to the eleventh century and is apparently derived from a sermon on the Nativity of Our Lord from St. Leo the Great. This prayer remains in the offertory of the *Novus Ordo* as follows: "By the mystery of this water and wine may we come to share in the divinity of Christ, who humbled himself to share in our humanity." See also the preface for the Ascension.

[25] St. Leo the Great, *Sermo 21 in nat. Dom.*, 3, PL 54:192C.

CHAPTER 10

The Portrait of the Church in the Acts of the Apostles

After considering the four marks of the Church separately, let us reflect on the lineaments of the Messianic Kingdom as it is first made visible in the Acts of the Apostles, which gives us an inspired portrait of the apostolic Church in her first thirty years of existence. St. Luke centers his account on the activity of the Apostles in preaching and building up the Kingdom of God, which is the Church, through the power of the Holy Spirit. The main protagonists of Acts are the Apostles, especially Peter and Paul, the Church, and the Holy Spirit. Two other centers of interest in Acts are Israel, from whose bosom the Kingdom comes forth and to whom it is first preached, and the Gentiles, who are also called to enter into the Kingdom.

The book of Acts, therefore, treats the Church in a very profound way, focusing (a) on the foundation of the Church, which is the Apostles; (b) on the divine soul of the Church, which is the grace of the Holy Spirit impelling the Apostles and disciples in their mission; and (c) the relation between Jewish roots of the Church and her universal mission to extend to all the Gentiles.

It is no accident that Acts begins and ends with the preaching of the Kingdom of God, which is the Church. It begins with the Risen Christ teaching the Apostles about the Kingdom of God in Israel:

> In the first book, O Theophilus, I have dealt with all that Jesus began to do and teach, until the day when he was taken up, after he had given commandment through the Holy Spirit to the apostles whom he had chosen. To them he presented himself alive after his passion by many proofs, appearing to them during forty days, and speaking of the *kingdom of God*.

Acts ends with St. Paul under house arrest in Rome, preaching first to the Jews and then to the Gentiles about the Kingdom of God (Acts 28:23–30):

> And he expounded the matter to them from morning till evening, testifying to the *kingdom of God* and trying to convince them about

159

Jesus both from the law of Moses and from the prophets. And some were convinced by what he said, while others disbelieved. So, as they disagreed among themselves, they departed, after Paul had made one statement: ". . . Let it be known to you then that this salvation of God has been sent to the Gentiles; they will listen." And he lived there two whole years at his own expense, and welcomed all who came to him, preaching the *kingdom of God* and teaching about the Lord Jesus Christ quite openly and unhindered.

The Acts of the Apostles was written by Luke around the year 62 AD, which is the date in which Paul's first imprisonment in Rome came to a close. If Acts had been written much later, then St. Luke would certainly have included four momentous events that occurred five to eight years later: Nero's persecution, the martyrdoms of Peter and Paul, and the destruction of Jerusalem. However, there is not a word about any of these events.

Acts therefore gives us a picture of the apostolic Church written only thirty years after Jesus' death and Resurrection. Furthermore, the author is a close disciple and companion of St. Paul, who accompanied Paul on various stages of his missionary voyages, as we can see from the "we" sections of Acts.

The Missionary Expansion of the Church

One of the main themes of Acts is the missionary expansion of the Church, moving from Jerusalem to the ends of the earth, through the power of the Holy Spirit. We see this fundamental theme proclaimed already in Acts 1:6–8. Just before Jesus' Ascension into heaven the Apostles ask Him if He will "at that time restore the Kingdom to Israel." Jesus does not correct their error concerning the temporal restoration of Israel, but simply responds that it is not for them "to know times or seasons which the Father has fixed by his own authority. But you shall receive power when the Holy Spirit has come upon you; and *you shall be my witnesses in Jerusalem and in all Judea and Samaria and to the end of the earth*." This is the last saying of Jesus recorded by St. Luke, and it marks the principal theme of the Acts of the Apostles.

The disciples were asking about the Kingdom based, most probably, on the erroneous idea that it would restore Israel to her glorious condition under David and Solomon. They failed to see the full extent of the newness of the Kingdom of the New Covenant and the true spiritual nature of its glory.

Jesus' answer compresses a great content into few words. First, He indicates that the Church is not given to know the precise "times or seasons that the Father has fixed by his own authority." The Apostles are not told when Jesus will come again to complete the constitution of the Kingdom in glory. He thus implies that the Kingdom that He has founded on Peter, to whom He has entrusted its keys, is not yet constituted in a state of glory and will not receive its full glorification until the season that the Father has appointed for it—the Second Coming—, the day and hour of which no one knows and which Christ has not revealed.

Secondly, Christ promises the Apostles a "power," which is not temporal but utterly supernatural—the spiritual power conferred by the Holy Spirit and the fullness of His gifts: "You shall receive power when the Holy Spirit has come upon you." This spiritual power conferred by the Spirit involves the expansion of the Kingdom from Jerusalem to the ends of the earth, but not, of course, by temporal means such as military conquest or shrewd diplomacy. The Kingdom is to expand through the power of the Holy Spirit that is manifested in the interior transformation of the Apostles and disciples, and which gives witness to Christ, who, with the Father, sends the Spirit to His Church.

The itinerary of Acts follows the prophecy of Jesus: "You shall be my witnesses in Jerusalem and in all Judea and Samaria and to the end of the earth." Acts begins in Jerusalem, in which the great miracle of Pentecost took place. The action moves to Samaria and other parts of Judea (such as Joppa) in chapters 8–11. Giving witness to the ends of the earth begins in the second half of chapter 11 with the foundation of the church in Antioch, and especially with St. Paul's missionary voyages that begin in chapter 13. It is not by chance that Acts ends in Rome, the then capital of the world and its temporal power.

This missionary expansion of the Church from Jerusalem to the ends of the earth also reflects the great theme of the relation between Israel and the Gentiles in salvation history. The Church which comes fully into being in Acts 2 in Jerusalem with the miracle of Pentecost is a Church entirely composed of Israelites. The Church is thus born out of the remnant of Israel and in the heart of Israel—David's capital. The cenacle in which the miracle of Pentecost occurred is in fact located above the tomb revered by Jews today as that of David. However, although composed entirely of Jews, the Kingdom at Pentecost already spoke all languages through the miracle of tongues, thus foreshadowing the future catholicity of the Church.

The first opening of the Gospel to non-Jews occurred with the conversion of the Samaritans in Acts 8, through the preaching of the deacon Philip. (The Samaritans, although considered a heretical and impure sect, were still part of Israel and descendants of Jacob.) The next step, recounted in Acts 10, was Peter's preaching of the Gospel to the God-fearing centurion Cornelius Joppa and his household, followed by the administration of Baptism and Confirmation. Cornelius and his household were the first non-Jews who entered the communion of the Church.

The Church's transition from being composed entirely of Jewish members to a Church composed principally (in numerical terms) of Gentile members is symbolically represented in the figures of the Apostles Peter and Paul. The first half of the book of Acts centers on the figure of Peter, who is clearly the main protagonist of Acts 1–12. However, in the second half of Acts (13–28), Paul becomes the central figure, with Peter mentioned only once in Acts 15 at the Council of Jerusalem. The book of Acts is composed and structured, as it were, through this narrative device of focusing first primarily on Peter, and then primarily on Paul.

Although both are Apostles chosen by Christ (although in two very different ways), and thus given a universal mission, they nevertheless have two quite distinct missionary roles, with Peter focusing (at least at first) on the mission to the Jews, and Paul on the mission to the Gentiles. St. Paul states this in Galatians 2:7–8: "I had been entrusted with the gospel to the uncircumcised, just as Peter had been entrusted with the gospel to the circumcised, for he who worked through Peter for the mission to the circumcised worked through me also for the Gentiles." It follows that the narrative shift from Peter to Paul in the Acts of the Apostles mirrors the shift in the Church's missionary emphasis from Israel to the nations, and from Jerusalem and Judea to the ends of the earth.

In exercising his mission to the Gentiles, however, St. Paul always first addressed himself to the synagogue in each of the Gentile cities to which he brought the Gospel. In every city, the Jews would thus be the first recipients of the Gospel, followed by the God-fearing Gentiles who also frequented the synagogue, and then finally the rest of the Gentiles.[1] This preference shown to the Jews in the preaching of the Gospel was a matter of justice, fulfilling God's promises to Abraham, Isaac, and Jacob, and their descendants. It also respected God's work in salvation history of preparing Israel in a unique way as a people to receive the Messiah and give Him to the world. In order to give Him to the world, however, the Gospel had to be preached also to the Gentiles.

The Role of the Holy Spirit in Acts

This missionary expansion of the Church could not be explained by human means alone, but is clearly the work of the Holy Spirit. This is the reason why the Church herself, in her miraculous spread, her

---

[1] See Acts 13:13–48; 14:1–2; 16:13; 18:4; 18:19.

unbroken interior unity, her holiness, catholicity, and apostolicity, is one of the greatest motives of credibility for the truth of the Catholic faith.

St. Luke emphasizes this by pointing out the decisive presence of the Holy Spirit in all the key events of the Acts of the Apostles. Acts opens, as we have seen, with the Risen Christ's promise of the Holy Spirit and His power. The promise is fulfilled in the great event of Pentecost, by which the Apostles and the nascent Church are totally transformed and sanctified.

Although already constituted in most of her essential elements by Jesus before His Ascension, the Church was still lacking the full outpouring of the Holy Spirit through the sacrament of Confirmation, which is the sacrament of spiritual maturity. This sacrament was first given to the Church and her members in an altogether extraordinary way on Pentecost (Acts 2:1–11).

We know that the Apostles were immature in their faith before the Resurrection and even on the day of the Ascension, as they asked about the restoration of the kingdom of Israel. However, that immaturity vanished through the impetus of the extraordinary outpouring of the Holy Spirit. We can see those gifts in action and the Apostles' consciousness of this, in Peter's address to the crowds amazed by the miracle:

> Peter, standing with the eleven, lifted up his voice and addressed them, "Men of Judea and all who dwell in Jerusalem, let this be known to you, and give ear to my words. For these men are not drunk, as you suppose, since it is only the third hour of the day; but this is what was spoken by the prophet Joel: 'And in the last days it shall be, God declares, that I will pour out my Spirit upon all flesh, and your sons and your daughters shall prophesy.'"[2]

Peter then preaches Christ to the crowd with a degree of courage unimaginable before:

> Men of Israel, hear these words: Jesus of Nazareth, a man attested to you by God with mighty works and wonders and signs which God did through him in your midst, as you yourselves know—this Jesus, delivered up according to the definite plan and foreknowledge of God, *you crucified and killed by the hands of lawless men.* But God raised him up, having loosed the pangs of death, because it was not possible for him to be held by it.[3]

---

[2] Acts 2:14–17.
[3] Acts 2:22–24.

The crowds are "cut to the heart" and ask Peter what they should do. He responds that they should "repent, and be baptized every one of you in the name of Jesus Christ for the forgiveness of your sins; and you shall receive the gift of the Holy Spirit. For the promise is to you and to your children and to all that are far off, every one whom the Lord our God calls to him" (Acts 2:38–39). As we know, about three thousand Jews responded to this call and were baptized on that day.

This conversion fulfills the two principal meanings of the Old Testament feast of Pentecost. Falling fifty days (seven weeks) after Easter (hence the name Pentecost, or, in Hebrew, *Shavuot*[4]), Pentecost celebrated the giving of the Law on Mt. Sinai. It also was the celebration of the first fruits of the first harvest of the land of Israel. The first Christian Pentecost fulfilled both aspects. First of all, the full outpouring of the gifts of the Holy Spirit is essentially the new Law of the New Covenant, by which alone the moral law proclaimed to Israel in the double commandment of love and the Ten Commandments is capable of being fully observed. Jeremiah, in 31:31–33, proclaims: "Behold, the days are coming, says the Lord, when I will make a *new covenant* with the house of Israel. . . . *I will put my law within them, and I will write it upon their hearts.*" This first occurred in an extraordinary way on the first Pentecost, and continues to occur in the Church through her sacraments and the supernatural life of grace and charity that they give us. Secondly, the first Christian Pentecost was a feast of first fruits: the first fruits of the harvest of souls that was to extend from Jerusalem to the ends of the earth and from that day until Jesus' Second Coming.

The Holy Spirit in Acts after Pentecost

The Holy Spirit's presence, however, is not confined to Acts 2. We see the extraordinary action of the Holy Spirit in all the key moments of Acts.[5]

An interesting example is in Acts 8:5–17, in which Samaria is converted by the deacon Philip. The Samarians received Baptism, and the Apostles Peter and John were sent to lay hands on them, that they might receive the Holy Spirit. This seems to be the first mention of the sacrament of Confirmation conferred by the Apostles (at Pentecost the sacrament was conferred on the Apostles by God Himself). The deacon Philip was able to baptize but not confer Confirmation with its fuller

---

[4] Pentecost comes from the Greek word for fifty, and *Shavuot* comes from the Hebrew for "weeks," referring to the seven weeks after Passover.

[5] See, for example, Acts 4:31; 5:32; 6:5; 7:55 (stoning of Stephen); 8:14–19; 9:17; 11:24; 13:1–2; 13:9; 13:52; 15:8; 15:28; 19:2–6; etc.

outpouring of the Holy Spirit because this sacrament is reserved to the fullness of Holy Orders, which the Apostles possessed.

> Now when the apostles at Jerusalem heard that Samaria had received the word of God, they sent to them Peter and John, who came down and prayed for them that they might receive the Holy Spirit; for it had not yet fallen on any of them, but they had only been baptized in the name of the Lord Jesus. Then they laid their hands on them and they received the Holy Spirit.[6]

The magician Simon was so impressed with the power of the Apostles to confer the Holy Spirit that he sought to buy that power from them. Hence the word "simony," which refers to the sacrilege of attempting to buy spiritual power (Acts 8:18–20).

We see the outpouring of the Holy Spirit on Saul in Acts 9:17. When Ananias laid his hands on Paul, he said, "Brother Saul, the Lord Jesus, who appeared to you on the road by which you came, has sent me that you may regain your sight and be filled with the Holy Spirit." The great importance of this conversion is shown in the fact that it is related three times in Acts in very similar words.[7]

The Holy Spirit is poured out on Cornelius and his family in Acts 10:44–46. As Peter was preaching the Gospel to them,

> The Holy Spirit fell on all who heard the word. And the believers from among the circumcised who came with Peter were amazed, because the gift of the Holy Spirit had been poured out even on the Gentiles. For they heard them speaking in tongues and extolling God. Then Peter declared, "Can any one forbid water for baptizing these people who have received the Holy Spirit just as we have?"

This event has a great importance for the life of the Church, for it was the first time a Gentile received Baptism and thus entered the Church. Its prominence is shown in that it is recounted again in chapter 11 and referred to in Acts 15:7, in which Peter addresses the Council of Jerusalem: "Brethren, you know that in the early days God made choice among you, that by my mouth the Gentiles should hear the word of the gospel and believe. And God who knows the heart bore witness to them, giving them the Holy Spirit just as he did to us." The Church's first expansion to the Gentiles thus does not come through human agency or planning, but through the decisive intervention of the Holy Spirit.

---

[6] Acts 8:14–17.

[7] See Acts 9; 22; 26.

The Holy Spirit is likewise the instigator of the first missionary voyage of St. Paul and Barnabas, as we read in Acts 13:1–2:

> Now in the church at Antioch there were prophets and teachers, Barnabas, Simeon who was called Niger, Lucius of Cyrene, Manaen a member of the court of Herod the tetrarch, and Saul. While they were worshiping the Lord and fasting, the Holy Spirit said, "Set apart for me Barnabas and Saul for the work to which I have called them." Then after fasting and praying they laid their hands on them and sent them off. So, *being sent out by the Holy Spirit*, they went down to Seleucia; and from there they sailed to Cyprus.

The Holy Spirit is also an invisible protagonist at the Council of Jerusalem. At the end of the Council, a letter is drafted to be sent to all the brethren (Acts 15: 28–29):

> For *it has seemed good to the Holy Spirit and to us* to lay upon you no greater burden than these necessary things: that you abstain from what has been sacrificed to idols and from blood and from what is strangled and from unchastity. If you keep yourselves from these, you will do well. Farewell.

The Gospel was first brought to Greece and thus to Europe through the intervention of the Holy Spirit, as recounted in Acts 16:6–10. On this occasion the action of the Spirit was negative at first, prohibiting them from gaining fruit in Asia Minor (present-day Turkey), so that they would turn to Greece.[8] Once again the mission of the Church to the Gentiles is shown to be not the work of human planning or apostolic strategy sessions, but of the action of the Holy Spirit, who is the soul of the Church.

In Acts 19:2–6, Paul arrives in Ephesus for the first time and meets several disciples who had only received the baptism of John the Baptist and were unaware of the existence of the Holy Spirit:

> And he said to them, "Did you receive the Holy Spirit when you believed?" And they said, "No, we have never even heard that there is a Holy Spirit." And he said, "Into what then were you baptized?" They said, "Into John's baptism." And Paul said, "John baptized with the baptism of repentance, telling the people to believe in the one who was to come after him, that is, Jesus." On hearing this, they were baptized in the name of the Lord Jesus. And when Paul had laid his hands upon them, the Holy Spirit

---

[8] As mentioned in chapter 4, Pope Benedict XVI commented on this key text in his famous Regensburg Lecture.

came on them; and they spoke with tongues and prophesied. There were about twelve of them in all.

St. Paul both baptized and confirmed these brethren. Confirmation seems to be indicated by St. Paul's laying on of hands. Ephesus subsequently became one of the great centers of the early Church with St. John residing there.

The Holy Spirit, finally, impels St. Paul to return to Jerusalem,[9] where he knows that he will be persecuted and imprisoned, and from which he will be sent to Rome. In Acts 20:22–23, he tells the disciples of Asia Minor who gathered to meet him in Troas: "And now, behold, I am going to Jerusalem, bound in the Spirit, not knowing what shall befall me there; except that the Holy Spirit testifies to me in every city that imprisonment and afflictions await me."

Paul's return to Jerusalem was the providential occasion for his eventual journey to Rome, the very heart of the Gentile world. As St. Paul worshiped in the Temple in Jerusalem to fulfill a Nazirite vow made at the request of St. James, a riot broke out as Paul was in the Temple, and he was arrested while he was almost torn limb from limb. He appealed to Caesar to escape persecution, and was finally sent to Rome.

When Paul arrived in Rome and was under house arrest waiting for his appeal to be heard, he preached to the Jewish community in Rome, who came to him in "great numbers" as he attempted to "to convince them about Jesus both from the Law of Moses and from the prophets. And some were convinced by what he said, while others disbelieved" (Acts 28:23–24). Acts concludes by stating that Paul stayed in Rome for two years, "preaching the kingdom of God and teaching about the Lord Jesus Christ quite openly and unhindered" (Acts 28:31).

Theme of Conversion in the Acts of the Apostles

As we have seen, the life of the Church in the Acts of the Apostles is all about conversion, which means a turning spiritually from self to the Lord. The miracle of Pentecost was a miracle of conversion, first in the Apostles and disciples and then in three thousand Israelites. The following chapters of Acts show the first fruits of that conversion in the Church's life of sanctity and communion. We see then the conversion of Samaria, the conversion of Saul (recounted three times), the conversion of the centurion Cornelius and his household (recounted twice), the

---

[9] See Acts 19:21: "Now after these events Paul resolved in the Spirit to pass through Macedonia and Achaia and go to Jerusalem, saying, 'After I have been there, I must also see Rome.'"

conversion of Gentiles in Antioch, the conversion of Cyprus and Asia Minor in Paul's first missionary journey, and the conversion of parts of Greece as well as Asia Minor in his second and third journeys. Acts 21 shows us the fruits of conversion among Jews in Judea, as James testifies: "You see, brother, how many thousands there are among the Jews of those who have believed; they are all zealous for the law" (Acts 21:20). Acts ends with many conversions in Rome itself.

The conversion of hearts and minds is the goal of the Church's missionary effort. Conversion is nothing other than a continual striving to accomplish God's will in one's life and in the world, through an ever more perfect realization of the double commandment of love.

Continuity between Israel and the Church in Acts

It is clear from what we have seen that another great theme of Acts is that of continuity and distinction between Israel and the Church. The continuity is revealed first of all in that the Church of Pentecost was entirely Jewish, and that the Gospel went out from Jerusalem to the ends of the earth, as foretold in Isaiah 2:2–3.

The Apostles continued to worship in the Temple, as we see in Acts 3, in which the lame man is healed at the "Beautiful Gate" as Peter and John were going to pray at the "hour of prayer" (the evening sacrifice).[10] We see it also in Acts 21, in which Paul goes to the Temple to pray and fulfill a Nazirite vow with four other Jewish Christians, a practice which involved animal sacrifices.[11] This was done at the request of James, because the Jewish Christians in the church in Jerusalem had become scandalized, hearing that Paul was teaching "all the Jews who are among the Gentiles to forsake Moses, telling them not to circumcise their children or observe the customs" (Acts 21:21). James therefore suggested to Paul that he unequivocally show that this was not the case by publicly purifying himself and four other men in the Temple so that "all will know that there is nothing in what they have been told about you but that you yourself live in observance of the law" (Acts 21:24). Paul complied with the request of James, but, far from appeasing the people, it ironically ended up precipitating a riot in which Paul was almost beaten to death, for it was thought that Paul had brought Gentile Christians with him into the Temple. This was the occasion of Paul's imprisonment, from which he appealed to Caesar and was subsequently sent to Rome.

---

[10] For the evening sacrifice, see Ex 29:39–42.

[11] Paul had also fulfilled this vow earlier in Acts 18:18 at Cenchreae. See Num 6:13–18.

With regard to circumcision, we know that Paul circumcised Timothy, whose mother was a Jewish "believer," although his father was a Greek.[12] Acts 16:3 explains that he did this "because of the Jews that were in those places, for they all knew that his father was a Greek." In other words, Paul performed the rite of circumcision to avoid scandalizing and alienating Jews, and to show that he was not contrary to an observance of rites pertaining to the ceremonial law of Moses on the part of Jewish Christians, as long as it would not have the consequence of bring about an imposition of that law on Gentile Christians.

We know that the Apostles kept the kosher food laws until Peter went into the house of the centurion, Cornelius. A special revelation from heaven was needed for Peter to take this momentous step. Thus when Gentiles entered the Church at Antioch, the disciples no longer felt bound to the kosher laws and ate in the way of the Gentiles so as to maintain table fellowship with them and not cause a separation in the community. We know this from Paul's Letter to the Galatians (2:11–14), which describes his public disagreement with Peter on this issue, when Peter temporarily separated himself from table fellowship with the Gentiles so as not to scandalize some Jewish Christians who came to Antioch from the church in Jerusalem:

> But when Cephas came to Antioch I opposed him to his face, because he stood condemned. For before certain men came from James, he ate with the Gentiles; but when they came he drew back and separated himself, fearing the circumcision party. And with him the rest of the Jews acted insincerely, so that even Barnabas was carried away by their insincerity. But when I saw that they were not straightforward about the truth of the gospel, I said to Cephas before them all, "If you, though a Jew, live like a Gentile and not like a Jew, how can you compel the Gentiles to live like Jews?"

Paul opposed Peter's practice in this case because he thought that it would have the effect of leading the Gentile Christians to adopt the kosher laws in order to be able to share table fellowship with Peter and the other Jewish Christians.

Distinction of the Church from Israel

Although the Acts of the Apostles as a whole gives a picture of general outward conformity of the Church in Jerusalem with ancient Israel, we can see that there are also momentous differences, which at first could

---

[12] Acts 16:1.

remain partially hidden from outward view. First of all, there is the awareness manifested by the Apostles that man is not saved by works of the ceremonial Law of Moses, but by the grace of God granted through the Passion of Christ and communicated through faith and the sacraments that transmit a participation in Christ's life. Secondly, the new Israel of the New Covenant has a new hierarchical authority which rests not on the priesthood of Aaron, but on the foundation of the Twelve Apostles.

We see this new apostolic authority constantly at work through the Acts of the Apostles. We also see it clash with the old authority of the Sanhedrin in Acts 5:28–32, in which the High Priest charges them, saying:

> "We strictly charged you not to teach in this name, yet here you have filled Jerusalem with your teaching and you intend to bring this man's blood upon us." But Peter and the apostles answered, "We must obey God rather than men. The God of our fathers raised Jesus whom you killed by hanging him on a tree. God exalted him at his right hand as Leader and Savior, to give repentance to Israel and forgiveness of sins. And we are witnesses to these things, and so is the Holy Spirit whom God has given to those who obey him."

The clash is quieted for a moment due to the intervention of Gamaliel, but it resurges shortly afterwards with the stoning of Stephen, the persecution worked by Saul, the martyrdom of James in 42 AD, the imprisonment of Peter in the same year, and the later imprisonment of Paul in Acts 21.

We see the Apostles exercising supreme religious authority over the new Israel, in the name of the Messiah. "And with great power the apostles gave their testimony to the resurrection of the Lord Jesus" (Acts 4:33). Built on the Apostles, the new Israel has a new juridical and priestly authority and foundation, completely independent from that of the Old Covenant, by which it was prefigured. This change of religious and juridical authority is far more momentous than one might grasp at first sight. For a change in priesthood and ultimate religious authority allows the Church to prudently make all the gradual transitions necessary for the Gospel to reach from Jerusalem to the ends of the earth, as promised by Christ at His Ascension. The outward form of life appropriate to the Church in Jerusalem, in which all the believers are Jews, will clearly be different from that which comes to pass at Antioch and throughout the Gentile world. The fact that the Church has a living authority in the Apostles allows her to make the changes necessary in docility to the guidance of the Spirit.

Right after the miracle of Pentecost (Acts 2:42), a summary picture of the early Church is given: "And they devoted themselves to the apostles' teaching and fellowship, to the breaking of bread and the prayers." This sentence gives a remarkably concise statement of the essence of the life of the Church. It is founded first on the obedience of faith to the teaching of the Apostles, and to their power of governance. Secondly, it is built on the communion of charity that flows from the unity of faith. Third, it is built on the breaking of the bread, which is a reference to the Eucharistic sacrifice, which right from the beginning is shown to be the very center of the life of the Church.[13] Finally, it is built on prayer in common, which primarily must refer to the liturgy of the Church, which obviously is built on the liturgy of Israel and her psalms, but is now made to revolve around the saving work of Christ in the Paschal mystery.

The Eucharist/"breaking of the bread" appears associated especially with the "first day of the week" in Acts 20:7: "On the first day of the week, when we were gathered together to break bread, Paul talked with them, intending to depart on the morrow; and he prolonged his speech until midnight." The "first day of the week," according to the Jewish understanding, was Sunday. Thus it appears that Sunday was already the "day of the Lord" on which the Eucharist was celebrated with special solemnity.[14]

The Lord chose Sunday not only to rise from the dead, but also to appear solemnly to the Apostles gathered in the upper room (on Easter Sunday and on the following Sunday), and to give the Holy Spirit to the Apostles on Pentecost,[15] which in the Church's memory is always

---

[13] Together with the "breaking of the bread," the Apostolic Church was also founded on the other sacraments, especially Baptism, Confirmation, and Holy Orders.

[14] The expression, "Lord's day," is used in Rev 1:10. See John Paul II, apostolic letter *Dies Domini* 21 (1998).

[15] See John Paul II, *Dies Domini* 28: "Sunday, the day of light, could also be called the day of 'fire,' in reference to the Holy Spirit. The light of Christ is intimately linked to the 'fire' of the Spirit, and the two images together reveal the meaning of the Christian Sunday. . . . The outpouring of the Spirit was the great gift of the Risen Lord to his disciples on Easter Sunday. It was again Sunday when, fifty days after the Resurrection, the Spirit descended in power, as 'a mighty wind' and 'fire' (Acts 2:2–3), upon the Apostles gathered with Mary. Pentecost is not only the founding event of the Church, but is also the mystery which for ever gives life to the Church. Such an event has its own powerful liturgical moment in the annual celebration which concludes 'the great Sunday,' but it also remains a part of the deep meaning of every Sunday, because of its intimate bond with the Paschal Mystery. The 'weekly Easter' thus becomes, in a sense, the 'weekly Pentecost,' when Christians relive the Apostles' joyful encounter with the Risen Lord and receive the life-giving breath of his Spirit."

celebrated on Sunday.[16] This shows us that although the disciples in Israel continued to keep the Sabbath in accordance with the people of Israel, the privileged day for God's worship had already shifted to Sunday, in virtue of God's own choice in raising Jesus from the dead on Sunday rather than the Sabbath.[17]

Sunday, however, could not yet be observed as a public day of rest, either in Israel or in the Gentile cities of the Roman Empire. This would have to wait until the fourth century after the legalization of Christianity under Constantine.[18] In the meantime, however, we know from various sources, including Acts 20:7, that the Sunday Eucharist was celebrated before dawn, so that all could attend. Sunday, therefore, had already spiritually replaced the Jewish Sabbath, even when the Sabbath was still celebrated outwardly in the Church in Judea. Similarly, the breaking of the bread had spiritually replaced the rites of the Temple worship in the life of the Church, even though the Apostles still observed those rites together with those who did not believe in Christ, until the destruction of the Temple in Jerusalem made those rites impossible for all Jews.

---

[16] See Lev 23:15–16: "And you shall count from the morrow after the sabbath, from the day that you brought the sheaf of the wave offering; *seven full weeks* shall they be, counting *fifty days* to the morrow after the seventh sabbath; then you shall present a cereal offering of new grain to the Lord."

This text is ambiguous about the day in which the counting of fifty days was to begin, and there were different ways of reckoning it among different Jewish sects. The practice of the Sadducees was to count from the Sabbath during the Passover, in which case Pentecost would always occur on a Sunday, as in the Christian practice. The Pharisees, followed by rabbinical Judaism, counted fifty days from the Passover, according to which Pentecost always falls on the sixth day of the Jewish month of Sivan.

[17] John Paul II, *Dies Domini* 1–2: "It is *Easter* which returns week by week, celebrating Christ's victory over sin and death, the fulfilment in him of the first creation and the dawn of 'the new creation' (see 2 Cor 5:17). It is the day which recalls in grateful adoration the world's first day and looks forward in active hope to 'the last day,' when Christ will come in glory (see Acts 1:11; 1 Thess 4:13–17) and all things will be made new (see Rev 21:5). . . . Therefore, in commemorating the day of Christ's Resurrection not just once a year but every Sunday, the Church seeks to indicate to every generation the true fulcrum of history, to which the mystery of the world's origin and its final destiny leads.' See also no. 24: 'Christian thought spontaneously linked the Resurrection, which took place on 'the first day of the week,' with the first day of that cosmic week (see Gen 1:1–2:4), which shapes the creation story in the Book of Genesis: the day of the creation of light (see 1:3–5). This link invited an understanding of the Resurrection as the beginning of a new creation, the first fruits of which is the glorious Christ, 'the firstborn of all creation' (Col 1:15) and 'the firstborn from the dead' (Col 1:18)."

[18] See *Dies Domini* 64.

The outward participation of the Church in the ceremonial rites of ancient Israel, however, ran the danger of hiding the novelty of the New Covenant, sealed in the Blood of Christ on Calvary, made present on the altar in the "breaking of the bread," that is, in every valid Mass. Why continue to celebrate the figurative animal sacrifices of the Mosaic Covenant, when the Church has been given the one true Sacrifice of the Messiah, which alone is capable of redeeming the sins of the world, to which every other sacrifice points as a mere type or figure?

St. Thomas Aquinas has an interesting discussion on whether the ceremonial precepts of the Mosaic Law should have continued after Christ. In order to resolve the question, he establishes the general principle that external worship should be in accordance with the interior worship of the heart, which consists in faith, hope, and charity. However, our faith and hope are not exactly the same under the Mosaic Law and during the time of the Church. Under the Mosaic Law, there was a twofold hope: in the Redemption to be worked by the Messiah and in the heavenly beatitude of the world to come. In the time of the Church we still hope for heavenly beatitude, but we know through faith that the Redemption worked by the Messiah has already been realized. Since our interior worship is different from that of the Old Covenant, it is fitting that it should be differently expressed. For this reason the sacraments of the Church apply the power of Christ's Passion as something already present and operating in the world. The Eucharist, for example, makes Christ Himself present as the Victim who sacrifices Himself for the sins of the world. The rites of the Old Covenant were not able to do this because the Messiah had not yet come. The ceremonial law of Moses could only prefigure Christ's sacrifice through the sacrifice of animals and other created things. St. Thomas writes: "The ceremonies of the Old Law betokened Christ as having yet to be born and to suffer: whereas our sacraments signify Him as already born and having suffered."[19] Because He has already been born and suffered, His action and His very Person are able to touch us in the "breaking of the bread"—the Holy Eucharist, the sacrament that lies at the center of the Church's existence, unity, holiness, and missionary power.

The reason why the Apostles and the early Church from the circumcision continued to follow some of the observances of the Mosaic Law is clearly not because they regarded them as necessary for salvation, or intrinsically capable of communicating the grace won for us by Christ. This is true only of the sacraments of the Church. Rather, they continued to observe them, it seems, principally out of reverence

---

[19] St. Thomas Aquinas, *ST* I-II, q. 103, a. 4.

and love for the Old Covenant, out of devotion, and so as not to scandalize the Jewish community.[20]

The Council of Jerusalem

The Council of Jerusalem did not address the question of whether Jewish Christians were bound by the Law of Moses, but only that of whether Gentile converts should be required to observe the ceremonial or ritual precepts of the Law of Moses. Some of the Christians who were Pharisees held that all Christians had to follow the Law of Moses. As we know, the Council upheld the position taught by both Peter and Paul that the Gentiles did not have to be circumcised or follow the Mosaic ceremonial law. Peter made the decisive contribution to the debate, recalling how the pagan Cornelius and his household had received the Spirit without the works of the Law of Moses. James then says:

> Simeon has related how God first visited the Gentiles, to take out of them a people for his name. And with this the words of the prophets agree, as it is written, "After this I will return, and I will rebuild the dwelling of David, which has fallen; I will rebuild its ruins, and I will set it up, that the rest of men may seek the Lord, and all the Gentiles who are called by my name, says the Lord, who has made these things known from of old." Therefore my judgment is that we should not trouble those of the Gentiles who turn to God, but should write to them to abstain from the pollutions of idols and from unchastity and from what is strangled and from blood. For from early generations Moses has had in every city those who preach him, for he is read every sabbath in the synagogues.[21]

In order to make peace between Christians from Judaism and from the Gentiles, the Council of Jerusalem, following the advice of James, required all Gentile Christians to observe a very minimal ritual purity consisting in abstaining from animal blood (and, for the same reason, from animals killed by strangling). Abstaining from idols and unchastity was also part of the moral law, which of its very nature is binding on all

---

[20] See St. Thomas Aquinas, *ST* I-II, q. 103, a. 4, ad 1: "The reason why the Holy Spirit did not wish the converted Jews to be debarred at once from observing the legal ceremonies, while converted heathens were forbidden to observe the rites of heathendom, was in order to show that there is a difference between these rites. For heathenish ceremonial was rejected as absolutely unlawful, and as prohibited by God for all time; whereas the legal ceremonial ceased as being fulfilled through Christ's Passion, being instituted by God as a figure of Christ."

[21] Acts 15:14–21.

Christians. Abstaining from blood and meat that was strangled was a disciplinary and temporary measure, whose observance ceased when the circumstances that had produced it—tensions between Jewish and Gentile Christians—were no longer a major issue.[22]

It is very interesting that James, in Acts 15:12–18, cites Amos 9:11–12, a beautiful prophecy of the Messianic Kingdom, which is to be the spiritual "rebuilding" of the fallen "dwelling of David." The rebuilding of the Messianic Kingdom by the Messiah, the son of David, must be *catholic*, extending to all the Gentiles. As such, it is clear that it can no longer be bound by a ceremonial law partially designed to separate Israel from the nations until the Messiah had come, as well as serving to prefigure His coming.

In summary, the Church depicted in the Acts of the Apostles is a Church that is one in faith, government, and communion, holy in charity, incipiently universal or catholic, and absolutely apostolic—built on the foundation of the Apostles.

---

[22] For further discussion of this issue, see p. 237 below.

Chapter 11

The Church as the Body of Christ according to St. Paul

One of the great themes of the Letters of St. Paul is his presentation of the Church as the Body of Christ. This theme is hard for us to grasp in contemporary Western culture. We live in a very individualistic society, and it is foreign to the atmosphere that we breathe to believe that we form one body and that we are not simply our own masters. The Church is not merely an institution, or an "organized religion," or a collection of individuals who share the same customs or beliefs. The Church has a life bigger than the sum of all her members. At Baptism we are inserted into the life of Christ and become members of a spiritual and supernatural society that is the Church. The life of the Church is the life of Christ that continues in us. The Church is the means by which we have a share in Christ's own life, Christ who is the living Torah.

The germ of this teaching was made known to Saul when he was blinded on the road to Damascus and encountered Jesus, who said to him, "Saul, Saul, why do you persecute me?" (Acts 9:4). Saul was not persecuting Christ directly, for He had ascended to heaven several years before. Rather, he was persecuting Jews who were members of Christ's Church. Christ speaks of the persecution of the members of the Church as a persecution of Himself, for through Baptism and faith they are members of His Mystical Body and He lives in them. Christ could have said, "Why are you persecuting my followers, or my Church?" But instead He asks, "Why are you persecuting *me*?"

St. Paul later will be the great defender and preacher of this truth. He had an exemplary awareness of the union between Christ and the Christian—that Christ lives in him and he in and for Christ. In Galatians 2:19–20, he writes: "I have been crucified with Christ; it is no longer I who live, but Christ who lives in me; and the life I now live in the flesh I live by faith in the Son of God, who loved me and gave himself for me." Similarly, in Philippians 1:21 he writes that "for to me to live is Christ."

All Christians are called to this union of life, and it is truly realized in all who are in a state of grace. Christ promised that if we keep His commandments, He will come and dwell in us, with the Father and the Holy Spirit:

He who has my commandments and keeps them, he it is who loves me; and he who loves me will be loved by my Father, and I will love him and manifest myself to him. . . . If a man loves me, he will keep my word, and my Father will love him, and we will come to him and make our home with him.[1]

Christ founded the Church to prolong His life in the world until the end of time, so to speak, by living in His members and enabling His members to live in Him and to share in His interior life, which is charity, and in His mission, which is redemption and the building up of the Church.

Obviously, not all the members of the Church share equally in Christ's life. The Church contains dead members as well as living ones. Dead members are members of the Catholic Church who are living in a state of mortal sin, and in whom, consequently, Christ cannot indwell. The living members are those in a state of grace. Among the living members there is a great diversity of degrees of holiness. However, all are called to share in the sentiments of St. Paul (Gal 2:20): "It is no longer I who live, but Christ who lives in me."

He expresses the same idea by saying of the members of Christ that "we have the mind of Christ" (1 Cor 2:16). This is not an empty platitude. He exhorts all the Christians of Philippi to have the mind of Christ (Phil 2:5), which means that as He emptied Himself to be obedient unto death, so we are to empty ourselves with regard to our neighbor in charity and humility in like manner. Or again, he frequently expresses this idea by saying that the members of the Church are to "put on Christ." In Galatians 3:27, St. Paul says: "For as many of you as were baptized into Christ have put on Christ." In Romans 13:14, he says: "But put on the Lord Jesus Christ, and make no provision for the flesh, to gratify its desires."[2]

All the members of the Church are called to share the life of Christ, and in virtue of that union, to share in a common life with all the members of Christ. The Church thus is knit together by a dual union— vertical and horizontal. The vertical union is primary, uniting each living member with the Holy Trinity. The horizontal union presupposes the vertical and unites all the members among themselves on the model of Christ's love for all His members.

---

[1] Jn 14:21–23.

[2] This was the verse that worked St. Augustine's conversion, after he heard the boy saying "Take and read."

No member of the Church lives simply for himself.[3] Through Christ's grace, he lives first for God and then for the building up of the Body in charity. Just as the hand does not live for itself but for the sake of the head and the whole body, so each member of the Church is to live for Christ, who is the head, and for the whole Body, which is the Church.

Every Christian should strive to live as an *alter Christus*, another Christ, "putting on Christ" and seeking to imitate Him in charity. This could seem to be absurd presumption, and it would be indeed, if Christ did not give us the grace to live His life, and command us to follow Him, carrying our cross.

The Mystical Body of Christ in 1 Corinthians 12 and Romans 12

The Church is the Body of Christ in that, like every living body, it is composed of a vital union between the head and many other diverse members. Just as the other members of an animate body cannot live apart from their union with the head, which gives direction, so too in the Church. Every member of the Church lives spiritually from his union with Christ, the Head of the Body. In virtue of this union with the Head, the various members also live in communion and complementarity with one another.

St. Paul speaks of this intimate union of Christ and the Church, and of the complementarity of members in the Body of Christ in 1 Corinthians 12:12–20:

> For just as the body is one and has many members, and all the members of the body, though many, are one body, so it is with Christ. For by one Spirit we were all baptized into one body—Jews or Greeks, slaves or free—and all were made to drink of one Spirit. For the body does not consist of one member but of many. . . . As it is, there are many parts, yet one body.

He returns to the same theme in Romans 12:4–5: "For as in one body we have many members, and all the members do not have the same function, so we, though many, are one body in Christ, and individually members one of another."

The Body of Christ which results from our sacramental union with Him has both visible and invisible dimensions, in which the many members complement each other in a marvelous way. Visibly, the

---

[3] See Rom 14:7: "None of us lives to himself, and none of us dies to himself. If we live, we live to the Lord, and if we die, we die to the Lord; so then, whether we live or whether we die, we are the Lord's."

Church is hierarchically structured according to the sacrament of Holy Orders, according to the calling which some of the members of the Body have received. The Body is also structured by various charisms, such as the vocation to the consecrated or religious life, or the role of the laity, who also participate in complementary spiritual gifts for the building up of the Body of Christ, each according to his own circumstances, temporal activity, and apostolate.

Thus there is a diversity of roles in the Body, but the Body remains one through its living connection with the one Head of the Body, which is Christ, and through the one soul animating the Body, which is the Holy Spirit.

Preparation for the Mystical Body in Ancient Israel

Biblical Israel, understood not as a country but as the society of all Jews, also was (and continues to be) a spiritual society that could be spoken of as a mystical body. Jews, whether they recognize it or not, are members of a people that has a corporate destiny and spiritual purpose, which is principally to prepare for the coming of the Messiah. Even after Christ has come they continue to be tied to this corporate destiny. We know from St. Paul that the Chosen People will have a significant role to play in preparing for Christ's Second Coming.[4]

Ancient Israel was one body through sharing one Law revealed on Mt. Sinai, having one faith through the Law and the prophets (the written and the oral Torah). Israel had one hope in the Messiah and in the world to come. Israel had one worship as commanded in the Law and a common sacrifice. There was one ark of the covenant and one Temple in which all sacrifice was to be offered. Israel had one priesthood through Aaron and his sons. There was one supreme religious authority in the high priesthood and in the Sanhedrin composed of seventy of the most prominent men. In all these ways Israel was bound together as a kind of mystical body united in faith and hope in God and in the Messiah. Israel was thus a precursor of the Mystical Body which is the Church.

The Members of the Church Are Joined Sacramentally to Christ

The Church is one body in an even stronger way than Biblical Israel. She is bound together into a living body through supernatural channels of life, which we can compare to arteries, veins, nerves, and sinews. These channels of supernatural life are the seven sacraments of the Church,

---

[4] See Rom 11:15 and *CCC* 674. For a fuller treatment, see pp. 226ff. below.

through which the members of the Mystical Body are connected with the life of the Head—in sanctifying grace, faith, hope, and charity. Through the sacraments, beginning with Baptism and culminating in the Eucharist, the members of the Church are joined to Christ through mystical or sacramental bonds, which create a real supernatural union with Christ.

This union has two dimensions: baptismal character and sanctifying grace. In virtue of baptismal character, all the faithful receive a share in Christ's priestly, prophetic, and kingly office. This means that through Baptism we receive a spiritual power to participate in the offering of Christ's redemptive sacrifice (priestly office), to participate in the prophetic office of professing the true faith, and to cooperate in the ordering of all temporal realities according to the Law of God (kingly office), which is summarized in the bond of supernatural charity.

In virtue of sanctifying grace, not only are we joined to Christ's priestly, prophetic, and kingly mission, but we are also joined to Him in a real union of friendship and adopted sonship. All the members of Christ are thus made into one Mystical Body with Him.

The formation of the Mystical Body culminates in the Eucharist, which is the sacrament of union—with Christ and one another. Christ makes Himself present on the altar in His Body and Blood under the species of bread and wine to nourish the members of His Church with His very Body and thus to communicate a greater share in His interior life, as long as we receive Him worthily. At the same time, as a necessary consequence, the Eucharist also works to deepen our communion with one another in the Mystical Body, and thus it is the sacrament of ecclesiastical unity.[5] St. Paul states this in 1 Corinthians 10:17: "For we, being many, are one bread, one body, all that partake of one bread." The Eucharist binds us into one Mystical Body by strengthening our unity with Christ and with one another.

Who are the members of this Mystical Body? Pius XII gives a brief and clear answer:

> Actually only those are to be included as members of the Church who have been baptized and profess the true faith, and who have not been so unfortunate as to separate themselves from the unity of the Body, or been excluded by legitimate authority for grave faults committed. . . . It follows that those who are divided in faith or government cannot be living in the unity of such a Body, nor can they be living the life of its one Divine Spirit.[6]

---

[5] See St. Thomas Aquinas, *ST* III, q. 82, a. 2, ad 3.

[6] Pius XII, *Mystici Corporis* 22.

In other words, the members of the Mystical Body of Christ are the baptized faithful who have not become tragically separated through public schism, heresy, apostasy, or excommunication. Those visible members who have not separated in any of those ways, but are in a state of mortal sin, are still members of the Body, but not *living* members. Those who are unbaptized or who are outside of the visible communion of the Catholic Church are not visible members of the Mystical Body. If, however, they are invincibly ignorant of the true Church and are in a state of grace, they have an invisible spiritual bond with the soul of the Mystical Body, which is the Holy Spirit. If they die in that state they will be members of the Body for all eternity in the Church triumphant.

The Body of Christ and the Four Marks of the Church

St. Paul's teaching on the Mystical Body of Christ is intimately related to the four marks of the Church that we have examined in chapters 4 through 8 and which we profess in the Creed: the Church is one, holy, catholic, and apostolic.

The Church is *one* Mystical Body through her interior *unity*: through having one common spiritual life of faith, hope, and charity, given to us by Christ and uniting us spiritually to Him.

The Church is the Mystical Body of Christ through her *catholicity* (universality). The unity of faith, hope, and charity coexists with an extreme diversity of members, which is the catholicity of the Church. There is a place in the one Body for all nations, for all types of personalities, for all natural and spiritual gifts, for all professions and social classes, for all legitimate diversity. The catholicity of the Church fills up the Mystical Body.

The Church is the Mystical Body of Christ also through her mark of *apostolicity*. Every living animal body is hierarchically organized with a head that directs other members. The Church likewise has a hierarchical structure given her by Christ, in which the successors of the Apostles serve as the head of the body in every locality or diocese. The sacrament of Holy Orders gives to its recipients a sacramental share in Christ's headship.

Finally, the Church is the Mystical Body of Christ above all through her *holiness* which consists in participating in the very life and holiness of Christ Himself, through the grace of Christ given to us in the sacraments which vivify the Body of Christ as arteries, veins, and nerves vivify a natural body.[7]

---

[7] See Eph 2:21.

Diversity of Roles in the One Body of Christ

St. Paul uses the analogy of the Mystical Body of Christ to show three great truths: (a) the union of all the members of the Church with Christ the Head; (b) the union in faith, hope, and charity of all the members of the Body with one another; and (c) the complementarity of the various members. No one member is sufficient unto himself, for he needs the other members as well as the head. The hand or foot cannot get along by itself, but each member needs all the other members and is dependent on them.

St. Paul explains this diversity within the Body of Christ in 1 Corinthians 12:15–21:

> If the foot should say, "Because I am not a hand, I do not belong to the body," that would not make it any less a part of the body. And if the ear should say, "Because I am not an eye, I do not belong to the body," that would not make it any less a part of the body. If the whole body were an eye, where would be the hearing? If the whole body were an ear, where would be the sense of smell? But as it is, God arranged the organs in the body, each one of them, as he chose. If all were a single organ, where would the body be? As it is, there are many parts, yet one body. The eye cannot say to the hand, "I have no need of you," nor again the head to the feet, "I have no need of you."

Not all of the members can be the head or the eyes, but this does not make them of a lesser fundamental dignity. All the members of the Church share in the dignity of Christ Himself.

The Role of the Priesthood in the Mystical Body

The invisible Head of the Church is always Christ. However, the Body also needs a visible head who sacramentally represents Christ on earth. This headship is given to the Church through the sacrament of Holy Orders. The bishops represent Christ the Head of the Church in their respective dioceses, of which they are the visible heads. The priests represent Christ the Head in their respective parishes. The Pope represents Christ the Head in the entire universal Church.

Without bishops and priests the Church would be unable to administer the sacraments of the Eucharist, Penance, and Confirmation, and the Church would lose her arteries and channels of grace. Without priests, Christ's Body and Blood would not come onto our altars in the sacrifice of the Mass, and we could not receive Him in Holy Communion.

Without the Pope and his infallible teaching office, the Church would be unable to maintain her unity in the faith and she would splinter like the Protestant denominations. The Pope is not set over the Mystical Body, but ordained to serve all the servants of God by providing the ministry of unity.

The other members of the Mystical Body should not resent the fact that they were not called to be the head, but rather ears, hands, and feet. Every member needs all the other members for the good of the whole. And if we need all the other members, we are especially dependent on the head, and so we need to pray especially for those who are called to share in Christ's headship of the Church: Pope, bishops, and priests.

The Role of Religious in the Mystical Body

In addition to members who are distinguished by receiving Holy Orders, the Church is also endowed with some members called to follow Christ in a special way in religious life or consecrated life. Although not part of her hierarchical structure as the priesthood is, religious life is an essential part of the Church's sanctity and identity.[8]

Religious respond to a special calling by Christ to "imitate Him more closely"[9] in seeking the perfection of sanctity. They do this by voluntarily taking up the three evangelical counsels of poverty, chastity, and obedience, which are based on the form of life lived by Jesus Himself and to which He called the Apostles. By means of the three evangelical counsels, religious are "totally dedicated to God, loved beyond all things. In this way, that person is ordained to the honor and service of God under a new and special title."[10]

The Second Vatican Council, in the Dogmatic Constitution on the Church, *Lumen gentium*, speaks of religious as being called to a state of life that serves as a witness to the heavenly realities for which the Church lives in hope:

> The religious state, whose purpose is to free its members from earthly cares, more fully manifests to all believers the presence of heavenly goods already possessed here below. . . . Christ proposed to His disciples this form of life, which He, as the Son of God, accepted in entering this world to do the will of the Father. . . . The religious state clearly manifests that the Kingdom of God and its

---

[8] See Vatican II, *Lumen gentium* 44: "Thus, the state which is constituted by the profession of the evangelical counsels, though it does not belong to the hierarchical structure of the Church, nevertheless, undeniably belongs to its life and holiness."

[9] Vatican II, Decree on the Adaptation and Renewal of Religious Life, *Perfectae Caritatis* 1.

[10] *Lumen gentium* 43.

needs, in a very special way, are raised above all earthly considerations.[11]

The religious state has a special role in the Mystical Body, not by serving as head and governing, which is proper to the priesthood, but rather through the example of a life based, even in its outward form, on the imitation of Christ in poverty, chastity, and obedience. Religious are called to be a kind of model of what the entire Church is called to be: the Bride of Christ.

The Role of the Laity in the Mystical Body

Very often the laity have a very insufficient awareness of their role and dignity as living members of the Mystical Body of Christ. As members of the Body, they are called to live the life of Christ to the full in their own state of life and profession, and to help build up the Body of Christ wherever they find themselves.

The special role of the laity in the mission of the Church consists in giving a Christian spirit to all their activities: to the workplace, to family life, to education, to friendship, to the political and economic sphere, to culture and sports, etc. In this way they are called to animate all the honest activities of the world. By being a Christian witness in all their ordinary activities, the Christian laity are called to be salt of the earth and light of the world (together with priests and religious).

The Second Vatican Council put great emphasis on the role of the laity in building up the Church in the Dogmatic Constitution on the Church, *Lumen gentium*:

> The laity, by their very vocation, seek the kingdom of God by engaging in temporal affairs and by ordering them according to the plan of God. They live in the world, that is, in each and in all of the secular professions and occupations. They live in the ordinary circumstances of family and social life, from which the very web of their existence is woven. They are called there by God that by exercising their proper function and led by the spirit of the Gospel they may *work for the sanctification of the world from within as a leaven.* In this way they may make Christ known to others, especially by the *testimony of a life resplendent in faith, hope and charity.* Therefore, since they are tightly bound up in all types of temporal affairs it is their special task to order and to throw light upon these affairs in such a

---

[11] *Lumen gentium* 44.

way that they may come into being and then continually increase according to Christ to the praise of the Creator and the Redeemer.[12]

Lumen gentium explains that the laity are called to participate in the apostolate of the Church. The word "apostolate" refers to the activity entrusted by Christ to His Apostles and disciples to *"make disciples of all nations"* (Mt 28:19). Obviously, the apostolate is exercised in a special way by priests, who administer the sacraments and govern the Church in the person of Christ the Head. Nevertheless, the apostolate of the Church needs to be the work of the entire Body of Christ. All the members are crucial and each one has an irreplaceable role in being salt and light in his or her own environment. As stated in *Lumen gentium* 33–34:

> Now the laity are called in a special way to make the Church present and operative in those places and circumstances where only through them can it become the salt of the earth. Thus every layman, in virtue of the very gifts bestowed upon him, is at the same time a witness and a living instrument of the mission of the Church itself "according to the measure of Christ's bestowal". . . . Upon all the laity, therefore, rests the noble duty of working to extend the divine plan of salvation to all men of each epoch and in every land. Consequently, may every opportunity be given them so that, according to their abilities and the needs of the times, they may zealously participate in the saving work of the Church.

A beautiful example of lay apostolate can be seen in the Acts of the Apostles in the Jewish married couple Aquila and Priscilla, who collaborated with St. Paul in building up the Church in Corinth and Ephesus. Aquila was a tentmaker by profession like St. Paul. When Apollos came there to preach the Gospel after Paul had left Ephesus, Aquila and Priscilla took him "and expounded to him the way of God more accurately" (Acts 18:26). Apollos then became a great apostle of Christ in his turn. Lay people today are called to collaborate with priests in bringing the people that we come in contact with to a deeper understanding and love of the faith.

The Role of Suffering in the Mystical Body

Those who suffer also have a great role in the Mystical Body. All the sufferings of the members who are in a state of grace have a redemptive value that participates in the infinite merits of Christ's Passion. St. Paul teaches this in Colossians 1:24: "Now I rejoice in my sufferings for your

---

[12] *Lumen gentium* 31 (my italics).

sake, and in my flesh I complete what is lacking in Christ's afflictions for the sake of his body, that is, the church."

What does St. Paul mean when he speaks of "completing what is lacking in Christ's afflictions"? How could anything be lacking in Christ's suffering? Of course, nothing was lacking. Because of the infinite charity to which it was joined and the dignity of His divine Person, Christ's suffering was of infinite value, sufficient to redeem infinite worlds. Yet St. Paul says that something was "lacking" still. What is lacking is *our participation* in Christ's redemptive suffering. The Mystical Body must live the life of the Head of that Body. Christ manifested His love through redemptive suffering. He wills that we, the members of His Mystical Body, learn charity through the offering of our suffering, which will have redemptive value in and through Christ.

Obviously He does not need the merits of our redemptive suffering, but He wills to associate us with Him in the work of redemption so as to teach us to love more perfectly, for love is proved through suffering. It is easy to say that we love God. But it is harder to show that we mean it. Suffering shows the truth of love, in that it shows that we prefer to suffer pain rather than displease our beloved. Love is proved when we are willing to sacrifice for the sake of love. This was the ultimate reason for the superabundance of Christ's suffering in His Passion. He wished to show us the extent of His love through freely suffering an immensity of pain for our sake.

No man who lives in this vale of tears can avoid suffering. It comes to all of us. However, not all of us offer it up to God with love, with an inner smile. The good and the bad thief suffered equally, but only one redeemed his sufferings, uniting them with those of Christ at his side. Thus he merited to accompany Christ to heaven that very day. As the Curé of Ars says:

> There are two ways of suffering—to suffer with love and to suffer without love. The saints suffered everything with joy, patience, and perseverance, because they loved. As for us, we suffer with anger, vexation, and weariness, because we do not love. If we loved God, we should love crosses, we should wish for them, we should take pleasure in them. We should be happy to be able to suffer for the love of Him who lovingly suffered for us. . . . Worldly people are miserable when they have crosses, and good Christians are miserable when they have none. The Christian lives in the midst of crosses, as the fish lives in the sea.[13]

---

[13] St. John Vianney, *The Little Catechism of the Curé of Ars* (Rockford, IL: TAN Books, 1987), 67, 69.

Very often people who are seriously infirm are tortured with the thought that their lives are completely useless and that they are only a burden on society. This way of thinking is what people use to justify euthanasia. In reality the suffering members of Christ are the ones who are actually most active, although they do not know it, in building up the Body of Christ through the redemptive merit of their suffering offered in union with that of Christ.

The Role of Charismatic Gifts in the Mystical Body

Another beautiful aspect of St. Paul's teaching on the Mystical Body is the diversity of spiritual gifts or charisms. God gives these spiritual gifts for the good of the entire Church, and not just for the sanctification of the person who receives them. To one person He gives the gift of leadership, to another preaching, to another teaching, to another healing, etc. God divides His gifts up among the members of the Body so that all participate, each according to his own gift. St. Paul explains this in Romans 12:4–8:

> For as in one body we have many members, and all the members do not have the same function, so we, though many, are one body in Christ, and individually members one of another. Having gifts that differ according to the grace given to us, let us use them: if prophecy, in proportion to our faith; if service, in our serving; he who teaches, in his teaching; he who exhorts, in his exhortation; he who contributes, in liberality; he who gives aid, with zeal; he who does acts of mercy, with cheerfulness.

The Roles of Men and Women in the Mystical Body

Men and women have complementary and equal roles in the Mystical Body. Often people think that women are discriminated against in the Church because women cannot become priests or bishops. This is a misconception. Maleness is necessary for the priesthood because the priest acts in the person of Christ and *sacramentally* represents Him. Maleness is thus part of the matter of the sacrament of Holy Orders, as water is the matter of the sacrament of Baptism, and bread and wine of the Eucharist.

Women, however, have a great and irreplaceable role in the Body of Christ which makes them apt in a special way to be the *heart* of the Church, as they are of the family. God created man male and female, in such a way that each sex better manifests different aspects of God, and of our common humanity. This complementary character is summarized in the distinction between paternity and maternity to which man and woman, respectively, are called. God has endowed woman with a special aptitude for the particular virtues most intimately connected with her mission of maternity and man with those more particularly connected with his mission of paternity.

The special characteristics of woman consist in an aptitude for all that is oriented towards nurturing the new life that emerges from her womb. This entails a special attitude of attention to the personal sphere, to the concrete person in his totality, a special gift of empathy, intuition, and sensitivity to the other, to affectivity and the sphere of the heart. The gift of paternity, on the other hand, leads the male sex to be generally more oriented towards governance, production, and abstract thought. This seems to be related to the paternal task of providing sustenance for the family, by which they are oriented more to the objective than to the personal dimension.

The maternal aspect of woman's character has been developed perceptively by St. Edith Stein in a series of talks on the role of woman that she gave in the early 1930s, in which she said:

> Woman naturally seeks to embrace that which is *living, personal, and whole*. To cherish, guard, protect, nourish and advance growth is her natural, maternal yearning. Lifeless matter, the *fact*, can hold primary interest for her only insofar as it serves the living and the personal, not ordinarily for its own sake. Relevant to this is another matter: *abstraction in every sense* is alien to the feminine nature. The living and personal to which her care extends is a concrete whole and is protected and encouraged as a totality. . . . Her natural line of thought is not so much conceptual and analytical as it is directed intuitively and emotionally to the concrete. . . . This maternal gift is joined to that of *companion*. It is her gift and happiness to share the life of another human being and, indeed, to take part in *all things* which come his way in the greatest and smallest things, in joy as well as in suffering, in work, and in problems.[14]

---

[14] Edith Stein, "Ethos of Women's Professions," in *Essays on Woman*, trans. Freda Mary Oben (Washington: ICS Publications, 1987), 43–44 (italics original). See also *Essays on Woman*, 248–49: "1. Man appears more *objective:* it is natural for him to dedicate his faculties to a discipline (be it mathematics or technology, a trade or business management) and thereby to subject himself to the precepts of this *discipline. Woman's attitude is personal;* and this has several meanings: in one instance she is happily involved with her total being in what she does; then, she has particular interest for the living, concrete person, and, indeed, as much for her own personal life and personal affairs as for those of other persons. 2. Through submission to a discipline, man easily experiences a *one-sided development.* In woman, there lives a natural drive towards *totality* and *self-containment.* And, again, this drive has a twofold direction: she herself would like to become a *complete human being*, one who is fully developed in every way; and she would like to help others to become

Karol Wojtyla, with his great pastoral experience and insight, has described the natural temperament of woman as follows:

> Women are more feeling and intuitive people and become involved in things in a more sensitive and complete manner. This is why they need a support (for example, in the Gospel we find them "by Christ's side"), great maturity, and interior independence. . . . They are much more susceptible than men to things like psychological conditioning and must therefore gain this independence through an interior struggle which does not banish love from their lives but instead recognizes it as the underlying motivation in the Great Love of which they are capable.[15]

Men, on the contrary, are characterized by Wojtyla as follows:

> We are quite ready to take, or conquer, in terms of enjoyment, profit, gain, and success—and even in the moral order. Then comes the question of giving, and at this point we hang back, because we are not prepared to give. The element which is so characteristic under other forms in the spiritual portrait of women is barely perceptible in men. . . . In men the intellect has a certain supremacy over the heart.[16]

---

so, and by all means, she would like to do justice to the complete human being whenever she has to deal with persons."

See also Alice von Hildebrand, *The Privilege of Being a Woman* (Ann Arbor: Sapientia Press, 2002), 59–63; Dietrich von Hildebrand, *Man and Woman: Love and the Meaning of Intimacy* (Manchester, NH: Sophia Institute Press, 1992), 36.

[15] Karol Wojtyla, *The Way to Christ: Spiritual Exercises*, trans. Leslie Wearne (San Francisco: Harper & Row, 1984), 35–36 (exercises preached in 1962).

[16] Wojtyla, *The Way to Christ*, 51, 53. He returns to this theme of what is proper to the two sexes in the apostolic letter *Mulieris Dignitatem: On the Dignity and Vocation of Women*. In article 18, he draws out the particular characteristics of woman from her vocation to participate with God in a special way through the gift of *maternity*: "Motherhood involves a special communion with the mystery of life, as it develops in the woman's womb. The mother is filled with wonder at this mystery of life, and 'understands' with unique intuition what is happening inside her. In the light of the 'beginning,' the mother accepts and loves as a person the child she is carrying in her womb. This unique contact with the new human being developing within her gives rise to an attitude towards human beings—not only towards her own child, but every human being—which profoundly marks the woman's personality. It is commonly thought that women are more capable than men of paying attention to another person, and that motherhood develops this predisposition even more. The man—even with all his sharing in parenthood—always remains 'outside' the process of pregnancy and the baby's birth; in many ways he has to learn his own 'fatherhood' from the mother."

The special character of woman also comes from her "bridal" aspect. John Paul II writes: "The Bride is loved: it is she who receives love, in order to love in return."[17] Woman's special gift is to interiorize love and return it with fecundity. This ability to interiorize love is shown to us in the Gospels above all in Our Lady, who "hid these words in her heart."[18]

This complementarity between the sexes, which is as much spiritual as it is physical, is a source of great richness to humanity and to the Church.

The Role of Ethnic and Cultural Diversity in the Mystical Body

The diversity of the Mystical Body also concerns the dimension of human culture and ethnicity. Every culture is called to add to the richness of the Mystical Body of Christ. Christ's Bride is to be composed of all nations, and if some nations and cultures are under-represented, the splendor of the Catholic Body is diminished. Every nation brings the wealth of its own cultural traditions to Christ when the society becomes Christian.

For example, the separation of a great part of the Eastern Church in the eleventh century is an extraordinary tragedy for the Church, preventing the full assimilation of the treasures of the Eastern Church in the West, and vice versa. John Paul II spoke about this in a beautiful way by saying that Christian Europe needs to breathe with both lungs.[19]

The Role of Jews in the Mystical Body

If it is true that every nation has a unique and irreplaceable contribution to make to the Body of Christ, this is no less true of Jews in the Body of Christ. They have a full right of citizenship in the Body, and a duty to bring to the Body what is uniquely theirs. Indeed, of all nations, the Jews have a special place in the Mystical Body because they are the people God used to prepare for Christ's Advent. Jews in the Church bring something unique—a living contact with the culture that prepared for Christ's coming and into which Christ came and lived.

Hebrew Catholics bring to the Church a great love and knowledge of the treasures that God sowed in the Jewish people to make them disposed for their vocation as the Chosen People, the people of the

---

[17] John Paul II, *Mulieris dignitatem: On the Dignity and Vocation of Women* 29.

[18] Lk 2:19, 51. For reflections on how Mary exemplifies the feminine vocation, see St. Edith Stein, "Ethos of Women's Professions," in *Essays on Woman*, 45–46; Alice von Hildebrand, *The Privilege of Being a Woman*, pp. 99–106; John Paul II, *Mulieris dignitatem* 5, 19.

[19] See John Paul II, apostolic letter *Euntes in mundum* 12 (1988).

Preparation and Advent and of the Incarnation. For example, Jews have a special appreciation and love for the Torah, God's revealed Law. This is especially significant in the context of modern culture, in which the Law of God is generally seen in a negative light, as an opposition or limit to human freedom, which is seen as the absolute good. Hebrew Catholics also should have a special appreciation for the ways in which the Old Testament prefigures and prophesies the New. Thus they can help the whole Church have a better grasp of the totality of salvation history.

The Role of Charity in the Mystical Body

We have looked at the diversity of members in the Mystical Body; let us conclude by looking at the element of unity that binds all the members together—the bond of charity.

A beautiful expression of how charity is the supernatural invisible soul and life of the Church is given to us in the autobiographical writing of St. Therese of Lisieux, *Story of a Soul*. She was searching the Scriptures for insight into her particular vocation in the Church. She felt a great attraction to all the visible paths of sanctity and service in the Church: apostolate, teaching, missionary work, martyrdom, etc., and wanted to do all of these at once. She opened the Scriptures to 1 Corinthians 12, which speaks of the various visible vocations in the Church, saying that all are necessary for the common good, and that each complements the others:

> And God has appointed in the Church first apostles, second prophets, third teachers, then workers of miracles, then healers, helpers, administrators, speakers in various kinds of tongues. Are all apostles? Are all prophets? Are all teachers? Do all work miracles? Do all possess gifts of healing? Do all speak with tongues? Do all interpret? But earnestly desire the higher gifts. And I will show you a still more excellent way.[20]

Still, St. Therese had not found what she was looking for, and so she proceeded to St. Paul's marvelous hymn on charity in 1 Corinthians 13, in which he speaks of charity as a "higher gift." Here St. Therese found the hidden and invisible vocation of the entire life of the Church—supernatural charity:

> Considering the mystical body of the Church, I had not recognized myself in any of the members described by St. Paul, or rather I desired to see myself in them all. Charity gave me the key to my

---

[20] 1 Cor 12:28–31.

vocation. I understood that if the Church had a body composed of different members, the most necessary and most noble of all could not be lacking to it, and so I understood that the Church *had a Heart and that this Heart* was BURNING WITH LOVE. *I understood it was Love alone* that made the Church's members act, that if *Love* ever became extinct, apostles would not preach the Gospel and martyrs would not shed their blood. I understood that LOVE COMPRISED ALL VOCATIONS, THAT LOVE WAS EVERYTHING, THAT IT EMBRACED ALL TIMES AND PLACES. . . . IN A WORD, THAT IT WAS ETERNAL![21]

The Church lives through the supernatural charity that flows in her "veins," which is infused through the power of the sacraments. This is the living water of which Jesus spoke to the Samaritan woman at the well in John 4:10–14: "If you knew the gift of God, and who it is that is saying to you, 'Give me a drink,' you would have asked him, and he would have given you living water. . . . The water that I shall give him will become in him a spring of water welling up to eternal life."

In order to enable the impulses of the Holy Spirit and of charity to direct our lives in this way, the members of the Mystical Body need to pray regularly—daily. The members of the Mystical Body need to have a daily spiritual contact with the invisible Head of the Body, Christ. This kind of contact can only come through mental prayer, in which we *converse* with Christ daily about what is most important in our lives and seek to *contemplate* what was most important in His life.

One of the great spiritual problems in the Church in modern times is nominal Catholicism. Many members of the Church, perhaps the majority, live their lives without a serious life of prayer and without appreciating the great and inestimable gift that is given to us in making us *members of Christ* with sacramental access to the very love of God. We tend to think of membership in the Church as membership in some religious association, in cultural practices taught to us in our childhood, in following certain rules proper to Catholics, if we still do even that.

Through prayer, each one of us has to rediscover for himself what was so clear for St. Paul: "I have been crucified with Christ; it is no longer I who live, but *Christ who lives in me*; and the life I now live in the flesh I live by faith in the Son of God, who *loved me and gave himself for me*" (Gal 2:19–20).

---

[21] St. Therese of Lisieux, *The Story of a Soul: The Autobiography of St. Therese of Lisieux*, trans. John Clarke (Washington DC: ICS Publications, 1996), 194 (manuscript B).

CHAPTER 12

Justification and Sanctification in the Church

A reflection on holiness in the Church would not be complete without a consideration of the thorny problem of justification. How are the members of the Body of Christ justified and sanctified? What is the relationship between justification and holiness? Are the members of the Church made just through Baptism with a participation in the sanctity of God, or is justification merely the imputation of Christ's righteousness, leaving us interiorly unchanged? Are the members of the Church enabled to live the life of Christ, into whose Body they have been engrafted? Can the living members of the Church truly say with St. Paul, "It is no longer I who live, but *Christ who lives in me*" (Gal 2:20)? Can the members of the Church truly say God has put His law within them, has written it upon their hearts (cf. Jer 31:33), and has given them a new heart and put a new spirit within them (Ezek 36:26)?

All of these questions are bound up with the debate over justification, which is deeply relevant to a meditation on the nature of the Church. What is at stake in the debates over justification is the mark of holiness of the Church and her identity as the fulfillment of the Old Testament prophecies in which the Messianic Kingdom is described as a kingdom in which the Holy Spirit is given in abundance and the law of God is written on the hearts of the faithful.

Justification refers to the process by which a person in a state of original or mortal sin is brought into friendship with God, is made to share in some way in God's justice and holiness, and is made a child of God and heir of heaven. The term "justification" comes from the Hebrew *zadik*, which means "just" not in the restricted sense of the cardinal virtue of justice, but in the broader sense of being in the right relationship with God. It is in this sense that St. Joseph is said to be "a just man" in Matthew 1:19, and Abraham's faith is said to be "reckoned to him as righteousness (*zedakah*)" (Gen 15:6). Justification, therefore, is the process by which a person enters into the right relationship with God, exiting from the aversion to God entailed by grave sin. This consists in repenting for sin[1] and in lovingly subordinating one's reason

---

[1] See the fine description of repentance (*teshuvah*) by Moses Maimonides: "And what is *Teshuvah*? It occurs when the sinner forsakes his sin, and removes it from his thoughts, and concludes in his heart not to do it again, as it is said, 'Let the wicked

and will to God through reception of the gift of grace and the theological virtues: faith, hope, and charity. In virtue of this gift one leaves the unjust relationship of enmity with God and enters into *filial friendship* with Him, which is the essence of Biblical justice (*zedakah*).

The Council of Trent, in its famous *Decree on Justification*, defines justification as "not only a remission of sins but also the sanctification and renewal of the inward man through the voluntary reception of the grace and gifts whereby an unjust man becomes just and from being an enemy becomes a friend, that he may be an heir according to hope of life everlasting."[2]

It should not be surprising that great theological passions were raised around the subject of justification, for no theme could be of greater existential importance to us. Indeed, everything is at stake in justification, for an eternity of heaven or hell depends on its presence or absence.

The question of justification is very closely related to the theme of faith, hope, and charity. Are we justified by faith alone, or by faith, hope, and charity together? The answer to this question is crucial to the burning question of justification that rent the Church in the Reformation. If the question is posed in this way, I think that it can be clearly seen that justification is brought about by faith, hope, and love together, which are infused into our heart by the Holy Spirit, together with sanctifying grace.

Martin Luther, on the contrary, proposed that we are saved by *faith alone*, by which Christ's justice is imputed to us, and we are accounted by God to be righteous by Christ's own righteousness, without our becoming interiorly righteous. Faith is precisely that which enables Christ's justice to be imputed to us.

The key question is whether justification changes us interiorly or not. Does justification consist in God pouring His grace into our hearts, changing them radically and writing His Torah in them, or merely in imputing Christ's justice to us, without necessarily pouring grace into our hearts?

---

forsake his way, and the man of iniquity his thoughts' (Is 55:7) Let him also regret what has happened, as it is said, . . . (Jer 31:19). And let the sinner call to Him who knows all hidden things to witness that he will never return to sin." Moses Maimonides, *Hilkhot Teshuvah* II.2, cited in *Days of Awe: A Treasury of Jewish Wisdom for Reflection, Repentance, and Renewal on the High Holy Days*, ed. S.Y. Agnon (NY: Schocken Books, 1995), 119.

[2] Council of Trent, session 6, ch. 7, DS 1528 (D 799).

Justification by Faith, Not by Works

Luther's interpretation of justification was based in great part on St. Paul's repeated affirmation that we are justified by faith and not by "works of the law." For example, in Galatians 2:16, Paul writes: "We have believed in Christ Jesus, in order to be *justified by faith* in Christ, and not by works of the law, because by works of the law shall no one be justified."[3]

What does St. Paul mean, however, by "works of the Law"? This is a crucial question. St. Thomas Aquinas and other scholastic theologians distinguish the precepts of the Law of Moses into three fundamental categories: moral, ceremonial, and judicial. The moral law is expressed above all in the double commandment of love and in the Ten Commandments, as well as other subordinate moral precepts which clarify the commandments and what is implied by them. The ceremonial law refers to the precepts regarding divine worship and ritual purity. The judicial precepts give elements akin to a civil penal code.

When St. Paul says that the "works of the Law" do not justify, to which class of precepts is he referring? Does he mean that no one is justified by observing the double commandment of charity, or does he mean that we are not justified by observance of the ceremonial law, signified by circumcision? The context of the Letter to the Galatians supports the interpretation that he is referring to the ceremonial precepts of the Old Covenant, for the principal subject of the letter is the question of circumcision, and whether Gentile Christians should be circumcised.[4]

The observance of the ceremonial precepts, in and of themselves, cannot justify, any more than could the blood of goats and rams atone for sin. Justification requires the circumcision not of the flesh but of the heart, by which one becomes a "new creature" (Gal 6:15).[5] Hence Galatians 5:6 states that "in Christ Jesus neither circumcision nor uncircumcision is of any avail, but faith working through love."

A similar teaching is found in Romans 3:20–25:

> For no human being will be justified in his sight by works of the law, since through the law comes knowledge of sin. But now the righteousness of God has been manifested apart from law, although the law and the prophets bear witness to it, the

---

[3] See Luther's commentary on this text, for example, in *Lectures on Galatians* (1535), in *Luther's Works*, vol. 26 (Saint Louis: Concordia Publishing House, 1963), 139–41.

[4] See chapter 13 below.

[5] See Gal 6:15: "For neither circumcision counts for anything, nor uncircumcision, but a new creation."

righteousness of God through faith in Jesus Christ for all who believe. For there is no distinction; since all have sinned and fall short of the glory of God, they are justified by his grace as a gift, through the redemption which is in Christ Jesus, whom God put forward as an expiation by his blood, to be received by faith.

Here too the "works of the Law" are to be understood principally of the ceremonial law represented by circumcision. Hence St. Paul goes on to say that "we hold that a man is justified by faith apart from works of the law. Or is God the God of Jews only? Is he not the God of Gentiles also? Yes, of Gentiles also, since God is one; and he will justify the circumcised on the ground of their faith and the uncircumcised through their faith" (Rom 3:28–30).

Justification could not be brought about by any merely human works, even though commanded by God in the Mosaic Law, because it *must be something entirely supernatural.* Through justification, sin is forgiven, we are brought into union with God, and made heirs of heaven. No merely human and natural work could bring about such momentous changes in us!

Justification must principally be the work of God in us (although not without our cooperation). Thus justification must be through grace and through divine gifts: we "are justified by his grace as a gift" (Rom 3:24). Hence St. Paul says that boasting is excluded (Rom 3:27). The gratuitousness of justification is also clearly shown by Ephesians 2:8, in which he writes: "For by grace you have been saved through faith; and this is not your own doing, it is the gift of God."

It follows that our initial justification cannot possibly be merited by us through any human work. The heresy of Pelagianism consisted in thinking that justification could be caused by human works of asceticism and virtue, without the necessity of grace.[6] Justification requires both actual grace which prepares our soul by illuminating our mind and strengthening our will, and sanctifying grace, by which we are given a

---

[6] The Pelagian understanding of justification was condemned at the Council of Trent, session 6, in the first three canons on justification, DS 1551–53 (D 811–13): "Canon 1. If anyone says that man can be justified before God by his own works, whether done by his own natural powers or through the teaching of the law, without divine grace through Jesus Christ, let him be anathema. Canon 2. If anyone says that divine grace through Christ Jesus is given for this only, that man may be able more easily to live justly and to merit eternal life, as if by free will without grace he is able to do both, though with hardship and difficulty, let him be anathema. Canon 3. If anyone says that without the predisposing inspiration of the Holy Ghost and without His help, man can believe, hope, love or be repentant as he ought, so that the grace of justification may be bestowed upon him, let him be anathema."

share in the divine nature, according to 2 Peter 1:4, and made sons and daughters of God.

St. Bonaventure explains this second aspect well in his *Breviloquium*:

> No conceivable man is worthy to attain this supreme Good exceeding in every possible way the limits of human nature, unless he is lifted up above himself through the action of God coming down to him. Not that God would come down in His immutable essence: He does so through an influence that emanates from Him; nor that the soul would rise above itself by physical ascent: it is lifted up through a God-conforming disposition.[7]

The Council of Trent on Justification

The difficulty we have in understanding the work of our salvation lies in the fact that justification is a complex mystery with several complementary facets. Heresy consists in emphasizing one or more of these aspects while excluding others which are also integral. The problem lies not in what is affirmed but in what is excluded or denied.

The Council of Trent gave a beautiful and profound, as well as infallible, description of justification in its Decree on Justification, chapter 7. This teaching enables one to put in harmony the various complementary aspects of justification that we find brought out in different texts of St. Paul and throughout the New Testament.

The Council of Trent sought to bring clarity to this question by distinguishing the various aspects or causes of justification. The Council distinguished (1) the efficient cause that brings it about, which is the power of God; (2) the purpose (final cause), which is the glory of God and the gift of eternal life; (3) the meritorious cause that won justification for us, which is the Passion of Christ; (4) the instrumental cause by which it is applied to us, which is Baptism; and (5) the formal or interior cause by which we are made interiorly just, which is sanctifying grace and supernatural charity (which flows from sanctifying grace).[8] To these we should also add (6) the preparatory cause, which is

---

[7] St. Bonaventure, *Breviloquium*, 5.1.3, trans. José de Vinck (Paterson, NJ: St. Anthony Guild Press, 1963), 182.

[8] The *Catechism of the Catholic Church* 1992 summarizes this doctrine as follows: "Justification has been *merited for us by the Passion of Christ* who offered himself on the cross as a living victim, holy and pleasing to God, and whose blood has become the instrument of atonement for the sins of all men. Justification is conferred in Baptism, the sacrament of faith. It conforms us to the righteousness of God, who makes us inwardly just by the power of his mercy. Its purpose is the glory of God and of Christ, and the gift of eternal life."

faith, by which one seeks Baptism and without which "it is impossible to please God" (Heb 11:6).[9]

Justification is the result of all of these causes working together. It is produced in our souls by the power of God through the instrumentality of Baptism to which we come in faith. It was merited by Christ's Passion. It consists interiorly (formally) in the infusion of sanctifying grace and charity in our souls, conforming us interiorly to Christ. Its purpose is the communication of eternal life for the glory of God. The Council of Trent states this as follows:

> The causes of this justification are: the *final cause* is the glory of God and of Christ and life everlasting; the *efficient cause* is the merciful God who washes and sanctifies gratuitously, signing and anointing with the holy Spirit of promise, who is the pledge of our inheritance, the *meritorious cause* is His most beloved only begotten, our Lord Jesus Christ, who, when we were enemies (Rom 5:10), for the exceeding charity wherewith he loved us (Eph 2:4), merited for us justification by His most holy passion on the wood of the cross and made satisfaction for us to God the Father; the *instrumental cause* is the sacrament of baptism, which is the sacrament of faith, without which no man was ever justified.
>
> Finally, the *single formal cause* is the justice of God, not that by which He Himself is just, but that by which He makes us just, that, namely, with which we being endowed by Him, are renewed in the spirit of our mind (cf. Eph 4:23), and not only are we reputed but we are truly called and are just (cf. 1 Jn 3:1), receiving justice within us, each one according to his own measure, which the Holy Ghost

---

[9] This is treated in the Council of Trent, session 6, Decree on Justification, ch. 6: "Now, they [the adults] are disposed to that justice when, aroused and aided by divine grace, receiving faith by hearing (Rom 10:17), they are moved freely toward God, believing to be true what has been divinely revealed and promised, especially that the sinner is justified by God by his grace, through the redemption that is in Christ Jesus; and when, understanding themselves to be sinners, they, by turning themselves from the fear of divine justice . . . to consider the mercy of God, are raised to hope, trusting that God will be propitious to them for Christ's sake; and they begin to love Him as the fountain of all justice, and on that account are moved against sin by a certain hatred and detestation, that is, by that repentance that must be performed before baptism; finally, when they resolve to receive baptism, to begin a new life and to keep the commandments of God. Of this disposition it is written: 'For whoever would draw near to God must believe that he exists and that he rewards those who seek him' (Heb 11:6); and, 'Be of good faith, son, thy sins are forgiven thee' (Mt 9:2)."

distributes to everyone as He wills (cf. 1 Cor 12:11), and according to each one's disposition and cooperation.[10]

In Romans 3:25 we can see all of these complementary causes of justification put together:

Since all have sinned and fall short of the glory of God, they are justified by his grace as a gift, through the redemption which is in Christ Jesus, whom God put forward as an expiation by his blood, to be received by faith.

The final cause (or purpose) of justification is the restoration of the glory of God, trampled on by sin. The meritorious cause is "the redemption which is in Christ Jesus, whom God put forward as an expiation by his blood, to be received by faith." Faith is the cause preparing us for justification and leading us to Baptism (not mentioned but logically present).

The efficient cause is God by whom we are "justified by his grace as a gift." At the same time, this phrase indicates the formal (or interior) cause, which consists in the reception of grace in the heart.

General Agreement between Catholics and Protestants

Of these various causes of justification, where do Catholics and Protestants agree and disagree? As we shall see, there is agreement on the purpose of justification, its meritorious, efficient, and instrumental causes, but disagreement over the interior or formal cause.

First of all, Catholics and Protestants agree in the purpose of justification: the restoration of the glory of God trampled on by sin and the communication of the seed of eternal life.

Secondly, perhaps the most important area of agreement concerns the meritorious cause: Christ *merited* our salvation through His Passion and Death on the Cross, by which He *atoned* for all human sins.

St. Thomas Aquinas explains atonement for sin as offering to God something more pleasing or loveable than all sin is detested.[11] We

---

[10] Council of Trent, session 6, ch. 7, DS 1529 (D 799) (my italics).

[11] See St. Thomas Aquinas, *ST* III, q. 48, a. 2: "He properly atones for an offense who offers something which the offended one loves equally, or even more than he detested the offense. But by suffering out of love and obedience, Christ gave more to God than was required to compensate for the offense of the whole human race. First of all, because of the exceeding charity from which He suffered; secondly, on account of the dignity of His life which He laid down in atonement, for it was the life of one who was God and man; thirdly, on account of the extent of the Passion, and the greatness of the grief endured, as stated above. And therefore Christ's Passion was not only a sufficient but a superabundant atonement

cannot redeem ourselves because we cannot offer anything more pleasing to God than all sin is displeasing. The infinite charity with which Christ offered His life, on the contrary, was immeasurably more pleasing than all sin is displeasing to God. Thus Christ's death atoned for all sin and made superabundant satisfaction for it.

Scripture refers to the meritorious cause of our salvation in a great number of texts. In the First Letter to Timothy, St. Paul writes: "The saying is sure and worthy of full acceptance, that Christ Jesus came into the world to save sinners . . . the man Christ Jesus, who gave himself as a ransom for all" (1 Tim 1:15, 2:6). In 1 Corinthians 15:3 Paul says: "For I delivered to you as of first importance what I also received, that *Christ died for our sins* in accordance with the scriptures."

Significantly, the Old Testament, as the Apostle affirms, had already taught that the sufferings of the Messiah are the meritorious cause of our justification. Perhaps the clearest text is Isaiah 53:11, canticle of the Suffering Servant: "My just servant shall justify many and he shall bear their iniquities."[12]

Third, we agree on the fact that God alone is the efficient cause who alone produces justification in the soul. (An efficient cause is the agent who brings about an effect, like a sculptor who makes a statue.) Hence justification is the gratuitous work of God in us, and we are saved by grace. We also agree that Baptism has been established as the instrument by which God effectively justifies the soul.[13]

Salvation through Faith, Hope, and Charity

Finally, Catholics and Protestants also agree that faith plays a decisive and crucial role in opening the gate for justification, although we differ in the way in which this is understood. For Luther and his followers, faith alone is that which *grasps* and appropriates the salvation won for us by Christ. Catholics, on the contrary, hold that this occurs by "faith working through love" (Gal 5:6). Faith is the beginning of the work of justification because it is the precondition of hope and charity, and thus the foundation of the entire life of grace and conversion.

---

for the sins of the human race; according to 1 John 2:2: 'He is the propitiation for our sins: and not for ours only, but also for those of the whole world.'"

[12] Translation following the Neo-Vulgate.

[13] See *CCC* 1257–59. The justification efficaciously produced by the sacrament of Baptism is also made present by an upright desire for Baptism and Baptism of blood. Hence *CCC* 1258 states that "this *Baptism of blood*, like the *desire for Baptism*, brings about the fruits of Baptism without being a sacrament."

St. Paul often uses the word "faith" to encompass all three theological virtues: faith, hope, and charity. For example, in Galatians 2:20, he describes the Christian life by saying: "It is no longer I who live, but Christ who lives in me; and the life I now live in the flesh I live by *faith* in the Son of God, who loved me and gave himself for me." Clearly "faith" here also is meant to include Paul's hope in Christ, and his love for Him. Faith can be used to stand for the other two because it is their foundation and presupposition. No one can hope in or love a God in whom he does not believe. Faith shows us the promises of God in which we hope, and it shows us the exceeding goodness of God which we love through divine charity.

Thus St. Paul can say that we are saved through faith,[14] saved through hope (Rom 8:24), and saved through charity, as when he says that we are saved in "faith working through charity" (Gal 5:6).[15] 1 Corinthians 13:2 shows the insufficiency of faith without charity for salvation: "And if I have prophetic powers, and understand all mysteries and all knowledge, and if I have all faith, so as to remove mountains, but have not love, I am nothing." The Church teaches that we are saved through faith, hope and charity together.[16]

How Is Christ's Redemption Applied to Our Souls?

The principal disagreement between Protestants and Catholics with regard to justification concerns the way in which Christ's redemption has been applied to our souls by actually making us just before God. Or to put it another way, disagreement concerns the precise way we have been saved by grace and faith. In scholastic language, the disagreement concerns the *formal* cause of justification: in what does the *interior essence of justification* consist? A "formal cause" is an interior cause by which a thing is what it is. It may be easier to understand by referring to this as the *interior cause*. Does this consist in the mere imputation of Christ's justice through faith, or in the actual infusion of sanctifying grace and charity into the heart through the action of the Holy Spirit? The former

---

[14] See Rom 3:22; 5:1; Gal 2:16; Eph 2:8; etc.

[15] See also 1 Tim 1:14, which speaks of St. Paul's own justification through "the faith and love that are in Christ Jesus."

[16] See Council of Trent, session 6, Decree on Justification, ch. 7, DS 1531 (D 800): "For faith, unless hope and charity be added to it, neither unites one perfectly with Christ, nor makes him a living member of his body. For this reason it is most truly said that 'faith without works is dead,' and is of no profit, and 'in Christ Jesus neither circumcision availeth anything, nor uncircumcision, but faith, which worketh by charity.' This faith, in accordance with apostolic tradition, catechumens beg of the Church before the sacrament of baptism, when they ask for 'faith which bestows life eternal,' which, without hope and charity, faith cannot bestow."

is the answer of Martin Luther, and the latter that of the Catholic Church, as defined in the Council of Trent.

Luther's Understanding of Justification

Martin Luther maintained that what justifies us in the eyes of God is *nothing in ourselves*, but solely the justice of Jesus Christ that God *imputes* to us in a juridical way, as if it were ours, through faith. According to Luther, this imputation of Christ's justice *leaves the interior of the heart unchanged*, and changes only God's *judgment* of us. In other words, justification would really be more of a change in God than in us, so to speak. Justification is like putting on a *mask of Christ* through our faith, such that God sees Christ instead of us when He looks at us. Behind the mask there remains the sin and vice that were there before our justification, but they are "hidden" from God's wrath by our faith in Christ.[17]

This gives rise to Luther's doctrine that the justified person is *"simul peccator et justus,"* at once "totally a sinner" and "totally righteous."[18] Perhaps we could use Christ's description of the scribes and Pharisees (Mt 23:27) to describe this doctrine: "you are like whitewashed tombs, which outwardly appear beautiful, but within they are full of dead men's bones and all uncleanness."

This doctrine of Luther's lies behind the famous text from his letter to his disciple Melancthon of August 1, 1521:

> If you are a preacher of grace, then preach a true and not a fictitious grace; if grace is true, you must bear a true and not a fictitious sin. God does not save people who are only fictitious sinners. *Be a sinner and sin boldly, but believe and rejoice in Christ even more boldly*, for he is victorious over sin, death, and the world. As

---

[17] J.-B. Bossuet, in his *History of the Variations of Protestant Churches*, 1.7 (Fraser, MI: American Council on Economics and Society, 1997), 19, gave a good summary of Luther's position: "Justification is that grace which, remitting to us our sins, at the same time renders us agreeable to God. Till then, it had been believed that what wrought this effect proceeded indeed from God, but yet necessarily *existed in man*; and that to be justified—namely, for a sinner *to be made just*—it was necessary he should *have this justice in him; as to be learned and virtuous, one must have in him learning and virtue.* But Luther had not followed so simple an idea. He would have it, that what justifies us and renders us agreeable to God was *nothing in us*: but we were justified because God imputed to us the justice of Jesus Christ, as if it were our own, and because by faith we could indeed appropriate it to ourselves" (my italics).

[18] This doctrine is repeated in the *Joint Declaration on the Doctrine of Justification* (1999), par. 29. For a critique of certain aspects of this document (especially with regard to the formal cause of justification), see Christopher Malloy, *Engrafted into Christ: A Critique of the Joint Declaration* (New York: P. Lang, 2005).

long as we are here we have to sin. This life is not the dwelling place of righteousness, but, as Peter says, we look for new heavens and a new earth in which righteousness dwells. It is enough that by the riches of God's glory we have come to know the Lamb that takes away the sin of the world. *No sin will separate us from the Lamb, even though we commit fornication and murder a thousand times a day.* Do you think that the purchase price that was paid for the redemption of our sins by so great a Lamb is too small? Pray boldly—you too are a mighty sinner.[19]

According to Catholic doctrine, on the other hand, our sin is really abolished by justification which effects an *interior transformation*, infusing charity and sanctifying grace into our hearts. It is true that we can still sin venially and remain justified. Nevertheless justification is incompatible with mortal sin. Luther, unfortunately, lacked this distinction between venial and mortal sin! Mortal sin destroys the work of justification by expelling the gift of charity, which can only be restored through the power of the sacrament of Penance.

Luther's doctrine on justification through imputation of Christ's merits was solemnly condemned in the Council of Trent:

If anyone shall say that men are justified either by the sole imputation of the justice of Christ, or by the sole remission of sins, to the exclusion of grace and charity which is poured forth in their hearts by the Holy Spirit and remains in them, or also that the grace by which we are justified is only the favor of God, let him be anathema.[20]

The Essence of Justification: The Infusion of Sanctifying Grace and Charity

Given the fact that Luther claimed Scripture, and St. Paul in particular, as the source and foundation for his view of justification, we have to ask whether the letters of St. Paul, rightly understood, teach that justification essentially involves the infusing of charity in our hearts, as taught by the Council of Trent, or not.

In fact, St. Paul frequently speaks about justification in terms of the transformation of the human heart through the infusing of charity and the gift of the Spirit. This is in profound continuity with the Old Testament prophecies of the New Covenant and the outpouring of the Spirit.

---

[19] In *Luther's Works*, vol. 48, *Letters*, vol. 1, edited and translated by Gottfried Krodel (Philadelphia: Fortress Press, 1955), 281–82 (my italics).

[20] Council of Trent, session 6, canon 11, DS 1561 (D 821). See also canon 10.

In Ezekiel 36:24–27, justification, to be worked by Baptism, is described as the giving of a new heart which causes one to walk in the commandments of God:

> And I will vindicate the holiness of my great name. . . . And I will pour upon you clean water, and you shall be cleansed from all your filthiness, and I will cleanse you from all your idols. And I will give you a new heart, and put a new spirit within you, and I will take away the stony heart out of your flesh, and will give you a heart of flesh. And I will put my spirit in the midst of you, and I will cause you to walk in my commandments, and to keep my judgments, and do them.

Here we see various causes of justification mentioned by the Council of Trent. The final cause or purpose is the restoration of the glory of God; the efficient cause is the power of God who gives a new heart. The interior (or formal) cause is precisely the reception of the new heart and spirit, enabling one to walk in the commandments.

Jeremiah gives a similar description of justification in Jeremiah 31:31–33, according to which the New Covenant essentially consists in God writing the Law of God interiorly on human hearts:

> This is the covenant which I will make with the house of Israel after those days, says the Lord: I will put my law within them, and I will write it upon their hearts; and I will be their God, and they shall be my people. And no longer shall each man teach his neighbor and each his brother, saying, "Know the Lord," for they shall all know me, from the least of them to the greatest, says the Lord; for I will forgive their iniquity, and I will remember their sin no more.

Here Jeremiah connects three aspects of justification: it is (a) an interior rectification of the heart (on which the Law is interiorly "written"), by which (b) one becomes related to God in a new (filial) way, and through which (c) sin is forgiven.

St. Paul is in harmony with this prophetic witness when he stresses the role of the infusing of charity (a new heart) in the process of justification. This is especially prominent in three very significant texts which we shall briefly examine: Galatians 4:4–7, Romans 5:1–5, and Romans 8:1–17.

Galatians 4:4–7

In Galatians 4:4–7, St. Paul synthesizes the entire mystery of our Redemption in a few lines:

But when the fullness of time came, God sent his Son, born of a woman, born under the Law, that he might redeem those who were under the Law, that we might receive the adoption of sons. And because you are sons, God has sent the Spirit of his Son into our hearts, crying, "Abba! Father!" So through God you are no longer a slave but a son, and if a son then an heir.[21]

In this profound text, we have a dense presentation of the fundamental truths of salvation: the mystery of the three divine Persons of the Trinity; the mission of the Son into the world through the Incarnation, which marks the center of history (the fullness of time); the participation of the "woman"—Mary—through whom the Son comes into the world; the role of Judaism in preparing for the Messiah "born under the Law"; the redemption of mankind; our adoption as sons in the Son (divine filiation, which we receive through Baptism); and the sending of the Holy Spirit to give us the spirit of the Son by which we adore the Father as Christ has taught us.

The sequence of truths that Paul has presented above culminates in a description of justification. After being sent into the world by being born of the Virgin Mary, Christ redeemed mankind on Calvary. We are not justified, however, until Christ's redemptive work has been applied individually to our souls. This occurs when the Spirit of the Son is sent into our hearts so that we too can cry "Abba, Father!" In other words, we are made into sons of God by receiving filial love infused into our hearts by the Spirit. This reception of the spirit of filial love of God renders us like Christ by giving us a share in His interior sentiments.

Romans 5:5–10

Another synthetic statement of justification is given in Romans 5:5–10:

Hope does not disappoint us, because *God's love has been poured into our hearts through the Holy Spirit which has been given to us.* While we were still weak, at the right time Christ died for the ungodly. . . . But God shows his love for us in that while we were yet sinners Christ died for us. Since, therefore, we are now justified by his blood, much more shall we be saved by him from the wrath of God. For if while we were enemies we were reconciled to God by the death of his Son, much more, now that we are reconciled, shall we be saved *by his life.*

In this text, St. Paul speaks of justification under two aspects: Christ's dying for us (meritorious cause), and the infusion of God's love

---

[21] For Gal 4:4–6, I have used the translation of the Confraternity of Christian Doctrine (New York: Benziger Bros., 1958).

into our hearts by the Holy Spirit (formal or interior cause). By dying for us, Christ merited justification for us through His Blood. However, justification comes about in the soul insofar as one comes to live *Christ's life* (Rom 5:10), through the fact that "God's love has been poured into our hearts through the Holy Spirit which has been given to us" (Rom 5:5).

This text is one of the sources for the teaching of the Council of Trent that the essence of justification consists in the reception of the gift of sanctifying grace, from which charity flows into our hearts together with faith and hope. The Council of Trent teaches this as follows:

> For though no one can be just except he to whom the merits of the passion of our Lord Jesus Christ are communicated, yet this takes place in that justification of the sinner, when by the merit of the most holy passion, *the charity of God is poured forth by the Holy Spirit in the hearts (cf. Rom 5:5) of those who are justified and inheres in them*; whence man through Jesus Christ, in whom he is engrafted, receives in that justification, together with the remission of sins, *all these infused at the same time, namely, faith, hope and charity*.[22]

Justification therefore consists formally or properly in the infusion of charity (together with faith and hope) into the heart through the work of the Holy Spirit (infusing sanctifying grace), which infusion works the remission of sins.

Romans 8:1–17

Another very significant text which shows that justification consists essentially in the infusion of charity through the Holy Spirit is Romans 8:1–17:

> There is therefore now no condemnation for those who are in Christ Jesus. . . . Those who are in the flesh cannot please God. But you are not in the flesh, you are in the Spirit, if in fact the Spirit of God dwells in you. Anyone who does not have the Spirit of Christ does not belong to him. But if Christ is in you, although your bodies are dead because of sin, your spirits are alive because of righteousness. . . . For you did not receive the spirit of slavery to fall back into fear, but you have received the spirit of sonship. When we cry, "Abba! Father!" it is the Spirit himself bearing witness with our spirit that we are children of God, and if children, then heirs, heirs of God and fellow heirs with Christ.

---

[22] Council of Trent, Session 6, Decree on Justification, ch. 7, DS 1530 (D 800) (my italics).

The "spirit of sonship" by which we cry, "Abba, Father," is clearly the same love of God that "has been poured into our hearts through the Holy Spirit," mentioned earlier in Romans 5:5. For it is only through the gift of supernatural charity that we are given the power to love God as Father, on the pattern of Christ's own filial love.

In virtue of the infusion of the "spirit of sonship," the human person is justified by being interiorly conformed to Christ, whose filial spirit he has received, making the human person a "son in the Son," capable of crying, "Abba, Father!" The infusion of charity by the gift of the Holy Spirit makes the recipient a son of God, and thus a co-heir with Christ of His inheritance, which is eternal life. Clearly this is the essence of justification, which is the seed of glory.

The Infusion of Charity and the Indwelling of the Holy Spirit

The texts of St. Paul that we have just examined connect two closely related inconceivable and immeasurable gifts: the gift of charity infused into our hearts by the Spirit, and the gift of the Spirit Himself, who is given to us. The latter is referred to as the indwelling of the Holy Spirit, promised to us by Christ at the Last Supper.

For example, in Romans 5:5, St. Paul says: *"God's love has been poured into our hearts through the Holy Spirit which has been given to us."* God's love is poured into the soul, and, simultaneously, the Spirit Himself is given to the soul.

Supernatural charity is the supreme gift of the Spirit, and through this gift we are given the supernatural capacity to love God with a share or participation in the love of the Son for the Father. Through this supernatural love, God Himself becomes present in the soul in a new way: as the *Beloved* of our souls. Although sanctifying grace and charity are created realities in the soul (created grace), they truly cause God to be present in the soul as the Beloved (uncreated grace). At the Last Supper, Jesus revealed to the Apostles the great mystery of the divine indwelling:

> Judas (not Iscariot) said to him, "Lord, how is it that you will manifest yourself to us, and not to the world?" Jesus answered him, "If a man loves me, he will keep my word, and my Father will love him, and we will come to him and make our home with him" (Jn 14:22–23).

When a person receives charity and begins to love the Lord in a supernatural way, both the Father and the Son come and make their home with him. The Holy Spirit is also included in this promise of indwelling, as Christ specifies in John 14:26: "But the Counselor, the Holy Spirit, whom the Father will send in my name, he will teach you all things, and bring to your remembrance all that I have said to you."

The indwelling therefore is of all three divine Persons together, but it is attributed in a special way to the Holy Spirit because He is the divine Person who proceeds precisely as the fruit of the mutual love of the Father and Son.

St. Thomas Aquinas has given the classical theological explanation of the sending of the Holy Spirit and His indwelling in the souls of the just. He writes:

> The divine person is fittingly sent in the sense that He exists newly in any one; and He is given as possessed by anyone; and neither of these is otherwise than by sanctifying grace.
>
> For God is in all things by His essence, power and presence, according to His one common mode, as the cause existing in the effects which participate in His goodness. Above and beyond this common mode, however, there is one special mode belonging to the rational nature wherein God is said to be present as the object known is in the knower, and the beloved in the lover. And since the rational creature by its operation of knowledge and love attains to God Himself, according to this special mode God is said not only to exist in the rational creature but also to dwell therein as in His own temple. So no other effect can be put down as the reason why the divine person is in the rational creature in a new mode, except sanctifying grace. Hence, the divine person is sent, and proceeds temporally only according to sanctifying grace.
>
> Again, we are said to possess only what we can freely use or enjoy: and to have the power of enjoying the divine person can only be according to sanctifying grace. And thus the Holy Spirit is possessed by man, and dwells within him, in the very gift itself of sanctifying grace. Hence the Holy Spirit Himself is given and sent.[23]

The Moral Law and Justification

In John 14:23, we have seen that the indwelling of the divine Persons is connected by Christ with two conditions: love for Him and keeping His word. The divine indwelling presupposes the infusion of charity into our hearts through sanctifying grace, and our keeping the double commandment of charity and the Ten Commandments through the power of the grace that we have received.

---

[23] St. Thomas Aquinas, *ST* I, q. 43, a. 3.

As mentioned above, when St. Paul teaches that we are saved by faith and not by "works of the Law" (Gal 2:16), he clearly does not mean to say that it is irrelevant for justification that we observe the moral law, for he teaches the opposite in many texts, as does Jesus in dialogue with the rich young man who asked him about salvation: "If you would enter life, keep the commandments" (Mt 19:17). For example, in Galatians 5:14–21, St. Paul distinguishes between "works of the flesh" and "works of the Spirit," and says that those who do the former cannot inherit the Kingdom of God:

> For the whole law is fulfilled in one word, "You shall love your neighbor as yourself." . . . But I say, walk by the Spirit, and do not gratify the desires of the flesh. For the desires of the flesh are against the Spirit, and the desires of the Spirit are against the flesh. . . . Now the works of the flesh are plain: fornication, impurity, licentiousness, idolatry, sorcery, enmity, strife, jealousy, anger, selfishness, dissension, party spirit, envy, drunkenness, carousing, and the like. I warn you, as I warned you before, that those who do such things shall not inherit the kingdom of God.[24]

It is clear from this that justification involves the reception of a new spirit, by which one is enabled to walk according to the Spirit. This new spirit can be nothing other than the infusion of charity into our hearts together with sanctifying grace. Through these gifts the Spirit Himself comes to dwell in the soul, as long as we do not chase Him out through mortal sin, signified here by St. Paul in the "works of the flesh."

Growth in Justification

Protestants commonly distinguish between justification and sanctification. Justification would consist in the imputation of Christ's merits to us and the consequent remission of sins. Sanctification would refer to the gradual process by which one grows in the works of the Spirit.

For Catholics, justification already is inchoate sanctification, precisely because justification consists in receiving the infusion of sanctifying grace. The gift of justifying grace, however, is not something static and fixed, but destined to grow throughout the Christian life, if we cooperate with God's grace. Hence St. Paul speaks of "measures" of grace, which are given so that we may tend to the "measure of the stature of the fullness of Christ" (Eph 4:13). The initial gift of sanctifying grace that we receive upon our first justification will grow to greater and greater fullness, if we cooperate with the gift of God.

---

[24] See also Rom 1:28–32.

Can Good Works Merit an Increase of Grace and Eternal Life?

Although purely human works cannot merit justification in any way, as we have seen, it is different with regard to works moved by charity that God has gratuitously poured into our hearts through the Holy Spirit, as merited by the Blood of Christ. A purely human work is in no way proportionate to eternal life, and so cannot possibly merit it. However, a human act motivated by supernatural charity is in a quite different condition. By stemming from supernatural charity, it is no longer completely disproportionate with eternal life, for charity is the essence of eternal life.

In order to rightly understand the value of good works, it is crucial therefore to distinguish two different kinds of "good works": natural and supernatural. In a person in a state of mortal sin, there can still be "good works" according to natural human virtue. Thus a person in a state of mortal sin can still love his family, be generous to others in need, work for the common good of his country, even die for his country in military service. In addition, a person in mortal sin can have faith and hope (dead faith and dead hope).[25] However, none of these works, since they are not inspired by supernatural charity, are meritorious for eternal life. Hence St. Paul says that "if I have prophetic powers, and understand all mysteries and all knowledge, and if I have all faith, so as to remove mountains, but have not love, I am nothing. If I give away all I have, and if I deliver my body to be burned, but have not love, I gain nothing" (1 Cor 13:2). Such works done without charity may be naturally good, but they are not proportioned to eternal life, which is the life of God, who is love.

Works moved and inspired by supernatural charity, on the contrary, are "good works" in a far higher sense. Because they stem from God's own gift of love, they can merit an increase of that same gift of love. Thus they contribute to a growth in justification/sanctification and merit eternal life, in accordance with the words of St. Paul to Timothy shortly before his death: "Henceforth there is laid up for me the crown of righteousness, which the Lord, the righteous judge, will award to me on that Day, and not only to me but also to all who have loved his appearing" (2 Tim 4:8).[26]

---

[25] See James 2:17; *CCC* 1815; St. Thomas Aquinas, *ST* II-II, q. 4, a. 4.

[26] See also the Council of Trent, Decree on Justification, canon 32, DS 1582 (D 842): "If anyone says that the good works of the one justified are in such manner the gifts of God that they are not also the good merits of him justified; or that the one justified by the good works that he performs by the grace of God and the merit of Jesus Christ, whose living member he is, does not truly merit an

Conclusion

We have seen that the Messianic Kingdom is characterized by the prophets as a kingdom in which the Holy Spirit is given so that the Law of God is written interiorly on the heart. The dispute over justification is ultimately a dispute over the reality of the fulfillment of these prophecies. Does the Church possess channels of grace by which the Spirit is given and the Law of God is written on our hearts? Is she the kingdom of the New Covenant spoken of by Jeremiah 31:31 and Ezekiel 36:25–27?

The reality of sin in the members of the Church might lead one to doubt or deny it. The answer of the Catholic tradition, however, is a resounding affirmative. The Church, despite the sins of her members, is the locus of the giving of the Holy Spirit through her sacraments, through which Christians are made into a "new creation," as long they do not block the transforming action of God's grace through obstinate resistance and unrepentant mortal sin.

---

increase of grace, eternal life, and in case he dies in grace, the attainment of eternal life itself and also an increase of glory, let him be anathema."

CHAPTER 13

Israel and the Church in the Letter to the Galatians

Letter to the Galatians: Salvation through the Cross

St. Paul treats the mysterious subject of the relationship between Israel and the Church in God's plan of salvation above all in the Letter to the Galatians, and in Romans 9–11. In this chapter we shall examine Galatians.

St. Paul wrote this letter principally to counter the position that Gentile converts had to be circumcised and observe the Law of Moses, which was being taught among the Galatians by certain other disciples who claimed apostolic authority for their doctrine, whom St. Paul refers to as "false brethren" (Gal 2:4). To show the gravity of the issue, St. Paul writes:

> I am astonished that you are so quickly deserting him who called you in the grace of Christ and turning to a different gospel—not that there is another gospel, but there are some who trouble you and want to pervert the gospel of Christ. But even if we, or an angel from heaven, should preach to you a gospel contrary to that which we preached to you, let him be accursed. As we have said before, so now I say again, If any one is preaching to you a gospel contrary to that which you received, let him be accursed.[1]

St. Paul seeks to counter the error of the "false brethren," by showing his apostolic authority, the centrality of faith in Christ's Cross for salvation, and the relationship between Israel and the Church.

The key theme of the Letter to the Galatians (and of Catholic theology), is that man is redeemed from the dominion of sin and its consequences by the Passion of Christ. For this to benefit man, however, he must believe it in faith, from which hope and charity are enkindled. Salvation, therefore, comes through the foundation of faith in Christ and His Paschal mystery.

---

[1] Gal 1:6–9.

212

Salvation could not come from a human work of divine worship commanded by the Mosaic Law, because satisfaction for sin in strict justice is beyond the reach of any merely human work. *Without the Passion of Christ, human merit could never equal the weight of human sin,* or repair in justice and truth the offense given to God by sin. The Passion of Christ alone allows the scale to be turned and sin to rise in the balance before it.

In virtue of the Incarnation, by which Christ is at once true and perfect man and true and perfect God, the Messiah was able to offer a sacrifice that was not only a symbol and figure of the homage and propitiation due to God (as were all the sacrificial offerings of animals offered under the Law) but a true homage and propitiation of infinite value. Christ's suffering and death on Calvary constitutes the one true sacrifice symbolized by all the bloody animal sacrifices.

The value of Christ's sacrifice comes from the fact, first of all, that it is the holocaust of a Person who has infinite dignity—God the Son, the divine Wisdom who has come to earth, and specifically to Israel, to converse with men[2] and offer Himself for them. Secondly, it has infinite value because the sacrifice of Calvary, unlike the offering of brute animals, was animated by an infinite charity. Christ suffered voluntarily out of absolute love for His Father, who is offended by the sins of the world, and out of love for all mankind, in order to reconcile them to God by offering satisfaction for all sin. Every man can say what was said by St. Paul in Galatians 2:20: the Son of God "loved me and gave Himself for me."

Furthermore, in the sacrifice of Calvary, victim and priest are one, and thus both have a divine dignity animated by infinite charity. The sacrifice of Calvary thus is capable of offering a true satisfaction for sin by *giving to God something more pleasing than all sin is displeasing.* The absolute charity with which the infinite dignity of His life was offered, in the midst of the most excruciating suffering borne with absolute fidelity and love, outweighs in its goodness the heinousness of all human sin.

Finally, in the sacrifice of Calvary, Christ offered Himself in union with all human suffering, redeeming it, and giving to all human suffering a redemptive sacrificial value, if offered in communion with the suffering of Christ. "For," as we read in Hebrews 4:15, "we have not a high priest who is unable to sympathize with our weaknesses, but one who in every respect has been tempted as we are, yet without sin."

---

[2] See Baruch 3:36–37, which says that God "found the whole way to knowledge, and gave her [the divine wisdom] to Jacob his servant and to Israel whom he loved. Afterward she [the divine wisdom] appeared upon earth and lived among men."

Even though the Sacrifice of Calvary had not yet occurred, salvation through it was available to Israel before Christ's Passion through faith and hope in it according to God's promise. For Israel, therefore, salvation was through faith in the coming of Christ and His Redemption. For this reason, no work of the Mosaic Law could be salvific as such. The works of the Law (including circumcision) had meritorious value only through the faith, hope, and charity with which they were done. St. Paul explains this with the example of Abraham in Galatians 3:6–8:

> Thus Abraham "believed God, and it was reckoned to him as righteousness." So you see that it is men of faith who are the sons of Abraham. And the scripture, foreseeing that God would justify the Gentiles by faith, preached the gospel beforehand to Abraham, saying, "In you shall all the nations be blessed."

Once the Passion of Christ is known no longer through figures and types, but in the historical reality that we know through the Gospel, then it is possible to live a life of faith, hope, and charity nourished on the life and Passion of Christ. After coming to know Christ, one cannot simply live as one had before, centering one's hope on the ceremonial law of Moses. On the contrary, recognizing that God became man to die out of love for me, to expiate my sins, requires a radical conversion of heart and mind. Faith in the death of Christ for me requires a death to self and a new life—which is that of Christ—in the Holy Spirit. St. Paul states this beautifully in Galatians 2:19–21:

> For I through the law died to the law, that I might live to God. I have been crucified with Christ; it is no longer I who live, but Christ who lives in me; and the life I now live in the flesh I live by faith in the Son of God, who loved me and gave himself for me. I do not nullify the grace of God; for if justification were through the law, then Christ died to no purpose.

Paul says that he died to the law through the law, in that it was part of God's eternal plan that the ritual Law of Moses give way to a new liturgical law centering on the Sacrifice of Christ. In other words, it was God's plan that the Mosaic covenant should be followed by a new and eternal covenant sealed not with the blood of bulls and other beasts, but with the Blood of Jesus Christ—blood flowing from a heart beating with infinite charity. It is through faith in this new and eternal covenant—a faith operating through love—that all men, including the saints of the Old Testament, are, were, and shall be saved.

St. Paul continues in Galatians 3:1–5:

O foolish Galatians! Who has bewitched you, before whose eyes Jesus Christ was publicly portrayed as crucified? Let me ask you only this: Did you receive the Spirit by works of the law, or by hearing with faith? Are you so foolish? Having begun with the Spirit, are you now ending with the flesh? Did you experience so many things in vain?—if it really is in vain. Does he who supplies the Spirit to you and works miracles among you do so by works of the law, or by hearing with faith?

St. Paul converted the Galatians through preaching about the Cross of Christ, by which the world was redeemed. Thus he says that Jesus Christ was publicly portrayed before them as crucified. After faith in Christ crucified was given to them through the ministry of preaching, they received the Holy Spirit. The gift of the Spirit, evidently, would have come through the sacraments of Baptism and Confirmation, which presuppose faith, and, with regard to adults, are only administered to those who already have faith.[3] For this reason he asks them: "Did you receive the Spirit by works of the law, or by hearing with faith?" Obviously they did not receive the Holy Spirit in virtue of the ceremonial precepts of the Mosaic Law, but through faith in the redemptive power of Christ's Passion, and through the sacraments of the New Law by which the merit of the Passion is spiritually and efficaciously applied to the soul. The ceremonial rites of the Mosaic Law were incapable of doing this, for they were merely still obscure figures of Christ's sacrifice, which they foreshadowed as something yet to come.

Circumcision, for example, was a material and fleshly sign of a spiritual reality—the circumcision of the heart that is worked by the gift of the Holy Spirit. For circumcision of the heart means to walk not according to the desires of the flesh, but according to the impulses of the Spirit.[4]

Circumcision in the flesh is good in that it was commanded by God to be a material symbol of a spiritual gift that was to be given through faith and through the sacraments of faith of the New Law. Circumcision of the flesh was to be completed and fulfilled through receiving the circumcision of the heart worked by Baptism and Confirmation. The Galatians, however, were in danger of thinking that the circumcision of the flesh completes and fulfills the circumcision of the heart, instead of

---

[3] For this reason these sacraments are called "sacraments of faith" in the Christian Tradition. Infants are baptized in the faith of the Church.

[4] See Gal 5:19–23: "Now the works of the flesh are plain: fornication, impurity, licentiousness, idolatry, sorcery, enmity, strife, jealousy, anger, selfishness, dissension, party spirit, envy, drunkenness, carousing, and the like. . . . But the fruit of the Spirit is love, joy, peace, patience, kindness, goodness, faithfulness, gentleness, self-control; against such there is no law."

the other way around. Hence St. Paul says, "Having begun with the Spirit, are you now ending with the flesh?" Ancient Israel, through the divine pedagogy, began with the flesh, so as to end with the Spirit in the New Covenant.

The Law of Moses Is a Tutor Leading to Christ

In order to explain why the Galatians—and other Gentiles—do not need to be circumcised according to the Law of Moses, St. Paul explains the relation between Israel and the Church by means of an analogy between the state of a child under a tutor and that of a young man come to maturity. The ceremonial law of Moses is thus portrayed as a tutor leading Israel to Christ. The tutor was necessary before the coming of Christ, but is to pass away when the fullness comes:

> Now before faith came, we were confined under the law, kept under restraint until faith should be revealed. So that the law was our tutor until Christ came, that we might be justified by faith. But now that faith has come, we are no longer under a tutor; for in Christ Jesus you are all sons of God, through faith.[5]

The tutor spoken of in this text refers to a slave who would bring the children to school and discipline their conduct and studies. The tutor was not the principal teacher, but one who would bring them to the master, discipline them, and prepare them for the master. The Law of Moses served as a kind of tutor because it led the people of Israel to Christ and prepared them for Christ, in a time in which they were not yet able to fully understand the mystery of Christ because He had not yet come in the flesh and completed His mission of redemption.

The ceremonial law of Moses prefigured Christ's sacrifice and the sacraments in multiple ways through material and visible figures, such as animal sacrifices, bread offering, incense, laws of ritual purity, circumcision, etc. However, the exact meaning of these figures and the way that they prefigured Christ and His sacraments could not be fully understood under the Old Law. Their full meaning only becomes clear through faith in Christ as revealed through the preaching of the Church.

Similarly, a child does not understand the full meaning of the various rules that he has to observe. Since he does not fully understand, he has to be taught obedience through constraint or threat of punishment. The state of the Mosaic covenant, therefore, is imperfect like that of a child under a tutor. While it is very much better for a child to be under a tutor than left to himself, it is better still for the child to

---

[5] Galatians 3:23–26; I have used "tutor" rather than "custodian" to translate the Greek word *paidagōgos*.

reach the age in which he no longer needs the tutor because he can understand for himself.

Israel under the Law of Moses, therefore, was blessed in comparison with all other nations who did not have the Law as a tutor and were left to themselves. The Church, however, is still more blessed because she is no longer under a tutor, but has Christ as Master, known and understood through faith.

The righteous of Israel were saved through faith in Christ, to which they were led by the Law and the prophets. Now, however, a fuller faith in Christ is revealed so that the new Israel is no longer under the Law as a tutor. Jesus expresses this idea to the Apostles after the Last Supper in John 15:15: "No longer do I call you servants, for the servant does not know what his master is doing; but I have called you friends, for all that I have heard from my Father I have made known to you." The new Israel is no longer under a tutor because the full revelation of God has been made known to her in Christ.

A child, even though he is an heir, is still treated as a servant, in that he is told to do things without fully grasping the reasons for what he is doing. Israel under the Mosaic Law, although she had received the adoption of sonship through grace, was still treated as a servant, in that she was under a guardian and was not yet able to grasp the full meaning of the figures of Christ present in her history and Law.

The just of the New Covenant are not merely servants of God (although that is a very good thing) but friends of Christ through "faith working through love" (Gal 5:6). St. Paul expresses this contrast in the famous text of Galatians 4:1–7. In Galatians 4:1–3, he speaks of Israel:

> The heir, as long as he is a child, is no better than a slave, though he is the owner of all the estate; but he is under guardians and trustees until the date set by the father. So with us; when we were children, we were slaves to the elemental spirits of the universe.

The Jews under the Law of Moses were heirs, but because of their age—because Christ had not yet come—they were still under a certain kind of servitude to the tutor, which is the ceremonial law of Moses. This involved the use of material figures or types of spiritual things, as in animal sacrifices, observance of new moons, kosher laws, and the like. St. Paul speaks of this as bondage to the "elemental spirits of the universe." It was a *good bondage* in that it was designed by God as a tutor, but it was nevertheless an imperfection that was not to be retained when the fullness had come. The fullness here is spelled out as the Incarnation of the Son of God in Galatians 4:4–6:

> But when the fullness of time came, God sent his Son, born of a woman, born under the Law, that he might redeem those who were under the Law, that we might receive the adoption of sons. And because you are sons, God has sent the Spirit of his Son into our hearts, crying, "Abba! Father!"[6]

Christ's Incarnation marks the fullness of time in which the Son of God was born of a woman (the Blessed Virgin Mary), redeemed mankind, and gave us the gift of adoption as sons, as a participation in His Sonship. Our adoption is brought about through the gift of the Spirit, by which we progressively come to share in the mind and interior sentiments of Christ.

It is true that Israel received the gift of divine sonship through faith in Christ to come. However, that faith was yet incomplete, and made complete only in the fullness of time through the preaching of the Church. Thus the faith of the Church and her sacraments fully realize the gift of adoption as sons of God (divine filiation).

Now if the Galatians after having received the full adoption of sons in Christ were to return to the ceremonial precepts of the Old Covenant, it would be like returning to the bondage to material religious symbols (idols) by which they were held captive before their conversion:

> Formerly, when you did not know God, you were in bondage to beings that by nature are no gods; but now that you have come to know God, or rather to be known by God, how can you turn back again to the weak and beggarly elemental spirits, whose slaves you want to be once more?[7]

Even though the worship of false gods by the Galatians was incomparably worse than the liturgical practices of the Mosaic Law, both have in common that God is worshiped through material and sensible figures. Both, therefore, are inferior to the worship "of the Father in spirit and truth" (Jn 4:23) under the New Covenant in the fullness of faith.

Allegory of the Two Covenants

In Galatians 4:22–31, St. Paul continues to illustrate the difference between the Old and New Covenants through an allegorical reading of the Genesis story of Abraham's two sons: Ishmael and Isaac, and their mothers, Hagar the bondswoman and Sarah. All Jews, of course, see Isaac as their father and Sarah as their mother; and they see Ishmael as

---

[6] Confraternity of Christian Doctrine translation (NY: Benziger Bros., 1958).
[7] Gal 4:8–9.

the father of the Arab peoples. St. Paul turns this upside down through an allegorical reading, according to which Hagar and Ishmael symbolize the Old Covenant whereas Sarah and Isaac signify the New:

> For it is written that Abraham had two sons, one by a slave and one by a free woman. But the son of the slave was born according to the flesh, the son of the free woman through promise. Now this is an allegory: these women are two covenants. One is from Mount Sinai, bearing children for slavery; she is Hagar. Now Hagar is Mount Sinai in Arabia; she corresponds to the present Jerusalem, for she is in slavery with her children. But the Jerusalem above is free, and she is our mother. For it is written, "Rejoice, O barren one who does not bear; break forth and shout, you who are not in travail; for the children of the desolate one are many more than the children of her that is married." Now we, brethren, like Isaac, are children of promise. But as at that time he who was born according to the flesh persecuted him who was born according to the Spirit, so it is now. But what does the scripture say? "Cast out the slave and her son; for the son of the slave shall not inherit with the son of the free woman." So, brethren, we are not children of the slave but of the free woman.[8]

Hagar and Ishmael are connected with Mt. Sinai because Ishmael and his descendants—the Bedouin—lived in Arabia, in the region of Mt. Sinai. Since the Mosaic Covenant was given at Mt. Sinai, Hagar is equated allegorically with the Mosaic Covenant. Since Hagar was a slave, the Mosaic Covenant is allegorically connected with a kind of bondage. Sarah, in contrast, is the free woman, and she is allegorically connected with the New Covenant and the heavenly Jerusalem—the Church—which is said to be *free*.

In what sense is the New Covenant free? The Church is here said to be free in that she possesses the spiritual realities—the channels of grace to attain to heaven—that were only prefigured in the Old Covenant. The New Covenant is free, therefore, in the sense that it is able to achieve its true end.

This is not to denigrate the dignity of the Chosen People. Their dignity consisted in being specially prepared to receive the Messiah and Redeemer, and for this reason they were under the tutorship of the Law, an immense privilege. Nevertheless, the Mosaic Law was never meant to be an end in itself, but was always conceived by God as a preparation for the Church which was to issue forth from it.

---

[8] Gal 4:22–31.

St. Paul speaks of the Old Covenant as a bondwoman, bearing children for slavery, in the sense that, although it prepared for the Church and symbolically represented it, it did not yet attain to "the glorious liberty of the children of God" (Rom 8:21) in that it did not have the seven glorious sacraments of the New Law, which not only represent grace, but which actually confer grace to all those who pose no obstacle to their action. The Old Covenant is allegorically a servant because it only attained to the figure, and not to the spiritual reality signified by the figure, which is the treasure of the Church: ordinary channels of sanctifying grace.

All who attain to the faith and grace of the New Covenant are allegorically sons of Sarah, the free woman, and are set free by Christ with a spiritual freedom. Those who reject the spiritual liberty and maturity of the New Covenant are allegorically said to be sons of Hagar. However, as Isaac was persecuted by Ishmael and Jacob by Esau, so the Christian must expect to be persecuted by the world, which lives according to the flesh and cannot comprehend life according to the Spirit.

St. Paul's conclusion from all of this is that there is no reason for the Galatians—and gentile Christians in general—to receive circumcision, for it is merely the figure of the interior justice given by faith and the sacraments:

> For in Christ Jesus neither circumcision nor uncircumcision is of any avail, but faith working through love. . . . For neither circumcision counts for anything, nor uncircumcision, but a new creation. Peace and mercy be upon all who walk by this rule, upon the Israel of God. Henceforth let no man trouble me; for I bear on my body the marks of Jesus.[9]

In addition to circumcision, which he received on the eighth day, St. Paul implies that he has received the marks of Jesus' wounds on his body. Although he could be referring to stigmata as St. Francis and St. Pio received it, he is usually understood to be referring to the manifold sufferings that he has borne in the service of the Gospel, scarring his body. The Greek word here is *stigmata*, which referred to the brand borne by slaves to show their subjection to their owner. St. Paul's subjection to Christ is purely spiritual.

The new creation that he speaks of refers to the supernatural life given through Baptism, working the forgiveness of sins and the infusion of sanctifying grace, from which charity flows. The new creation realized by Baptism should be manifested in the fact that one dies to the works

---

[9] Gal 5:6; 6:16–17.

of the flesh and lives according to the works of the Spirit, which is "faith working through love" (Gal 5:6). Living according to the Spirit means having the law of the double commandment of charity written on the heart through grace.

Conclusion

The relationship between Israel and the Church as set forth in the Letter to the Galatians shows both a fundamental continuity and a radical transformation. The continuity is given by the fact that Israel and the Church are compared as two different states of one person, who begins as a child and is transformed into an adult. Israel under the Old Covenant was already the son and heir but was not yet able to receive the full formation given by the Master who is Christ, because He had not yet come into the world and revealed Himself directly.

For St. Paul, the life of Israel under the Old Covenant was a participation in the life of Christ through the means of the material figures of the ceremonial law of Moses. The life of the New Covenant is a greater participation in the life of Christ through a fuller faith in that life already present in the world and communicated through the seven sacraments. The state of the heir under a tutor or guardian is good, but not to be preferred to that of the young man come to maturity. The maturity here is the interior possession of the mind and heart of Christ.[10]

The ceremonial law of the Old Testament retains a *permanent value of Revelation* in that it prefigures Christ. However, St. Paul says that through the death of Christ on the Cross, the Christian has "died to the Law" that he might "live to God" (Gal 2:19). This means that the ceremonial law of Moses is no longer the life-giving channel of worship currently desired by God, as it was formerly, for its role was to prefigure and prepare for the grace of Christ. Thus in God's plan it was "eclipsed," so to speak (but without losing its revelatory value), when Christ came in the flesh and completed His sacrifice on Calvary, and gave us the means to "live unto God" in the Church through faith and the sacraments, which are like rivers of grace.

---

[10] See 1 Cor 2:16; Gal 2:20; Phil 2:5.

CHAPTER 14

Israel and the Church:
Continuity and Discontinuity

As we have seen in our analysis of Galatians, St. Paul presents profound elements both of continuity and discontinuity between Israel and the Church. The discontinuity, however, should not be understood as a break but as a radical fulfillment. The Church fulfills the promises given to the Patriarchs and their descendants. In this chapter we shall reflect in a more systematic way on the elements both of continuity and discontinuity between Israel and the Church.

Elements of Continuity

Let us begin by looking at the elements of continuity between Israel and the Church. A key text in this regard is Romans 9:1–5. St. Paul begins this section of the letter (chapters 9–11) by expressing his most profound interior anguish over the fact that much of Israel has not come to faith in Jesus Christ as the Messiah and Lord:

> I have great sorrow and unceasing anguish in my heart. For I could wish that I myself were accursed and cut off from Christ for the sake of my brethren, my kinsmen by race. To them belong the *sonship, the glory, the covenants, the giving of the law, the worship, and the promises; to them belong the patriarchs, and of their race, according to the flesh, is the Christ,* who is over all, God, blessed for ever.

St. Paul here enumerates the great and awesome privileges of the Chosen People: the gift of divine sonship by which they were adopted as the People of God, the glory of God's Revelation, the covenants, the gift of the Law, a revealed form of divine worship, the promises of blessing and inheritance, the Patriarchs to whom those promises were made, and the fact that Christ, who is God, was made man in the offspring of Abraham, Isaac, and Jacob. All of these gifts obviously culminate in the inconceivable glory of the Incarnation, to which they were ordered and for which they prepared.

People of God Adopted as Children of God

The first gift mentioned is the adoption as children of God. This is of great importance, for it is the beginning of the undoing of the consequences of Adam's Fall. Through the Fall, divine sonship (filiation) was lost to the children of Adam, who are born "children of wrath" (Eph 2:3). To be adopted as a son of God means that one is restored to intimacy with God, incorporated into His "family," and made heir of His eternal inheritance, which is eternal life. Israel's adoption as sons was made known to Moses in Exodus 4:22–23, when God commanded him to say to Pharaoh: "Thus says the Lord, Israel is my first-born son, and I say to you, 'Let my son go that he may serve me.'"

Adoption as a child of God, although this was not made expressly known to ancient Israel, also means that one is made an adopted brother of the Son of God, who was to become incarnate as the Messiah of Israel. The gift of divine sonship was given to Israel in view of the Incarnation of the Son of God. However, the full glory of this sonship was not yet revealed to her. Hence, as we have seen, St. Paul in Galatians 3:24–26 speaks of the Israelites as being children under a tutor, which was the Law, until the coming of Christ.

Although St. Paul does not explain this further in Romans 9:4, the gift of divine sonship must include the gift of justification and the reception of sanctifying grace, by which one is given a share in the divine life (2 Pt 1:4). Although the Son had not yet become incarnate, the Jewish people would have received the spirit of adoption through grace and faith.[1]

It follows that the gift of divine sonship received in the Church at Baptism is a glorious extension of the divine filiation already granted in germ to Abraham and his descendants in the Old Covenant. As Joseph Ratzinger has profoundly stated, speaking of the relation between Israel and the Church: "The history of Israel should become the history of all, Abraham's sonship is to be extended to the 'many.'"[2]

Revelation

Secondly, the Chosen People received the revelation of God and His glory. All the other peoples who worshiped according to the natural religions of the world were groping in search of God, whereas God Himself went in search of Israel, as it were, revealing to them the secrets of His providence and His will through the witness of the prophets.

---

[1] See also Rom 8:14–17; Gal 4:6–8.

[2] Joseph Ratzinger, *Many Religions—One Covenant: Israel, the Church and the World* (San Francisco: Ignatius Press, 1999), 27.

This glory of Revelation forms a most powerful bond of continuity between Israel and the Church, for the latter is built not only on the Apostles, but also on the prophets (see Eph 2:20). The revelatory mission of the prophets, however, centered on Christ.

The *Catechism of the Catholic Church* 528, reflecting on the mystery of the Adoration of the Magi, draws attention to this great privilege of Israel as the recipient of God's Revelation and promises:

> The magi's coming to Jerusalem in order to pay homage to the king of the Jews shows that they seek in Israel, in the messianic light of the star of David, the one who will be king of the nations. Their coming means that pagans can discover Jesus and worship him as Son of God and Savior of the world only by turning toward the Jews and receiving from them the messianic promise as contained in the Old Testament.

Like the Magi, if the pagans are to have access to the promises of God, they must "come to Jerusalem," as it were, and receive the messianic promise contained in the Revelation of God to Israel in the Old Testament.[3] In the Church, the history of Israel becomes the history of all nations—of Abraham's sons and daughters according to the spirit.[4]

Covenants

Third, God sealed covenants of promise with the Chosen People. In the covenant sealed with Abraham in Genesis 15:18–21, Abraham received the promise of the *land*:

> On that day the Lord made a covenant with Abram, saying, "To your descendants I give this land from the river of Egypt to the great river, the river Euphrates, the land of the Kenites, the Kenizzites, the Kadmonites, the Hittites, the Perizzites, the Rephaim, the Amorites, the Canaanites, the Girgashites and the Jebusites."

Although in the literal sense, the land was the physical territory of Israel, in a spiritual sense, the promise of the land refers to the Kingdom of

---

[3] See Ratzinger, who comments on *CCC* 528 in *Many Religions—One Covenant: Israel, the Church and the World* (San Francisco: Ignatius Press, 1999), 26: "The star of the religions points to Jerusalem, it is extinguished and lights up anew in the Word of God, in the Sacred Scripture of Israel. The Word of God preserved herein shows itself to be the true star without which or bypassing which the goal cannot be found."

[4] Ibid., 27.

God of universal dimensions, which will be consummated in heaven.[5] The land of Israel is a figure of the Kingdom of God: the Church militant and the Church triumphant. We see this in Hebrews 11:9–10: "By faith he [Abraham] sojourned in the land of promise, as in a foreign land, living in tents with Isaac and Jacob, heirs with him of the same promise. For he looked forward to the city which has foundations, whose builder and maker is God."

The covenant of Sinai established Israel as God's own people, as according to Exodus 19:5–6: "Now therefore, if you will obey my voice and keep my covenant, you shall be my own possession among all peoples; for all the earth is mine, and you shall be to me a kingdom of priests and a holy nation." St. Peter quotes this in 1 Peter 2:9, applying it to the Church:

> But you are a chosen race, a royal priesthood, a holy nation, God's own people, that you may declare the wonderful deeds of him who called you out of darkness into his marvelous light. Once you were no people but now you are God's people; once you had not received mercy but now you have received mercy.

The Church stands thus in profound continuity with Israel in the privilege of being chosen by the grace of God to be His own people. As Israel was gratuitously chosen from all the peoples of the earth to be made God's people through the covenant with Abraham and that of Sinai, so the Church and all her members are the recipients of a completely gratuitous grace of election into the Body of Christ under the blessings of the New Covenant.

Promises

The Church is bound together with Biblical Israel by being her continuation not simply as the People of God, but as the fulfillment of the promises given to her. These promises centered on the establishment of the Messianic Kingdom in which all the nations of the world would be blessed.[6] *God's fidelity to Israel, therefore, is shown precisely in the very existence of the Church*, which He promised as the Messianic Kingdom in which the Son of David would rule forever.[7]

---

[5] In Matthew 5:5, the word "land" clearly refers to the Kingdom of heaven: "Blessed are the meek, for they shall inherit the land."

[6] See, for example, Gen 12:3; 18:18; 22:18; 26:4; 28:14; 49:10; Ps 72:17.

[7] See Lucien Cerfaux, *The Church in the Theology of St. Paul*, trans. Geoffrey Webb and Adrian Walker (NY: Herder and Herder, 1959), 35: "What we call the New Testament is the realization of the promise [to Abraham in Gen 15:18], and the actual taking possession of the inheritance. As soon as Christ arrives on the scene, everything that God has to give belongs to him."

Sometimes it is forgotten by Christians that the Messianic Kingdom was promised to Israel as *her* kingdom. For example, Jeremiah 31:31–33 gives the promise of a "new covenant" precisely to "the house of Israel and the house of Judah." Similarly, in Ezekiel 36:24–27, the promise of the Messianic Kingdom founded on the sacrament of Baptism is clearly given to the house of Israel:

> And I will vindicate the holiness of my great name. . . . For I will take you from among the Gentiles, and will gather you together out of all the countries, and will bring you into your own land.[8] And I will pour upon you clean water, and you shall be cleansed from all your filthiness. . . . And I will give you a new heart, and put a new spirit within you.

For this reason, St. Paul says that the Gospel proclamation is first for the Jews, and then for the Gentiles. It belonged to the Jews by promise, and was thus owed by God's justice and fidelity. Hence in Romans 15:8–9, St. Paul writes: "For I tell you that Christ became a servant to the circumcised to show God's truthfulness, in order to confirm the promises given to the patriarchs, and in order that the Gentiles might glorify God for his mercy."

Christ Is Born of the Jewish People

The Church is bound up with Israel, finally, in that the Church is founded on Christ, who was born in the bosom of Israel as the promised offspring of Abraham, Isaac, Jacob, Judah, and David. As St. Paul emphasizes, "of their race, according to the flesh, is the Christ, who is God over all blessed forever" (Rom 9:5). Indeed Israel was called precisely to be the people who would bear Christ and give Him to the world, so that all nations would be blessed in the offspring of Abraham. Christ was "born under the law" (Gal 4:4), a member of Israel, out of God's fidelity to His promise made to Abraham and the Patriarchs.

Israel and the Church as God's Olive Tree

The profound elements of continuity given in Romans 9:4–5 are further developed in Romans 11 through the image of Israel and the Church as an olive tree planted by God. St. Paul's purpose is to show that the Jewish people have not been entirely cast off from God, despite the fact that many have failed to believe in the realization of the promises of God in Christ.

---

[8] The Catholic tradition understands this ingathering in the land as signifying incorporation into the Church, the Kingdom of God.

Israel is pictured here as God's sacred olive tree, rooted in the promises given to the Patriarchs, into which Gentiles have been engrafted through faith in Christ and through Baptism, and from which unbelieving members (Jew or Gentile) have been cut off through disbelief. Nevertheless, Jews that have been cut off through disbelief still retain a unique relation to the tree, in that it is *their tree*. They are "natural branches," whereas the Gentile Christians are branches of a wild olive tree engrafted into the holy tree of Israel. Thus the natural branches can surely be engrafted back by the power of God:

> If the root is holy, so are the branches. And even the others, if they do not persist in their unbelief, will be grafted in, for *God has the power to graft them in again*. For if you have been cut from what is by nature a wild olive tree, and grafted, contrary to nature, into a cultivated olive tree, how much more will these natural branches be grafted back into their own olive tree. Lest you be wise in your own conceits, I want you to understand this mystery, brethren: a hardening has come upon part of Israel, until the full number of the Gentiles come in, *and so all Israel will be saved*; as it is written, "The Deliverer will come from Zion, he will banish ungodliness from Jacob"; "and this will be my covenant with them when I take away their sins." As regards the gospel they are enemies of God, for your sake; but as regards election they are beloved for the sake of their forefathers. *For the gifts and the call of God are irrevocable.* Just as you were once disobedient to God but now have received mercy because of their disobedience, so they have now been disobedient in order that by the mercy shown to you they also may receive mercy. For God has consigned all men to disobedience, that he may have mercy upon all.[9]

This text of St. Paul contains the great prophecy that the Jewish people will receive the mercy to be grafted back into the Body as natural branches. This will come after "the full number of Gentiles come in" (Rom 11:25), which means when the Gospel is preached to the entire world, as predicted by Christ in Matthew 24:14: "And this gospel of the kingdom will be preached throughout the whole world, as a testimony to all nations; and then the end will come."[10]

---

[9] Rom 11:16–32 (my italics).

[10] See St. Cyril of Alexandria's commentary on Rom 11:26 in *Explanation of the Letter to the Romans*, PG 74:849: "Israel will also be saved eventually, a hope which Paul confirms by quoting this text of Scripture. For indeed, Israel will be saved in its own time and will be called at the end, after the calling of the Gentiles." Quoted in *Ancient Christian Commentary on Scripture*, vol. 6, *Romans*, ed. Gerald Bray (Downers Grove, IL: InterVarsity Press, 1998), 299.

The engrafting of the natural branches is spoken of in Romans 11:15: "For if their rejection means the reconciliation of the world, what will their acceptance mean but life from the dead?" It thus seems to be intimately connected with the *parousia* and the consequent general resurrection.

There also seems to be an additional meaning to this mysterious reference to "life from the dead." It seems to refer not only to *physical* life from the dead in the general resurrection, but also to *spiritual* life from the dead, indicating a renewal in the life and faith of members of the Church who will have fallen away in the great apostasy, predicted by St. Paul in 2 Thessalonians 2:3. St. Thomas Aquinas comments on Romans 11:15 as follows:

> If the loss of the Jews provided the occasion for the reconciliation of the world, in that through the death of Christ we are reconciled with God, what will their acceptance be but life from the dead? That is, that the Jews are received again by God. . . . *What will that reception accomplish, if not that the Gentiles be made to rise unto life?* For the Gentile faithful will grow cold, according to Matthew 24:12: "And because wickedness is multiplied, most men's love will grow cold." Or also those who completely fall—deceived by the Antichrist— will be *restored to their pristine fervor by the converted Jews.* And thus as through the fall of the Jews the Gentiles were reconciled after being enemies, so after the conversion of the Jews, the end of the world being imminent, there will be the general resurrection, through which men will go from death to immortal life.[11]

St. Thomas thus holds that the conversion of the Jews in the last times will be the stimulus for a spiritual rising of the Gentile Christians who have fallen from Christian hope into tepidity, nominal Catholicism, or apostasy.[12] This will be soon followed—in God's time—by the *parousia* and the general resurrection of the dead.

---

[11] St. Thomas Aquinas, commentary on Rom 11:15, in *Super epistolas S. Pauli lectura*, ed. Raphael Cai (Turin: Marietti, 1953), 1:166, n. 890. My translation and italics.

[12] This interpretation of St. Thomas is developed by Charles Journet, "The Mysterious Destinies of Israel," in *The Bridge: A Yearbook of Judaeo-Christian Studies*, ed. John Oesterreicher, vol. 2 (New York: Pantheon Books, 1956), 84–85: "Now, must one assume that Israel's reintegration will mark the end of history, giving the signal for the Last Judgment and for the final restoration of the universe? Or may one assume that Israel's return will take place within the very web of historic time, that indeed it is meant to influence the course of the centuries to come after it? Both opinions are found within the Church, but the second seems to me to correspond better with the two pertinent texts of St. Paul. Impossible, he declares in the first, that Israel's restoration should not be of inestimable benefit to the other

The theme of the prophesied conversion of the Jewish people is treated in the *Catechism of the Catholic Church* 674:

> The glorious Messiah's coming is suspended at every moment of history until his recognition by "all Israel," for "a hardening has come upon part of Israel" in their "unbelief" toward Jesus.[13] St. Peter says to the Jews of Jerusalem after Pentecost: "Repent therefore, and turn again, that your sins may be blotted out, that times of refreshing may come from the presence of the Lord, and that he may send the Christ appointed for you, Jesus, whom heaven must receive until the time for establishing all that God spoke by the mouth of his holy prophets from of old."[14] St. Paul echoes him: "For if their rejection means the reconciliation of the world, what will their acceptance mean but life from the dead?"[15] The "full inclusion" of the Jews in the Messiah's salvation, in the wake of "the full number of the Gentiles,"[16] will enable the People of God to achieve "the measure of the stature of the fullness of Christ," in which "God may be all in all."[17]

Vatican II on the Continuity between Israel and the Church

The Second Vatican Council took up this theme of the continuity between Israel and the Church as expressed in Romans 9–11 in the Declaration on the Relation of the Church to Non-Christian Religions, *Nostra aetate* 4:

> As the sacred synod searches into the mystery of the Church, it remembers the bond that spiritually ties the people of the New Covenant to Abraham's stock.
>
> Thus the Church of Christ acknowledges that, according to God's saving design, the beginnings of her faith and her election are found already among the Patriarchs, Moses and the prophets. She professes that *all who believe in Christ*—Abraham's sons according to faith (see Gal 3:7)—*are included in the same Patriarch's call*, and likewise that the salvation of the Church is mysteriously foreshadowed by the chosen people's exodus from the land of

---

peoples, since even its stumbling marvelously profited them. . . . According to this second view, Israel's entry will provoke within the Church such a resurgence of love as could be compared to a return of the dead to life."

13 Rom 11:20–26; cf. Mt 23:39.

14 Acts 3:19–21.

15 Rom 11:15.

16 Rom 11:12, 25; see Lk 21:24.

17 Eph 4:13; 1 Cor 15:28.

bondage. The *Church, therefore, cannot forget that she received the revelation of the Old Testament through the people with whom God in His inexpressible mercy concluded the Ancient Covenant. Nor can she forget that she draws sustenance from the root of that well-cultivated olive tree onto which have been grafted the wild shoots, the Gentiles* (see Rom 11:17–24). Indeed, the Church believes that by His cross Christ, Our Peace, reconciled Jews and Gentiles, making both one in Himself (see Eph 2:14–16).

The Church keeps ever in mind the words of the Apostle about his kinsmen: "Theirs is the sonship and the glory and the covenants and the law and the worship and the promises; theirs are the fathers and from them is the Christ according to the flesh" (Rom 9:4–5), the Son of the Virgin Mary. She also recalls that the Apostles, the Church's mainstay and pillars, as well as most of the early disciples who proclaimed Christ's Gospel to the world, sprang from the Jewish people. . . . *God holds the Jews most dear for the sake of their Fathers; He does not repent of the gifts He makes or of the calls He issues*—such is the witness of the Apostle (see Rom 11:28–29). In company with the Prophets and the same Apostle, the Church awaits that day, known to God alone, on which all peoples will address the Lord in a single voice and "serve him shoulder to shoulder" (Zeph 3:9).[18]

Since the spiritual patrimony common to Christians and Jews is thus so great, this sacred synod wants to foster and recommend that mutual understanding and respect which is the fruit, above all, of biblical and theological studies as well as of fraternal dialogues.

True, the Jewish authorities and those who followed their lead pressed for the death of Christ; still, what happened in His passion cannot be charged against all the Jews, without distinction, then alive, nor against the Jews of today. *Although the Church is the new people of God, the Jews should not be presented as rejected or accursed by God, as if this followed from the Holy Scriptures.*[19]

Nostra aetate 4, closely following Romans 9–11, affirms a delicate balance. The Church is indeed the new People of God, founded on the mystery of Christ and participation in His Body. However, this new People of God finds "the beginnings of her faith and her election" in that of "the Patriarchs, Moses and the prophets." The new People of God results from an engrafting into the sacred olive tree rooted in the promises given to the Patriarchs. Many of the branches that have been engrafted are wild ones—Gentiles—but they have been engrafted into a tree whose trunk is natural.

---

[18] See Is 66:23; Ps 65:4; Rom 11:11–32.
[19] Vatican II, *Nostra aetate* 4 (my italics).

The text of Romans 11:28–29 is recalled and given great importance in the Council's affirmation that "God holds the Jews most dear for the sake of their Fathers; He does not repent of the gifts He makes or of the calls He issues." We cannot regard the Jewish people as rejected, accursed, or abandoned by God. This view, as we know, was the cause of terrible anti-Semitism throughout the centuries.

The Church therefore cannot be regarded as simply replacing Israel as the People of God. The people of Israel according to the flesh are still especially beloved of God on account of the Patriarchs, as were their fathers in Biblical Israel. Even more, they are uniquely beloved as a people on account of Mary, the archetypical "daughter of Zion," and on account of her divine Son, "born under the Law" (Gal 4:4).

The people of Israel, therefore, should be regarded as conserving their mysterious election in God's providential plan. Their role is not finished until they corporately come to receive the fulfillment of God's promises to them, through a great outpouring of His mercy, by which "all Israel will be saved" (Rom 11:26). It follows that Israel's election remains tied to the Messiah in whom all of God's promises are fulfilled.[20]

In the meantime Israel is a continual and impartial witness before the world of God's plan of salvation that culminates in the Messiah and His Church. St. Augustine wrote of the Jews that "by the evidence of their own Scriptures they bear witness for us that we have not fabricated the prophecies about Christ."[21] The existence and continued fidelity of the Jewish people to the covenant of Sinai, through so many centuries without a land, through so much persecution, tragedy, and trial, is a clear sign of a special providence and predilection of God in their behalf and of the special role that they continue to play in His plans, until they shall finally come to recognize their Messiah.

Elements of Discontinuity

Christocentrism of the Church

The relationship between Israel and the Church, however, is not only one of continuity, just as the butterfly is not only in a relation of continuity with the caterpillar. There is a profound distinction which comes from God's providential plan for the unfolding of salvation history. For the Church is the *Messianic Kingdom* of Israel, and the prophetic witness does not present the Messianic Kingdom simply as a

---

[20] See 2 Cor 1:20: "For all the promises of God find their Yes in him."

[21] St. Augustine, *The City of God*, 18.46, trans. Henry Bettenson (NY: Penguin Books, 1984), 827.

continuation of Biblical Israel. The promises of the Kingdom would not be worthy of God if their fulfillment did not exceed all expectation.

Discontinuity of the Church with Biblical Israel (as it existed under the Mosaic covenant) comes from the fact that the Church is entirely founded on Christ and the mysteries of His life: born of a woman, born under the Law, who suffered, died, rose from the dead, ascended into heaven, from whence He has sent the gift of His Spirit. The existence of the Church, in the full and proper sense of the word, presupposes the historical accomplishment of the entire work of the Paschal mystery, on which she is based and into which she is engrafted and made a participant. Christ, in His death and resurrection, is her foundation, cornerstone, eternal High Priest, and Head.

In Ephesians 2:19–21, St. Paul says that the Church is the "household of God, built upon the foundation of the apostles and prophets, Christ Jesus himself being the cornerstone, in whom the whole structure is joined together and grows into a holy temple in the Lord." The Church is entirely Christocentric, and thus it immensely exceeds the horizons of ancient Israel.

The Church Is the Body of Christ

St. Paul, as we have seen above, presents the Messianic Kingdom precisely as the *Body of Christ* (Body of the Messiah).[22] One does not enter into Christ's Body by physical birth into the people, as in Israel, but by spiritual birth through the sacrament of Baptism, which gives us a participation in the mystery of Christ's death and Resurrection, so that we die unto sin and rise unto new life in the Spirit.

Ancient Israel under the covenant of Sinai was made into the People of God, but was not yet the Body of Christ. Thus it could not be endowed yet with the fullness of the Spirit of the Son, which is the soul of the Mystical Body. As we have seen, the Messianic Kingdom was foretold by the prophets to be characterized by a fuller outpouring of the Holy Spirit onto all flesh.[23] Since the Holy Spirit is the Spirit of the Son, the Body of Christ—into which we enter by Baptism—must be animated by that same Spirit. In 1 Corinthians 12:12–13, St. Paul writes: "For just as the body is one and has many members, and all the members of the body, though many, are one body, so it is with Christ. For by one Spirit we were all baptized into one body—Jews or Greeks, slaves or free—and *all were made to drink of one Spirit.*"

---

[22] See Rom 12:5: "So we, though many, are one body in Christ."
[23] See Joel 2:28–29; Jer 31:31–33; Ezek 36:24–27.

The Church Has Sacramental Channels of Supernatural Life

The outpouring of the Holy Spirit in the Body of Christ, as we have seen, is realized through the ordinary channels of grace, which are the seven sacraments of the Church. These are the arteries and veins of the Mystical Body, by which "the whole structure is joined together and grows into a holy temple in the Lord" (Eph 2:21).

Israel was not yet provided with stable conduits of grace that were efficacious in themselves in imparting spiritual gifts and the Spirit Himself. The sacred rites of Israel were like the sacramentals of the Church. Sacramentals, such as blessings and devotions, do not directly confer the grace of the Holy Spirit but, through the prayer of the Church, prepare and dispose us to receive those graces.[24] Similarly, the sacred rites of Israel, although they could not directly give the Holy Spirit, disposed the people of God to receive His graces. For example, the baptism of repentance of John the Baptist did not confer the Holy Spirit as Baptism does, but prepared the people to receive the grace of Christ's Baptism. Hence the words of John the Baptist (Mt 3:11): "I baptize you with water for repentance, but he who is coming after me is mightier than I. . . . He will baptize you with the Holy Spirit and with fire."

The Church Is Catholic

As seen above, the fullness of the Spirit made available in the Church was intended by God to reach all mankind in the Church.[25] God says in Joel 2:28 that "it shall come to pass afterward, that I will pour out my spirit on all flesh."

St. Paul was called precisely to be the "chosen instrument" (Acts 9:15) to bring the Gospel to the Gentiles so that they might be engrafted into the Body, according to the Messianic prophecies.[26] The calling of Gentiles is said to be the "mystery hidden for ages in God" (Eph 3:9). St. Paul gives a dramatic description of this engrafting in Ephesians 2:11–22:

> Remember that at one time you Gentiles in the flesh, called the uncircumcision by what is called the circumcision, which is made in the flesh by hands—remember that you were at that time separated from Christ, alienated from the commonwealth of Israel, and strangers to the covenants of promise, having no hope and without God in the world. But now in Christ Jesus you who once were far off have been brought near in the blood of Christ. For he

---

[24] See *CCC* 1670.
[25] See chapter 4 above.
[26] See Is 49:6; Is 60:3–13; Ps 72:8–17; and Dan 2:35.

is our peace, who has made us both one, and has broken down the dividing wall of hostility, by abolishing in his flesh the law of commandments and ordinances, that he might create in himself one new man in place of the two, so making peace, and might reconcile us both to God in one body through the cross, thereby bringing the hostility to an end. And he came and preached peace to you who were far off and peace to those who were near; for through him we both have access in one Spirit to the Father. So then you are no longer strangers and sojourners, but you are fellow citizens with the saints and members of the household of God, built upon the foundation of the apostles and prophets, Christ Jesus himself being the cornerstone, in whom the whole structure is joined together and grows into a holy temple in the Lord; in whom you also are built into it for a dwelling place of God in the Spirit.

The New Priesthood of the New Covenant

The Church has a new religious authority, distinct from that given in the Mosaic Law. This authority is constituted by apostolic succession through the sacrament of Holy Orders in its highest grade: the episcopacy. The bishops are the successors of the Apostles, the foundation of the Church (Eph 2:20). Of the Apostles, Peter was singled out to be the head: "You are Peter, and on this rock I will build my Church" (Mt 16:18). This new religious authority supplants the authority of the High Priests and the Sanhedrin.

In a similar way, the New Covenant has a new priesthood, distinct from that of Aaron and his sons, and which consists in a participation of the priesthood of Christ. The Letter to the Hebrews (7:11–8:1) discusses the distinction between the Aaronic priesthood and that of Christ and the New Covenant:

> Now if perfection had been attainable through the Levitical priesthood (for under it the people received the law), what further need would there have been for another priest to arise after the order of Melchizedek, rather than one named after the order of Aaron? For when there is a change in the priesthood, there is necessarily a change in the law as well. . . . For it was fitting that we should have such a high priest, holy, blameless, unstained, separated from sinners, exalted above the heavens. He has no need, like those high priests, to offer sacrifices daily, first for his own sins and then for those of the people; he did this once for all when he offered up himself. . . . Now the point in what we are saying is this: we have such a high priest, one who is seated at the right hand of the throne of the Majesty in heaven.

Christ is the eternal high priest of the New Covenant. However, since He is no longer visible to us, the sacrament of Holy Orders enables men who are called to act in the person of Christ to make Him sacramentally present in the power of His priesthood.

As Hebrews 7:12 mentions, the change in the priesthood in the "new People of God"[27] implies a change in the entire ceremonial law and the covenant. Christ's priesthood mediates a far better covenant, "enacted on better promises" (Heb 8:6). Citing Jeremiah 31:31–33, Hebrews 8:6–13 speaks of the corresponding change between the Old and New Covenants:

> Christ has obtained a ministry which is as much more excellent than the old as the covenant he mediates is better, since it is enacted on better promises. For if that first covenant had been faultless, there would have been no occasion for a second. For he finds fault with them when he says: "The days will come, says the Lord, when I will establish a new covenant with the house of Israel and with the house of Judah; . . . This is the covenant that I will make with the house of Israel after those days, says the Lord: I will put my laws into their minds, and write them on their hearts, and I will be their God, and they shall be my people. . . ." In speaking of a new covenant he treats the first as obsolete. And what is becoming obsolete and growing old is ready to vanish away.

The Church therefore is the Messianic Kingdom of the New Covenant, founded on the promises of grace, the giving of the Spirit, and eternal life, merited through the sacrifice of Christ, which is made present continually in the sacrifice of the Mass.

The Ceremonial Law Is Replaced by the Liturgy of the Church

In the New Covenant, the ceremonial and judicial precepts of the Mosaic Law are no longer in force. We have seen above[28] that the Catholic theological tradition makes a distinction between three types of precepts in the Law of Moses: (a) moral precepts that contain and formulate the natural moral law, (b) ceremonial precepts that legislate the worship of God and ritual purity, and (c) judicial precepts that served as a kind of civil penal code for ancient Israel.

All three kinds of precepts are fulfilled by Christ, according to His words in the Sermon on the Mount in Matthew 5:17–18: "Think not that I have come to abolish the law and the prophets; I have come not to abolish them but to fulfill them. For truly, I say to you, till heaven and

---

[27] Vatican II, *Nostra aetate* 4.

[28] See p. 43.

earth pass away, not an iota, not a dot, will pass from the law until all is accomplished."

Christ fulfills the Law of Moses, however, in different ways, according to the type of precept one is considering. The moral precepts are fulfilled through Christ in three ways. First, through the spiritual power imparted by the sacraments, He gives us the grace to observe the whole moral law in charity, as God desires. Second, He fulfills them by giving us the perfect example of His own life and teaching.[29] Third, He fulfills them by endowing His Church with the authority to infallibly teach the obligations of the moral law to all nations and throughout all ages.

The ceremonial law is also completely fulfilled by Christ in His Paschal mystery, but in a different and mystical sense. He fulfills it by accomplishing the reality of salvation that the ceremonial precepts of the Old Law merely prefigured or symbolized. For example, He is the true Paschal Lamb who takes away the sins of the world, prefigured by the millions of paschal lambs sacrificed under the Law; He embodies the true circumcision of the heart, symbolized in the carnal circumcision He received on the eighth day; He accomplished the true Atonement, symbolized in the sacrifices of the Day of Atonement; and He embodies the true spiritual purity signified in the ritual purity commanded in the Law. It is fitting therefore that the ceremonial law of Moses be replaced by a new ceremonial law of the Church that draws its efficacy from and explicitly commemorates the Incarnation and the Paschal mystery already accomplished. This is the liturgy of the New Covenant.

The judicial precepts, finally, are also abrogated, in that civil penal law is left to temporal society (and to canon law), as guided by the Magisterium of the Church. In this way the judicial precepts can be adapted to the exigencies of different historical and cultural circumstances. Christ fulfilled the judicial precepts by founding His Church to be the light of the nations.

The ceremonial and judicial precepts of the Mosaic Law had the practical effect of separating Israel from the nations. This separation is no longer fitting under the New Covenant, precisely because it is destined to include all nations and cultures within its bosom. Thus St. Paul, in Ephesians 2:14–16, writes:

> He is our peace, who has made us both one, and has broken down
> the dividing wall of hostility, by abolishing in his flesh the law of
> commandments and ordinances, that he might create in himself
> one new man in place of the two, so making peace, and might

---

[29] See *CCC* 1968.

reconcile us both to God in one body through the cross, thereby bringing the hostility to an end.

Obviously St. Paul does not mean that Christ has abolished the moral precepts, for He says the contrary in numerous places. Christ has "abolished" in His flesh on the Cross only the ceremonial and judicial precepts. Because the ceremonial and the judicial precepts are no longer binding in the Church, it can be said that the Old Law has been abrogated in that regard. Indeed it has been abrogated precisely because it has been perfectly fulfilled by Christ.

Pius XII explains this abrogation in his encyclical on the Church, *Mystici Corporis* 29–30:

> And first of all, by the death of our Redeemer, the New Testament took the place of the Old Law which had been abolished; then the Law of Christ together with its mysteries, enactments, institutions, and sacred rites was ratified for the whole world in the blood of Jesus Christ. For, while our Divine Savior was preaching in a restricted area—He was not sent but to the sheep that were lost of the house of Israel—the Law and the Gospel were together in force;[30] but on the gibbet of his death Jesus made void the Law with its decrees (Eph 2:15), fastened the handwriting of the Old Testament to the Cross (Col 2:14), establishing the New Testament in His blood shed for the whole human race (Mt 26:28; 1 Cor 11:25). "To such an extent, then," says St. Leo the Great, speaking of the Cross of our Lord, "was there effected a transfer from the Law to the Gospel, from the Synagogue to the Church, from many sacrifices to one Victim, that, as our Lord expired, that mystical veil which shut off the innermost part of the temple and its sacred secret was rent violently from top to bottom."[31] On the Cross then the Old Law died.

The Old Law can be said to have "died" by being fulfilled in the New, such that its moral precepts are given new strength and its ceremonial precepts are subsumed into the liturgy of the Church.

The Use of Elements of the Ceremonial Law under the New Covenant

The fact that the ceremonial precepts of the Law of Moses are no longer binding in the Church does not mean that it is unlawful for them to be followed in any way, as long as one does not put one's hope in them as

---

[30] See St. Thomas Aquinas, *ST* I-II, q. 103, a. 3, ad 2.
[31] St. Leo the Great, Sermon 68.3, *PL* 54, 374.

if they were believed to be still necessary for salvation.[32] We know that the Apostles and the Jewish Christians of the first century continued to worship in the Temple and observe the ceremonial law in many ways.[33]

An interesting document of Pope Benedict XIV in the mid-eighteenth century sheds light on this subject. The document is about the approval of a book of liturgical prayers (Euchologion) used in the Eastern rite by the Greek Uniates. The liturgical prayers contained certain elements of the ceremonial law of Moses that were still customary in parts of Eastern Christianity, although no longer in the West. Some theologians wanted those elements to be eliminated.[34] Benedict XIV decided, however, not to modify the prayer book in that regard, reasoning that elements of the ceremonial law could be observed *as long as there was some utility in their observance.* He notes that some elements of the ceremonial law were imposed on the early Christians by the Council of Jerusalem (Acts 15) for the purpose of establishing peace between Jews and Gentiles in the Church. Those laws were retained longer in the Eastern Church than in the West. Hence the judgment of Benedict XIV was that some elements of the ceremonial precepts can be retained or observed, subject to the mind of the Church:

> Although the ceremonial precepts of the old Law have come to an end with the promulgation of the Gospel, and the new Law does not contain any precept which distinguishes between clean and unclean foods, nevertheless the Church of Christ has the power of renewing the obligation to observe some of the old precepts for just and serious reasons, despite their abrogation by the new Law.[35]

---

[32] See the Council of Florence, Bull of Union with the Copts *Cantate Domino* (1442), DS 1348 (D 712): "Whoever, after the passion, places his hope in the legal prescriptions and submits himself to them as necessary for salvation and as if faith in Christ without them could not save, sins mortally." However, *Cantate Domino* goes further and states that any use whatever by Christians of the rites of the ceremonial Law of Moses—such as circumcision—is illicit, even if one does not believe them necessary for salvation. This should be understood, however, in the light of later Magisterial teaching, such as Benedict XIV, *Ex quo primum*, discussed below. As Benedict XIV implies, this text should be considered to be a particular disciplinary measure binding only in those circumstances, as was the ruling of the Council of Jerusalem.

[33] See, for example, Acts 21:20–24.

[34] In this they were following the Council of Florence, *Cantate Domino*, DS 1348 (D 712).

[35] Benedict XIV, encyclical *Ex quo primum*, on the Euchologian, of March 1, 1756, n. 63, in *The Papal Encyclicals 1740–1878*, ed. Claudia Carlen (Wilmington, NC: McGrath Publishing, 1981), 99. Benedict XIV goes on to say that he did not think it would be expedient to restore elements of the ceremonial law of Moses whose

Although in this encyclical Benedict XIV was not considering the situation or practice of Hebrew Catholics, the principle he lays down is significant with regard to the practice of celebrating the Passover *seder* and other elements of Jewish prayer, to which many Hebrew Catholics are rightly attracted. This is legitimate as long as one recognizes the primacy of Christ and the Church, and defers to her judgment. The prudential decision as to which aspects of the ceremonial law of Moses could be taken up in some way by the Christian faithful depends on the changing conditions of history, as evaluated by the successors of the Apostles.

It seems to this writer that practices of Jewish prayer such as the Passover *seder, when done in the context of Christian faith,*[36] can be quite beneficial in manifesting the continuity of God's plan of salvation history and in aiding the faithful to grasp the divine pedagogy by which events in the Old Testament, commemorated in the liturgy of Israel, prefigure the Paschal mystery of Christ, the Church, and her sacraments. In the eyes of Christian faith the ceremonial rites and prayer of Israel take on a new meaning, which is precisely the light of their fulfillment in the New Covenant. Just as the messianic prophecies do not lose their importance from the fact that they have been fulfilled in Christ—but rather are magnified by that fulfillment—so too it seems that the ceremonial rites of Israel can retain a prophetic value which is not annulled by their being fulfilled in Christ. The obligatory quality of those rites has passed away, but their prophetic, typological, and revelatory value remains.

---

purpose was to prefigure the Sacrifice of Christ: "However, precepts whose main function was to foreshadow the coming Messiah should not be restored, for example, circumcision and the sacrifice of animals. . . . Precepts regarding external discipline and cleanliness of body, the kind which contain the precepts on clean and unclean foods, may be restored. The Western as well as the Eastern Church assumed this practice; this is documented from the earliest centuries" (ibid.).

[36] See *Ex quo primum* 67, in which Benedict XIV quotes a theologian (Leo Allatius) and approves of his reasoning: "It cannot be absolutely asserted that that man judaizes who does something in the Church which corresponds to the ceremonies of the old Law. 'If a man should perform acts for a different end and purpose (even with the intention of worship and as religious ceremonies), not in the spirit of that Law nor on the basis of it, but either from personal decision, from human custom, or on the instruction of the Church, he would not sin, nor could he be said to judaize. So when a man does something in the Church which resembles the ceremonies of the old Law, he must not always be said to judaize.'"

Conclusion

In conclusion, the relationship between Biblical Israel and the Church cannot be simply categorized as replacement (supersessionism), nor as separation (two parallel covenants). The New Covenant replaces the ceremonial precepts of the Old Covenant by making present the life-giving mystery of Christ's Passion and Resurrection, which the Old could only prefigure. However, the new People of God of the New Covenant does not simply replace the People of the Old Covenant, as if the latter had been rejected by God! First of all, it must be remembered that Christ, the Apostles, and the entire Church of Pentecost were Jewish. Never was the Church more beautiful than when, at her inception, she was entirely Jewish.[37] Second, Israel was not rejected, for God is faithful to His promises and calling. As St. Paul says in Romans 11:28–29: "As regards election they are beloved for the sake of their forefathers. For the gifts and the call of God are irrevocable." Third, Israel has not been rejected, for the Church is the *fulfillment* of the promises given to the Patriarchs and prophets. The Church is the Messianic Kingdom of Israel. Fourth, if Israel were rejected, the Gentiles could not be said to be engrafted into her as "God's cultivated olive tree," as St. Paul describes in Romans 11:16–24.[38] The Jews remain natural branches, even if they separate themselves from their tree through unbelief. Finally, Jews have not been rejected, for they still have a great role to play in the history of salvation, as they are reinserted as natural branches into God's olive tree, causing the Gentiles who are falling away to revive, and preparing the way for the *parousia*.

---

[37] See Acts 2:43–47; 4:32–35. See also Charles Journet, "The Mysterious Destinies of Israel," in *The Bridge: A Yearbook of Judaeo-Christian Studies*, ed. J. Oesterreicher, 2:58: "Never again, I think, will the Church on earth be so fervent, so loving, so pure, as when she was Jewish; never again in the course of the ages will she find sanctity like that of Mary or even like that of the apostles. One of the reasons for this, her initial excellence, was the task entrusted to her as she came forth from the hands of the messiah. The great things she did under His immediate influence were perfect, so that they could serve as models to the faithful of every century till the end of the world."

[38] See Joseph Ratzinger, *Many Religions—One Covenant: Israel, the Church and the World*, 26.

CHAPTER 15

Mary, Mother of Israel's Hope and Mother of the Church

The Messianic Kingdom cannot be fully understood without looking at Mary, Mother of the Church and of all the members of the Mystical Body. Mary is the Mother of the Church and of all Christians precisely because she is the Mother of Christ. Since she is the Mother of the Head of the Mystical Body, it is fitting that she also become the Mother of the whole Mystical Body and of all its members. By being chosen to be the Mother of Israel's hope, who is Christ, it is fitting that she become the mother of all those who come to share in the hope of Israel.

This theme of Mary's maternity with regard to the Church and all Christians is a subject that is, on the one hand, of extraordinary beauty and importance for the spiritual life. On the other hand, it is a subject that the Protestant world has failed to grasp and often vehemently rejects. Thus it is very important for Catholics to understand the doctrine, both for its own sake and to help meet Protestant objections.

What are the principal reasons for the Catholic understanding of Mary's spiritual maternity with regard to the Church and all Christians?

God's Constancy

God is constant and universal in His mode of action in the world. We see this throughout the cosmos and its natural laws. God does not change them capriciously. Hence we should expect the same order to be followed by God in the accomplishment of His plans.

God did not have to come into the world through a human mother or through a chosen people. He is completely free. He could have become man without any human mediation—without parents or a people from which He was to be born. However, we know that He chose to freely use human mediation. He was born into a people prepared for two thousand years to receive Him. And He was born of a mother who was prepared to receive Him through being immaculately conceived, free from the taint of Adam's Fall from the first moment of her conception.

God prepares for His great acts in a manner worthy of His infinite wisdom. As Israel was prepared to receive Christ through the great gifts of the Law and the prophets, so Mary—through her Immaculate Conception and her perfect faith in Israel's hope—was prepared to receive Him in her womb and give Him birth.

Now if the Head of the Body needed a Mother perfectly prepared to receive Him and give Him birth, so too the members of the Body of Christ are in no less need of a perfect Mother. That Mother is the Church, who engenders and continually nourishes the life of grace in us through her sacraments. We do not become members of the Church simply through our own effort and merit. However, that Mother is also Our Lady, who is the Mother of the Church. As Christ was born from the Chosen People and born from the Virgin Mary, so the Church is born from the Chosen People, and is born from Mary.

God's constancy is shown in this: the same means are chosen to bring Christ's Mystical Body into the world as were chosen to bring Christ into the world. Mary Immaculate is that chosen channel. As she was chosen to be the mother of the Son of God in the fullness of time, so she is chosen to be the spiritual Mother of those called to be made sons and daughters of God in Christ. As God willed to use the human mediation of the Chosen People and the Virgin Mary in His birth, so He wills to use the human mediation of Mary in the spiritual birth of His Body, the Church, and of all her members. As Christ chose to be dependent on His mother Mary in His coming into the world and was obedient to her for thirty years, so it is fitting that she retain her maternity over His Body, the Church.

Genesis 3:15

Mary's intimate association with her Son and His Mystical Body can be seen in the first Messianic prophecy at the dawn of time: Genesis 3:15. To protect Adam and Eve from the danger of despair, God reveals the future coming of a Redeemer, a descendant born of their lineage, who will triumph over the devil. After the Fall, God speaks to the three protagonists of that event: the serpent, Eve, and Adam. To the serpent He says: "I will put enmity between you and the woman, and between your seed and her seed; he [the seed of the woman] shall bruise [crush] your head, and you shall bruise his heel."

Christ the Messiah is obviously the "seed of the Woman" who will crush the head of the serpent, who indicates the devil. But who is the Woman? And why is she given so much prominence in this prophecy? At first sight she would seem to be Eve. But Eve was not in enmity with the serpent. Quite the contrary, she had become his accomplice, being obedient to his word rather than to God's.

The woman must refer to another woman whom Eve prefigures as universal mother of mankind. The prophecy indicates that there will be another woman like Eve who recapitulates her sex, who will give birth to one who will crush the head of the serpent, thus crushing the power of sin and Satan. That woman, of course, is Mary, who gives birth to Christ, whose Passion destroyed the power of Satan.

We see here that the work of salvation is pictured as coming through both a man and a woman, just as the original sin had been the work of both a man and a woman. As Adam and Eve had worked the Fall through obedience to the word of the devil, so a new Adam and a new Eve will repair the Fall and overcome the devil, untying the knot tied by the first couple. The Redeemer is the new Adam, but the "woman," the new Eve, is His mother. Thus it is fitting to think that as Eve was the "mother of all the living" according to our physical life, as she is called in Genesis 3:20, the new Eve will be the "mother of all the living" in a higher and better sense—in the life of the spirit.

This doctrine of Mary as the new Eve has great importance in understanding Mary's role in salvation history. The Fathers and the great Scholastic Doctors justify many of their Mariological doctrines on the basis of the typology of Mary as the new Eve. This can be seen in relation to the Immaculate Conception, Mary's perpetual virginity, the association of Mary in the work of Redemption, the universal spiritual motherhood of Mary, and Mary as Mediatrix of all graces. As Eve was created innocent in a state of grace, so Mary, the new Eve, is immaculate from the beginning, created in sanctifying grace. As Eve was a virgin before her fall, so Mary is perpetually virgin. As Eve was created to be a fitting companion and associate for Adam, so Mary is intimately associated with Christ, the new Adam, in His labor of redemption, and thus Mary is Co-Redemptrix (in a subordinate sense).[1] As Eve was mother of all the living (men) on the natural level,[2] so Mary is the

---

[1] St. Simeon prophesied Mary's co-redemption already at the Presentation, only forty days after the birth of Jesus: "A sword will pierce through your own soul also" (Lk 2:35). On Mary's subordinate co-redemption, see, for example, Pius XII, encyclical *Mystici corporis* 110: "It was she, the second Eve, who, . . . offered Him on Golgotha to the Eternal Father for all the children of Adam, sin-stained by his unhappy fall, and her mother's rights and her mother's love were included in the holocaust. Thus she who, according to the flesh, was the mother of our Head, through the added title of pain and glory became, according to the Spirit, the mother of all His members."

[2] See Gen 3:20.

spiritual mother of all men in the order of grace.[3] And insofar as she is spiritual mother in the order of grace, we can deduce that she is the Mediatrix of all graces, just as our physical mothers mediate God's natural gifts.[4]

St. Justin Martyr is the first to make this Marian typology explicit, which, from then on, became very common in the Fathers. In his *Dialogue with the Jew Trypho*, Justin writes:

> He became man by the Virgin, in order that the disobedience which proceeded from the serpent might receive its destruction in the same manner in which it derived its origin. For Eve, who was a virgin and undefiled, having conceived the word of the serpent, brought forth disobedience and death. But the Virgin Mary received faith and joy, when the angel Gabriel announced the good tidings to her that the Spirit of the Lord would come upon her, and the power of the Highest would overshadow her: wherefore also the Holy Thing begotten of her is the Son of God; and she replied, "Be it unto me according to thy word." And by her has He been born.[5]

St. Irenaeus perhaps gives the most eloquent exposition to this theme in *Against Heresies*:

> In accordance with this design, Mary the Virgin is found obedient, saying, "Behold the handmaid of the Lord; be it unto me according to your word" (Lk 1:38). But Eve was disobedient; for she did not obey when as yet she was a virgin. And even as she, having indeed a husband, Adam, but being nevertheless as yet a virgin . . . having become disobedient, was made the cause of death, both to herself and to the entire human race; so also did Mary, having a man betrothed [to her], and being nevertheless a virgin, by yielding obedience, become the cause of salvation, both to herself and the whole human race. . . . And thus also it was that the knot of Eve's disobedience was loosed by the obedience of Mary. For what the

---

[3] See St. Pius X, encyclical *Ad diem illum* 10 (1904): "For is not Mary the Mother of Christ? Then she is our Mother also. . . . Hence, though in a spiritual and mystical fashion, we are all children of Mary, and she is Mother of us all."

[4] See ibid., 13: "It cannot, of course, be denied that the dispensation of these treasures is the particular and peculiar right of Jesus Christ, for they are the exclusive fruit of His Death, who by His nature is the mediator between God and man. Nevertheless, by this companionship in sorrow and suffering already mentioned between the Mother and the Son, it has been allowed to the august Virgin to be the most powerful mediatrix and advocate of the whole world with her Divine Son."

[5] St. Justin, *Dialogue with Trypho* 100, *ANF* 1:249.

virgin Eve had bound fast through unbelief, this did the virgin Mary set free through faith.[6]

In this text, St. Irenaeus shows the fittingness of Mary's part in our Redemption (as Co-Redemptrix) through Biblical typology. Just as the original sin was the work not of Adam alone, but of the virgin Eve and Adam together, so it is fitting that the redemption from original sin likewise be worked not by the new Adam (Christ) alone, but rather by the new Adam together with the cooperation of the new Eve, Mary. Just as Eve collaborated with Adam in our Fall, so the new Eve collaborates with Christ in our rise, although in a way that is totally subordinate to her Son. And as Eve was a virgin in her collaboration in the Fall, so the new Eve must likewise be a virgin in her collaboration. However, there is also opposition. The original Eve collaborated in the Fall through disobedience to God and disbelief in His word. This is set right by the collaboration of Mary in perfect obedience and faith, expressed in her *fiat*: "Let it be done unto me according to your word" (Lk 1:38).

And as Adam is the head of humanity according to the flesh, Eve is his partner in this, being the "mother of all the living." Likewise, Christ the new Adam is the new head of humanity, which He recapitulates, and Mary is the new Eve, the mother of all those who receive the new life of Christ.

St. Irenaeus restates this idea later in the same work:

That the Lord then was manifestly coming to His own things, and was sustaining them by means of that creation which is supported by Himself, and was making a recapitulation of that disobedience which had occurred in connection with a tree, through the obedience which was [exhibited by Himself when He hung] upon a tree, [the effects] also of that deception being done away with, by which that virgin Eve, who was already espoused to a man, was unhappily misled,—was happily announced, through means of the truth [spoken] by the angel to the Virgin Mary, who was [also espoused] to a man. For just as the former was led astray by the word of an angel, so that she fled from God when she had transgressed His word; so did the latter, by an angelic communication, receive the glad tidings that she should bear God, being obedient to His word. And if the former did disobey God, yet the latter was persuaded to be obedient to God, in order that the Virgin Mary might become the patroness (*advocata*) of the virgin Eve. And thus, as the human race fell into bondage to death by means of a virgin, so is it rescued by a virgin; virginal disobedience having been balanced in the opposite scale by virginal obedience.

---

[6] St. Irenaeus, *Against Heresies* 3.22.4, *ANF* 1:455.

For in the same way the sin of the first created man receives amendment by the correction of the First-begotten, and the coming of the serpent is conquered by the harmlessness of the dove, those bonds being unloosed by which we had been fast bound to death.[7]

Mary as the new Eve cooperates with the work of Christ the new Adam, for the benefit of the children of Eve. St. Proclus, a Father of the fifth century, writes: "Let us call out to her . . . who alone cured the pain of Eve; who alone wiped off the tears from the one who was groaning; who alone carried the ransom of the world."[8] Or again: "Blessed are all women on account of her. The female race is no longer under a curse. For it produced an offspring that excels even the angels in glory. Eve has been cured."[9]

Mary at the Wedding at Cana

Mary's maternal mediation is shown in a beautiful and mysterious way in the wedding at Cana in John 2:1–10:

On the third day there was a marriage at Cana in Galilee, and the mother of Jesus was there; Jesus also was invited to the marriage, with his disciples. When the wine failed, the mother of Jesus said to him, "They have no wine." And Jesus said to her, "O woman, what have you to do with me? My hour has not yet come." His mother said to the servants, "Do whatever he tells you." Now six stone jars were standing there, for the Jewish rites of purification, each holding twenty or thirty gallons. Jesus said to them, "Fill the jars with water." And they filled them up to the brim. He said to them, "Now draw some out, and take it to the steward of the feast." So they took it. When the steward of the feast tasted the water now become wine, and did not know where it came from (though the servants who had drawn the water knew), the steward of the feast called the bridegroom and said to him, "Every man serves the good wine first; and when men have drunk freely, then the poor wine; but you have kept the good wine until now."

The text is very rich in its mystical meaning. Jesus is at the wedding feast on account of His mother. When the wine fails, she intercedes with her Son on behalf of the wedding party, seeking the miracle that He

---

[7] *Against Heresies* 5.19.1, *ANF* 1:547.

[8] *Homily* 5.3, *PG* 65:720C, in *Proclus, Bishop of Constantinople: Homilies on the Life of Christ*, trans. Jan Harm Barkhuizen (Brisbane: Centre for Early Christian Studies, Australian Catholic Univ., 2001), 95.

[9] Ibid., 94.

then performs, which, as John tells us, is the very first that He performed to inaugurate His public ministry.

It is of great significance that John shows us that Jesus' first miracle, like His coming into the world, is tied to and prepared for by the intercession of Mary, extraordinarily attentive to the needs of men. We see Mary's absolute faith in her Son in requesting something that she had never seen any sign of in the thirty years in which He had been obedient to her. That faith is then further manifested by Jesus' reply to her: "O woman, what have you to do with me? My hour has not yet come."

Why does He call her "woman"? Is He repudiating her maternity in His regard? It seems extraordinarily harsh, which shows us that there is a mystery hidden here. The word "woman" should remind us of Genesis 3:15: "I will put enmity between you and the woman." Jesus seems to be distancing Himself from a merely human tie, a tie merely of blood, to reveal a far deeper tie between Mother and Son. Mary is the woman associated with Christ's hour in which He will crush the head of the serpent. However, that hour has not yet come. Three years of the public ministry still lie ahead.

One would think that Mary would feel rebuffed in her request by her Son's mysterious answer, yet she is not deterred in the slightest! She does not take it as a refusal, for she knows her Son perfectly. With absolute faith she says to the servants: "Do whatever he tells you." These are Mary's last words in the Gospel and her testament. They show her role in salvation history: to bring Christ to birth in us through obedience to His Word.

Christ then works the miracle of turning the water for the Jewish rite of purification into the finest wine. This miracle is a figure of the New Covenant that succeeds the Old. The comment of the steward of the bridegroom expresses the relationship between the covenants: "Every man serves the good wine first; and when men have drunk freely, then the poor wine; but you have kept the good wine until now."

Mary's role of intercession in this miracle, which prefigures the entire New Covenant, is surely not accidental. The Fathers of the Church see the wedding feast at Cana to which Mary was invited as the wedding between mankind and God. That matrimony was begun in Israel and is to be consummated in the Church.[10] Mary was there, and through her, Jesus came to be there. And it is Mary who intercedes on

---

[10] See the Syrian Father, St. Ephrem, *Hymn on the Lord's Mysteries*, 34.1: "The bride is Thy holy Church, the guests at table are Thy guests, and the triumph of the miracle looks forward to Thy coming in majesty." Quoted in Hugo Rahner, *Our Lady and the Church*, trans. Sebastian Bullough (Bethesda, MD: Zaccheus Press, 2004), 55–56.

behalf of mankind: "They have no wine." She is still interceding with her Son, until the end of time, on behalf of all peoples still deprived (at least in part) of the wine of the Gospel.

The changing of the water into wine signifies not only the transformation of the Old into the New Covenant, but also the elevation of nature through grace, the transformation of the sons of Adam and Eve into sons and daughters of God in Christ. And "the mother of Jesus was there" (Jn 2:1), interceding on our behalf.

Mary at the Foot of the Cross

The hour of Jesus that had not yet come at the wedding in Cana, finally came three years later on Calvary. And again, "the mother of Jesus was there," standing at the foot of the Cross. This was the hour of her co-redemption through suffering, in which her intercession on our behalf was consummated. Her plea on our behalf in the first miracle at Cana had led to Calvary, in which the wine of God's grace would be merited for all mankind:

> But standing by the cross of Jesus were his mother, and his mother's sister, Mary the wife of Clopas, and Mary Magdalene. When Jesus saw his mother, and the disciple whom he loved standing near, he said to his mother, "Woman, behold, your son!" Then he said to the disciple, "Behold, your mother!" And from that hour the disciple took her to his own home. After this Jesus, knowing that all was now finished, said (to fulfill the scripture), "I thirst. . . . It is finished"; and he bowed his head and gave up his spirit.[11]

While dying of asphyxiation on the Cross, Christ finds the strength to give His mother to His beloved disciple. Mysteriously, again, He calls her not "mother" but "woman." If ever He should have called her by the sweetest name of "mother," we would have thought that it should have been then. It is clear that it is not through lack of filial affection that He calls her "woman." He does this to show that He is not tied to her merely by a tie of blood, as important as that is. He is tied to her as the original woman was tied to the original man, because it was not good for the man to be alone. Mary is tied to Christ as the companion or associate of the New Adam. She is the woman who sums up or recapitulates her sex and restores what was distorted by the first woman. She is "the woman" as He is "the Son of man."[12]

---

[11] Jn 19:25–30.
[12] See, for example, Mt 12:8; 16:13; 16:27; 17:22; 25:31; 26:64.

And He then enlarges her maternity. He entrusts His beloved disciple to her as her son, and the beloved disciple then takes her into his home. Only at this point is Christ's work of redemption completed, and He can say: "It is finished."

The entire Tradition of the Church has seen the beloved disciple—John—as a figure for all the beloved disciples of Christ, and for all who are called to be beloved disciples, that is, all men. Christ's last act during His earthly life was to entrust all His future disciples, and thus potentially all humanity, to Mary's enlarged maternity.

For Mary it was a disadvantageous trade. Instead of the perfect Son of God, she received sons and daughters filled with every kind of spiritual leprosy. Yet a mother loves her handicapped children no less than the healthy ones, for they need her care still more.

Mary and the Church in Revelation 12

The word "woman" is applied to Mary once more at the end of the New Testament in Revelation 12:1–17:

> And a great sign appeared in heaven: a woman clothed with the sun, and the moon was under her feet, and upon her head a crown of twelve stars. And being with child, she cried out in her travail and was in the anguish of delivery. And another portent appeared in heaven; behold, a great red dragon, with seven heads and ten horns, and seven diadems upon his heads. His tail swept down a third of the stars of heaven, and cast them to the earth. And the dragon stood before the woman who was about to bear a child, that he might devour her child when she brought it forth. She brought forth a male child, one who is to rule all the nations with a rod of iron, but her child was caught up to God and to his throne, and the woman fled into the wilderness. . . . Then the dragon was angry with the woman, and went off to make war on the rest of her offspring, on those who keep the commandments of God and bear testimony to Jesus.

The woman is shown to be both the Mother of Christ and the Mother of the Church. As in Genesis 3:15, she is in enmity with the great serpent, who is Satan.

Who is the child to whom she gives birth in travail? At first sight it appears to be Christ. However, Mary was spared the pains of childbirth in her delivery of Jesus at Bethlehem. She did not bring Him forth in travail as other women do, who have inherited the consequences of the fall of Eve. Mary was in travail not in Bethlehem but on Calvary, in which she stood at the foot of the Cross and was given another, larger maternity—all the disciples of her Son redeemed by the blood that poured from her Son's wounds.

The Fathers of the Church tell us that the child with whom Mary is in travail in Revelation 12 is Christ's Mystical Body, the "whole Christ," which includes all His members. This is also taught by St. Pius X in his encyclical on Mary, *Ad diem illum*:

> Everyone knows that this woman signified the Virgin Mary, the stainless one who brought forth our Head. The Apostle continues: "And, being with child, she cried travailing in birth, and was in pain to be delivered" (Rev 12:2). John therefore saw the Most Holy Mother of God already in eternal happiness, yet travailing in a mysterious childbirth. What birth was it? Surely it was the birth of us who, still in exile, are yet to be generated to the perfect charity of God, and to eternal happiness. And the birth pains show the love and desire with which the Virgin from heaven above watches over us, and strives with unwearying prayer to bring about the fulfillment of the number of the elect.[13]

Mary is our spiritual mother and brings us to birth in sorrow for our sorrows, in travail for our sins and sufferings, full of anguish for our offenses to God, full of mercy and heartbreak for her poor leprous offspring.

Mary is the mother of compassion and mercy. "Compassion" etymologically means "sharing" in the passion of someone. Mercy is the special love that we give to those who are in need of our compassion and benevolence.

The Apparition of Our Lady of Guadalupe and Mary's Universal Maternal Care

We are given a glimpse of the immense care and solicitude of our heavenly mother for the welfare of the souls of her children in the brief dialogue of Our Lady of Guadalupe with St. Juan Diego when she appeared to him in Mexico in 1531. It is not accidental that Mary appeared on the tilma of St. Juan Diego in the way that she appears in Revelation 12:1—clothed in the sun with the moon under her feet, surrounded with stars. Thus she appeared as the Mother of the Church and the mother of all humanity called to find salvation in the Church.

In her first message to Juan Diego, the Virgin said that she intensely desired her sanctuary to be erected in that place so that she could manifest her Son to the people:

---

[13] Pius X, encyclical on the Immaculate Conception, *Ad diem illum laetissimam* (Feb. 2, 1904), n. 24.

Where I will offer Him to all the people with all my love, my compassionate gaze and my help, my salvation. Because I am truly your merciful mother, yours and mother of all who live united in this land, and of all the other peoples of different ancestries, of all those who love me, of those who cry to me, of those who search for me, of those who have confidence in me. There I will listen to their cry, to their sadness, so as to curb all their different pains, their miseries and sorrow, to remedy and alleviate their sufferings.[14]

Here we clearly see the two aspects of Mary's maternity. She is the Mother of Jesus and wishes to give Him to the people of Mexico. However, by doing this, she exercises her spiritual maternity with regard to us. For we are generated in the order of grace by coming to know and love Jesus Christ through faith, hope, and charity, and by receiving Jesus into our hearts and souls through Baptism and the Eucharist. Mary wishes to give birth to us spiritually by giving Jesus to us.

Indeed, this is exactly what she did with regard to the Indians of Mexico in the decade of the 1530s. The vast majority did not yet know Christ. Through her apparition, the news of which quickly spread throughout the land, she made Jesus manifest to some eight to ten million Indians who were subsequently received into the Church, the Mystical Body of Christ. And so she gave birth to them in the order of grace.

Let us notice that she says that she will give Him to the people with her personal love. In the Annunciation, Mary conceived Jesus first with her heart, and then in her body. She is not a mere biological mother of Jesus! She conceived Him with all her personal love, which overshadowed that of all of the angels. Likewise, she is our mother in that she gives Jesus to us with her personal love.

At this point, Mary explains her desire to bring Jesus to the Indians and all peoples by stating directly that she is our "merciful mother." She

---

[14] *Nican Mopohua*, which is the earliest account of the apparitions by Don Antonio Valeriano, written in the Aztec language around 1548. English translation by Fr. Real Bourque, O.M.I., which depends on the translation into Spanish by Mario Rojas. Another translation, which is less Christocentric, is given by Lisa Sousa, C. M. Stafford Poole, and James Lockhart, *The Story of Guadalupe: Luis Laso de la Vega's Huei tlamahuicoltica of 1649* (Stanford, CA: Stanford University Press, 1998), 65–67: "where I will manifest, make known, and give to people all my love, compassion, aid, and protection. For I am the compassionate mother of you and of all you people here in this land, and of the other various peoples who love me, who cry out to me, who seek me, who trust in me. There I will listen to their weeping and their sorrows in order to remedy and heal all their various afflictions, miseries, and torments."

is not the mother of the Europeans only, but "yours . . . and of all who live united in this land." Mary thus beautifully affirms the universal nature of her maternity. First she says that she is the mother of Juan Diego personally. Then she states that she is the mother of all the people who live together in the land. This means that she is equally the mother of the Indians, in all their different warring tribes, and of the Spaniards.

This affirmation was of crucial importance in 1531, as the Indians were in danger of being enslaved, exterminated, and treated as sub-humans, as happened later to the North American Indians. For this reason, they were also in danger of rejecting the Gospel brought by the Spaniards, many of whom were coming to be identified as persecutors. Our Lady sought to create peace by affirming that all were brothers, children of one common Mother.

Mary then extends her spiritual motherhood to all peoples, "*all the other people of different ancestries.*" However, she implies that her spiritual maternity is especially exercised with regard to those who correspond to her love by loving her in return and seeking her intercession. She is especially the mother of "those who love me, of those who cry to me, of those who search for me, of those who have confidence in me." Clearly she is inviting us to be counted in this group of her lovers who cry to her, seek her, and trust in her, so as to experience the full extent of her merciful maternal care. She is the mother of all, but so many of her sons and daughters do not love her, nor seek her, and thus she is not able to exercise all the maternal care that she would love to lavish on us.

Let us look now at the discourse of Our Lady on December 12, 1531. Juan Diego was supposed to return to Mary on Tepeyac on the morning of December 11 to receive the sign that would convince the bishop to build the sanctuary. This therefore would have been the decisive apparition that would ensure the success of Juan Diego's mission. But what happened? Juan Diego arrived home on the evening of December 10 to find that his uncle had become seriously ill, in danger of death. The native doctors came at once and were unable to do anything because the illness had already progressed too far.

On the morning of Monday, December 11, it appears that Juan Diego had either *forgotten* about his appointment with the Virgin of Guadalupe to receive the decisive sign, or, more probably, he decided that he would have to postpone it for a few days to take care of his uncle first.

His uncle, however, got worse and was near death, and on the morning of Tuesday, December 12, he sent Juan Diego to fetch a priest to give him the last sacraments. To go to the parish, Juan Diego would have to pass by the hill of Tepeyac where Mary would be waiting for him. Juan Diego obviously felt some guilt about his missing the appointment with Our Lady on the previous day. However, instead of rectifying matters, he sought to evade her gaze by taking a back route around the other side of the hill. He apparently thought that Mary would not see him that way.

It is interesting to observe these realistic details of the immature faith of Juan Diego, which give greater credibility to the account. Who could have invented this extraordinary encounter which Juan Diego sought to avoid? He obviously did not realize that Mary knows all things through the beatific vision.

At this point Our Lady came down the back side of the hill and addressed Juan Diego. We might have expected some sort of reprimand, but instead she tenderly said: "Well, my youngest child, where are you going? Where are you headed?"[15]

After Juan Diego made known his excuse, Our Lady took the opportunity to reaffirm the message of her spiritual maternity that she had begun in her first message on December 9. However, this time it was even more exquisite because of the concrete circumstances in which it occurred and the solemn and poetic words chosen by Our Lady:

> Hear and let it penetrate into your heart, my dear little son; let nothing discourage you, nothing depress you. Let nothing alter your heart, or your countenance. *Am I not here who am your Mother? Are you not under my shadow and protection? Am I not your fountain of life? Are you not in the folds of my mantle? In the crossing of my arms? Is there anything else that you need?* Do not fear any illness or vexation, anxiety or pain. Let not the illness of your uncle afflict you, because he is not going to die now of what he has in himself. Be sure that he will get well.[16]

Let us analyze this brief paragraph. She begins with an introduction to show the importance of what she is about to say: "Hear and let it penetrate into your heart, my dear little son." Mary wants her words to penetrate into our hearts, in imitation of the way in which she conserved the words of her Son in her heart. For example, after narrating the events of the nativity, presentation, and loss of the Child Jesus in the Temple, St. Luke tells us that Mary "kept all these things in her heart" (Lk 2:51).

She then gives him a spiritual counsel that is quite radical. She tells him *never to allow anything to discourage or afflict him, to alter his heart and his*

---

[15] Sousa et al., trans., *The Story of Guadalupe: Luis Laso de la Vega's Huei tlamahuicoltica of 1649*, 77.

[16] Translation of Fr. Real Bourque, slightly modified.

countenance. She is referring evidently to the mortal illness of his uncle, as well as his anxiety over the fact that he neglected to keep his appointment with the Virgin, putting in jeopardy the success of his mission with the Bishop, etc.

This counsel is of the greatest importance in the spiritual life. We are not to allow ourselves to become depressed or discouraged, to lose peace of heart. But how can we avoid it? The Stoic philosophers of pagan antiquity sought to banish all such passions by sheer force of will and by philosophical reasoning. Their goal was to become *impassible, passionless*. Buddhism also puts forth a similar ideal. Buddha's recipe for happiness is to avoid desire of any kind so as to avoid the affliction of frustrated desires and cares.

Our Lady gives us a very different and extremely simple recipe for curing affliction of soul. Depression and affliction of heart comes ultimately from lack of childlike faith and confidence in divine Providence. It comes from lack of confidence in the fatherhood of God who watches over our every step and whose omnipotence is capable of turning to some greater good every evil He permits.

However, human children need not only paternity, but also maternity. It is the care of a mother that is most comforting to the little child. And we are all little children in the order of grace. Divine Providence has therefore provided us with a Mother through whom we should receive every care that God the Father wishes to give us. He willed that we should receive every grace—of which He is the source and which Christ merited on the Cross—through maternal hands, the maternal hands of Mary.

Mary therefore gives us a most efficacious motive for confidence in divine Providence by reminding us that she is our Mother in the order of grace who watches over every event in our lives.

When Mary says that she is our "fountain of life," it seems that she is referring to sanctifying grace. Of course, it is God who is the true fountain of grace and life, but Mary is also a fountain of grace, by bringing Christ into the world. Now, as two thousand years ago, she brings Christ to birth in the souls of the faithful. How does she do this? Simply through intercession on our behalf, and because God has willed that every grace come to us through her prayers, and be distributed through her maternal hands.

Mary and the Mediation of All Graces

As Mary interceded for the wedding party at Cana, so the Church believes that she continues to intercede for all the needs of humanity throughout all time. As our mother, will she not be forever interceding for all our needs before her Son? Could we ever be in need and she fail to say to her Son on our behalf: "They have no wine"? And as Jesus was ever obedient to Mary while on earth, even when He said that it was not yet His hour, how could He fail to be obedient to Mary's intercession in heaven? It is for this reason that the Church believes that every grace that is given by Christ to humanity throughout the centuries is given with the participation of Mary's merciful intercession.

Protestants argue that Christ does not need Mary's intercession, for He too knows our needs. Of course this is true. But did Christ need Mary's intercession at Cana? Did He not know that there was no wine? Of course He would know, but He preferred to act through the maternal intercession of Mary.

God does not need humanity's participation, but He wants to make use of that participation wherever possible, because that is the purpose of creation—to bring His rational creatures into a sharing in His kingship. God has no need of Mary or of any other creature in order to distribute His graces into our hearts, for He is omnipotent, but He wills to make use of Mary in distributing every grace because it is fitting for our frail human condition to grow through maternal care. We grow in confidence in God through childlike confidence in Mary our Mother.

Of course, Mary is a mere creature and thus in no way omnipotent, for she is infinitely less than God. Nevertheless, the Doctors and Fathers of the Church consider her to be omnipotent in a certain sense: through her prayer and intercession with God, who always hears her, as Christ did at the wedding in Cana. During His earthly life, Our Lord obeyed her and was subject to her and St. Joseph. Now that He has entered into His glory, is it reasonable to think that He will cease to do what she asks of Him? She is the Mother of God, the Bride of the Holy Spirit, the most beloved daughter of God the Father. Her prayers are certainly all-powerful with the Blessed Trinity.

Although it has not yet been infallibly defined that every grace comes to us through the mediation of Mary, this is taught by the ordinary Magisterium of the Church,[17] and is contained in her liturgy and Tradition. It is a truth that is "proximate" to being defined and could be done whenever the Holy Father deems it opportune. It is thus theologically certain that *every grace comes to us from God through Mary*. She is the universal channel or aqueduct of every grace. Thus she is our fountain of life, by bringing us to the source of living waters which is her Son.

St. Pius X writes in this regard:

---

[17] See St. Pius X, encyclical on the Immaculate Conception of February 2, 1904, *Ad diem illum* 12–15.

Mary, as St. Bernard justly remarks, is the channel; or, if you will, the connecting portion the function of which is to join the body to the head and to transmit to the body the influences and volitions of the head—We mean the neck. Yes, says St. Bernardine of Siena, "she is the neck of Our Head, by which He communicates to His mystical body all spiritual gifts." She is the supreme Minister of the distribution of graces. Jesus "sitteth on the right hand of the majesty on high." Mary sitteth at the right hand of her Son—a refuge so secure and a help so trusty against all dangers that we have nothing to fear or to despair of under her guidance, her patronage, her protection.[18]

This great theological truth was taught by Our Lady to the Indian convert, Juan Diego. However, she did not present it through scholarly concepts but through the simplest words and images of maternal care. In the second part of Our Lady's admonition to Juan Diego, she gives us the essential meaning of the path to sanctity known as "spiritual childhood," which has been beautifully developed by St. Therese of Lisieux in her "little way."

Our Lady tells us that we are in the folds of her mantle, as an Indian mother carries her child wrapped in her shawl. The same image is repeated in other words: "Are you not in the crossing of my arms?" As she held the Child Jesus in her arms in Bethlehem and in the flight to Egypt, so she says that she has each one of us now in the fold of her mantle, and in the crossing of her arms. By stating this as a series of questions, she is inviting us to examine ourselves also to see if we truly believe this. Are we really aware of this grace that has been given us to be a child in Our Lady's arms? Do we rejoice in it, draw strength from it, and give frequent thanks to God for it? Do we rest secure in this knowledge? Is it a frequent subject of our meditation and prayer? Do we pray to Our Lady with the confidence that comes from knowing that we are in her arms, especially in our trials and afflictions, such as Juan Diego was having on that particular day when his uncle was dying?

This doctrine of "spiritual childhood" is frequently taught in the New Testament and lies at the very center of the Gospel. Jesus taught that "unless you be converted and become as little children, you shall not enter into the kingdom of heaven" (Mt 18:3). We have been adopted as children of God, and we must have the innocence, humility, simplicity, and confidence in our father and mother characteristic of little children. That confidence must be directed to God the Father, and God has willed that it also be directed to Mary our Mother, who brings her Son to birth in our hearts.

---

[18] Ibid., 13.

St. Paul tells us, "Because you are sons, God has sent the Spirit of His Son into your hearts, crying: 'Abba, Father!'" (Gal 4:6). However, in order to help us to grow in this filial and childlike love of God our Father, Mary shows us that she is our Mother who intercedes for us so that we may receive the Spirit of her Son into our hearts.

Conclusion

The writings of the Fathers of the Church very frequently bring Mary and the Church intimately together.[19] Mary is the great exemplar of the Church, and also the Mother of the Church. The same phrases that are used to describe Mary are used to describe the Church, and vice versa. Both Mary and the Church give birth to the Body of Christ. As Mary is ever Virgin and yet the most fruitful of mothers, so the Church is both Virgin and fruitful Mother. As Mary is immaculate, so the Church is immaculate in holiness, although her members may stray from her fold through sin. As Mary was the "woman of valor" of Proverbs 31,[20] so the Church is the "woman of valor." As Mary drew Christ down from heaven through her faith, so the Church calls continually to her Spouse: *Come, Lord Jesus!* (Rev 22:20).

If we wish to grasp the deepest nature of the Church, there is no better way than to go to Mary, the daughter of Zion, the most perfect archetype of all that the Church is and will be in her heavenly completion in the world to come. The Second Vatican Council concluded its Dogmatic Constitution on the Church, *Lumen gentium*, with a prayer to Mary:

> The entire body of the faithful pours forth instant supplications to the Mother of God and Mother of men that she, who aided the beginnings of the Church by her prayers, may now, exalted as she is above all the angels and saints, intercede before her Son in the fellowship of all the saints, until all families of people, whether they are honored with the title of Christian or whether they still do not know the Saviour, may be happily gathered together in peace and harmony into one people of God, for the glory of the Most Holy and Undivided Trinity.[21]

---

[19] See Hugo Rahner, *Our Lady and the Church.*

[20] Prov 31:10–14: "A woman of valor who can find? She is far more precious than jewels. The heart of her husband trusts in her, and he will have no lack of gain. She does him good, and not harm, all the days of her life. She seeks wool and flax, and works with willing hands. She is like the ships of the merchant, she brings her bread from afar."

[21] *Lumen gentium* 69.

Bibliography

The Apostolic Fathers: Greek Texts and English Translations. Edited by Michael W. Holmes. 3rd ed. Grand Rapids, MI: Baker Academic, 2007.

Augustine. *City of God*. Translated by Henry Bettenson. New York: Penguin Books, 1972.

_____. *The Confessions*. Translated by F. J. Sheed. New York: Sheed & Ward, 1943.

_____. *De doctrina christiana*. Translated by R. P. H. Green. Oxford: Clarendon Press, 1995.

Béchard, Dean P., ed. *The Scripture Documents: An Anthology of Official Catholic Teachings*. Collegeville, MN: The Liturgical Press, 2002.

Benedict XVI. Encyclical *Deus caritas est*: On Christian Love. 2005.

_____. Encyclical *Spe salvi*: On Christian Hope. 2007.

_____. *Regensburg Lecture*. September 12, 2006.

Boguslawski, Steven C. *Thomas Aquinas on the Jews: Insights into His Commentary on Romans 9–11*. New York: Paulist Press, 2008.

Bonaventure. *Breviloquium*. Translated by José de Vinck. Paterson, NJ: St. Anthony Guild Press, 1963.

Bossuet, J.-B. *History of the Variations of Protestant Churches*. Fraser, MI: American Council on Economics and Society, 1997.

Carroll, Warren. *The Building of Christendom*. Front Royal, VA: Christendom College Press, 1987.

Catechism of the Catholic Church. New York: Doubleday, 1994.

Cerfaux, Lucien. *The Church in the Theology of St. Paul*. Translated by Geoffrey Webb and Adrian Walker. New York: Herder and Herder, 1959.

The Church. Selected by the Benedictine Monks of Solesmes. Translated by E. O'Gorman. Series: Papal Teachings. Boston: St. Paul Editions, 1962.

Clement of Alexandria. *Stromateis: Books One to Three*. Translated by John Ferguson. Washington DC: Catholic University of America Press, 1991.

Compendium: Catechism of the Catholic Church. Washington DC: United States Conference of Catholic Bishops, 2006.

Congar, Yves. *The Meaning of Tradition*. Translated by A. N. Woodrow. San Francisco: Ignatius Press, 2004.

Congregation for the Doctrine of the Faith. Declaration *Dominus Jesus*. August 6, 2000.

_____. *Instruction on Certain Aspects of the "Theology of Liberation."* August 6, 1984.

_____. "Responses to Some Questions Regarding Certain Aspects of the Doctrine on the Church." June 29, 2007.

_____. Letter *Communionis notio*, on Some Aspects of the Church Understood as Communion. May 28, 1992.

Cyprian. *De Lapsis and De Ecclesiae catholicae unitate.* Translated by Maurice Bévenot. Oxford: Clarendon Press, 1971.

De Lubac, Henri. *Catholicism: Christ and the Common Destiny of Man.* Translated by Lancelot Sheppard and Elizabeth Englund. San Francisco: Ignatius Press, 1988.

_____. *Medieval Exegesis.* Vols. 1–2, *The Four Senses of Scripture.* Translated by Mark Sebanc. Grand Rapids, MI: William B. Eerdmans, 1998–2000.

_____. *The Motherhood of the Church.* Translated by Sergia Englund. San Francisco: Ignatius Press, 1982.

_____. *Scripture in the Tradition.* Translated by Luke O'Neill. New York: Herder and Herder, 2000.

_____. *The Splendor of the Church.* Translated by Michael Mason. San Francisco: Ignatius Press, 1986.

Dulles, Avery Cardinal. "The Church and the Kingdom: A Study of their Relationship in Scripture, Tradition, and Evangelization." *Letter & Spirit* 3 (2007): 23–38.

Dunn, James D. G. *The Parting of the Ways: Between Christianity and Judaism and their Significance for the Character of Christianity.* 2nd ed. London: SCM Press, 2006.

The Encyclopaedia of Judaism. Edited by Jacob Neusner, Alan J. Avery-Peck, and William Scott Green. 5 vols. New York: Continuum Publishing, 1999–2005.

Eusebius. *History of the Church.* Translated by G.A. Williamson. London: Penguin Books, 1989.

Feuillet, André. *The Priesthood of Christ and His Ministers.* Translated by Matthew J. O'Connell. Garden City, NY: Doubleday, 1975.

Fonck, Leopold. *The Parables of the Gospel: An Exegetical and Practical Explanation.* Translated by E. Leahy. New York: F. Pustet, 1915. Reprint under the title, *The Parables of Christ.* Fort Collins, CO: Roman Catholic Books [199?].

Francis de Sales. *Introduction to the Devout Life.* Translated by Michael Day. Westminster, MD: Newman Press, 1956.

Friedman, Elias. *Jewish Identity.* New York: The Miriam Press, 1987.

Gregory of Nyssa. *Life of Moses.* Translated by Abraham Malherbe and Everett Ferguson. New York: Paulist Press, 1978.

Hahn, Scott, ed. *Catholic Bible Dictionary.* New York: Doubleday, 2009.

Hahn, Scott. *Covenant and Communion: The Biblical Theology of Pope Benedict XVI.* Grand Rapids, MI: Brazos Press, 2009.

Howell, Kenneth J. *Ignatius of Antioch & Polycarp of Smyrna: A New Translation and Theological Commentary.* Zanesville, OH: CHResources, 2009.

Irenaeus. *Against Heresies.* Vol. 1 of *The Ante-Nicene Fathers.* Peabody, MA: Hendrickson Publishers, 1994.

Jerome. *Jerome's Commentary on Daniel.* Translated by Gleason L. Archer, Jr. Grand Rapids, MI: Baker Book House, 1958.

_____. *Commentary on Matthew.* Translated by Thomas Scheck. Washington DC: Catholic University of America Press, 2008.

The Jewish Enclopedia. Edited by Isidore Singer. 12 vols. New York: Ktav Publishing House, 1964.

John Paul II. Apostolic Exhortation *Christifideles laici:* On the Vocation and the Mission of the Lay Faithful in the Church and in the World. 1988.

_____. Apostolic Letter *Dies Domini:* On Keeping the Lord's Day Holy. 1998.

_____. Encyclical *Fides et ratio:* On the Relationship between Faith and Reason. 1998.

_____. Apostolic Letter *Mulieris dignitatem:* On the Dignity and Vocation of Women. 1988.

_____. Encyclical *Redemptoris missio:* On the Permanent Validity of the Church's Missionary Mandate. 1990.

Josephus. *Complete Works.* Translated by William Whiston. Grand Rapids, MI: Kregel Publications, 1978.

Journet, Charles. "The Mysterious Destinies of Israel." In *The Bridge: A Yearbook of Judaeo-Christian Studies.* Edited by John Oesterreicher. Vol. 2, 35–90. New York: Pantheon Books, 1956.

_____. *The Theology of the Church.* Translated by Victor Szczurek. San Francisco: Ignatius Press, 2004.

Justin Martyr. *The First and Second Apologies.* Translated by Leslie Willaim Barnard. New York: Paulist Press, 1997.

_____. *Dialogue with the Jew Trypho.* Vol. 1 of *The Ante-Nicene Fathers.* Peabody, MA: Hendrickson Publishers, 1994.

Kevane, Eugene. *The Lord of History: Christocentrism and the Philosophy of History.* Boston: St. Paul Editions, 1980.

Kinzer, Mark S. *Post-Missionary Messianic Judaism: Redefining Christian Engagement with the Jewish People.* Grand Rapids, MI: Brazos Press, 2005.

Klausner, Joseph. *The Messianic Idea in Israel: From Its Beginning to the Completion of the Mishna.* Translated by W. F. Stinespring. New York: Macmillan, 1955.

Klyber, Arthur. *The One Who Is to Come: A Collection of Writings of Father Arthur B. Klyber, Hebrew Catholic Priest.* Edited by Matthew McDonald. New Hope, KY: Remnant of Israel, 2000.

Kugelman, Richard. "Hebrew, Israelite, Jew." In *The Bridge: A Yearbook of Judaeo-Christian Studies.* Edited by John Oesterreicher. Vol. 1, 204–24. New York: Pantheon Books, 1955.

Lagrange, M.-J. *Saint Paul Épitre aux Romains.* Paris: Libraire Lecoffre, 1950.

Leo XIII. Encyclical *Aeterni Patris:* On the Restoration of Christian Philosophy. 1879.

_____. Encyclical *Satis cognitum:* On the Unity of the Church. 1896.

Levering, Matthew. *Christ's Fulfillment of Torah and Temple: Salvation according to Thomas Aquinas.* Notre Dame, IN: University of Notre Dame Press, 2002.

_____. *Sacrifice and Community: Jewish Offering and Christian Eucharist.* Malden, MA: Blackwell Publishing, 2005.

Loisy, Alfred. *L'Évangile et l'Église.* Paris: Picard, 1902

Lustiger, Cardinal Jean-Marie. *The Promise.* Grand Rapids, MI: William B. Eerdmans, 2007.

Malloy, Christopher J. *Engrafted into Christ: A Critique of the Joint Declaration.* New York: P. Lang, 2005.

Manns, Frédéric. *Les Enfants de Rébecca. Judaïsme et christianisme aux premiers siècles.* Montrèal: Éditions Médiaspaul, 2002.

_____. *Jewish Prayer in the Time of Jesus.* Jerusalem: Franciscan Printing Press, 1994.

Marmion, Columba. *Christ the Life of the Soul.* Translated by Alan Bancroft. Bethesda, MD: Zaccheus Press, 2005.

Marshall, Taylor. *The Crucified Rabbi.* Dallas, TX: St. John Press, 2009.

Neusner, Jacob, ed. *The Babylonian Talmud: A Translation and Commentary.* 22 vols. Peabody, MA: Hendrickson Publishers, 2005.

_____. *The Oral Torah: The Sacred Books of Judaism: An Introduction.* San Francisco: Harper & Row, 1986.

_____. *A Rabbi Talks with Jesus.* Revised ed. Montreal: McGill-Queen's University Press, 2000.

Newman, John Henry. *Apologia pro vita sua.* London: J M Dent, 1993.

_____. *Discussions and Arguments on Various Subjects.* New York: Longmans, Green, and Co., 1897.

_____. *An Essay on the Development of Christian Doctrine.* Notre Dame: University of Notre Dame Press, 1989.

Odom, Robert Leo. *Israel's Preexistent Messiah.* New York: Israelite Heritage Institute, 1985.

Oesterreicher, John, ed. *The Bridge: A Yearbook of Judaeo-Christian Studies.* 4 vols. New York: Pantheon Books, 1955–61.

Pascal, Blaise. *Pensées.* Translated by A.J. Krailsheimer. New York: Penguin Classics, 1966.

Patai, Raphael. *The Messiah Texts.* Detroit: Wayne State University Press, 1979.

Paul VI, Encyclical *Ecclesiam suam:* On the Church. 1964.

Pius X. Encyclical *Ad diem illum:* On the Immaculate Conception. February 2, 1904.

Pius XII. Encyclical *Divino afflante spiritu:* On Promoting Biblical Studies. 1943.

_____. Encyclical *Humani generis*: Concerning Some False Opinions Threatening to Undermine the Foundations of Catholic Doctrine. 1950.

_____. Encyclical *Mystici Corporis*: On the Mystical Body of Christ. 1943.

Pontifical Biblical Commission. *The Jewish People and Their Sacred Scriptures in the Christian Bible.* May 24, 2001.

Prat, Fernand. *The Theology of Saint Paul.* Translated by John Stoddard. Westminster, MD: Newman Bookshop, 1952.

Pseudo-Dionysius: The Complete Works. Translated by Colm Luibheid. New York: Paulist Press, 1987.

Rahner, Hugo. *Our Lady and the Church.* Translated by Sebastian Bullough. Bethesda: Zaccheus Press, 2004.

Randellini, Lino. *La Chiesa dei Giudeo-cristiani.* Brescia: Paideia, 1968.

Ratzinger, Joseph. *Daughter Zion.* Translated by John M. McDermott. San Francisco: Ignatius Press, 1983.

_____. *Jesus of Nazareth: From the Baptism in the Jordan to the Transfiguration.* Translated by Adrian J. Walker. New York: Doubleday, 2007.

_____. *Many Religions—One Covenant: Israel, the Church, and the World.* Translated by Graham Harrison. San Francisco: Ignatius Press, 1999.

Refoulé, François. *"...Et ainsi tout Israël sera sauvé": Romains 11, 25–32.* Paris: Editions du Cerf, 1984.

Schauss, Hayyim. *The Jewish Festivals: A Guide to Their History and Observance.* New York: Schocken Books, 1996.

Schoeman, Roy. *Honey from the Rock.* San Francisco: Ignatius Press, 2007.

_____. *Salvation Is from the Jews.* San Francisco: Ignatius Press, 2003.

Scholem, Gershom. *The Messianic Idea in Judaism and Other Essays on Jewish Spirituality.* New York: Schocken Books, 1995.

Scholl, Andrew. *Completed Jew.* East Keilor, Vic.: Cosmoda Communications, 2002.

Skarsaune, Oskar, and Reidar Hvalvik, eds. *Jewish Believers in Jesus: The Early Centuries.* Peabody MA: Hendrickson Publishers, 2007.

Smith, Janet. *Humanae Vitae: A Generation Later.* Washington DC: Catholic University of America Press, 1991.

Smith, Janet, ed. *Why Humanae Vitae Was Right: A Reader.* San Francisco: Ignatius Press, 1993.

Stark, Rodney. *The Rise of Christianity: A Sociologist Reconsiders History.* Princeton, NJ: Princeton University Press, 1996.

Stein, Edith. *Essays on Woman.* Translated by Freda Mary Oben. Washington DC: ICS Publications, 1987.

Testa, Emmanuel. *The Faith of the Mother Church: An Essay on the Theology of the Judeo-Christians.* Translated by Paul Rotondi. Jerusalem: Franciscan Printing Press, 1992.

Thomas Aquinas. *Catena aurea.* Translated by John Henry Newman. 4 vols. Oxford: John Henry Parker, 1841–45. Reprinted with an introduction by Aidan Nichols. London: Saint Austin Press, 1997.

_____. *Commentary on the Gospel of St. John.* Part 1. Translated by James A. Weisheipl and Fabian R. Larcher. Albany, NY: Magi Books, 1966.

_____. *Commentary on St. Paul's Epistle to the Ephesians.* Translated and Introduction by Matthew L. Lamb. Albany, NY: Magi Books, 1966.

_____. *Commentary on the Epistle to the Hebrews.* Translated by Chrysostom Baer. South Bend, IN: St. Augustine's Press, 2006.

_____. *Commentaries on St. Paul's Epistles to Timothy, Titus, and Philemon.* Translated by Chrysostom Baer. South Bend, IN: St. Augustine's Press, 2007.

_____. *Commentary on Saint Paul's First Letter to the Thessalonians and the Letter to the Philippians.* Translated by F. R. Larcher and Michael Duffy. Albany, NY: Magi Books, 1966.

_____. *Commentary on Saint Paul's Epistle to the Galatians.* Translated by F. R. Larcher. Albany, NY: Magi Books, 1966.

_____. *Summa Contra Gentiles.* Translated by Anton Pegis. 4 vols. Notre Dame, IN: University of Notre Dame Press, 1975.

_____. *Summa theologiae of St. Thomas Aquinas.* 2nd ed. Translated by Dominican Fathers of the English Province. London: Burns, Oates, & Washbourne, 1920–1932.

_____. *Super epistolas S. Pauli lectura.* Edited by Raphael Cai. 2 vols. Turin: Marietti, 1953.

Vatican II. *The Sixteen Documents of Vatican II.* Boston, MA: Pauline Books and Media, 1999.

Wyschogrod, Michael. *The Body of Faith: Judaism as Corporeal Election.* New York: Seabury Press, 1983.

Zolli, Eugenio. *Before the Dawn.* New York: Sheed and Ward, 1954.

_____. *The Nazarene: Studies in New Testament Exegesis.* Translated by Cyril Vollert. New Hope, KY: Urbi et Orbi/Remnant of Israel, 1999.

Index

Roman Empire, 59, 130, 172
royal priesthood, 6, 7, 225

S

Sabbath, 150, 172
sacramentals, 233
sacraments, 9–11, 13, 24, 32, 43, 48,
    51, 75–77, 84, 116, 120, 126–29,
    134–35, 142, 145n, 155, 158, 164,
    170–73, 179–82, 185, 192, 211,
    215–16, 218, 220–21, 233, 236, 242
sacrifice of Christ, 7, 31, 128, 138, 199,
    213–14, 235
sacrifice of the Mass, 7, 29, 31, 73–74,
    128, 138, 173, 182, 235
saints of the Old Testament, 214
salvation outside the Church, 138–41
sanctification of work, 150–52
sanctifying grace, 9–10, 23, 25, 49, 125,
    158, 180, 194, 196–98, 201, 203,
    206–9, 220, 223, 243, 254
    and justification, 209
sanctity. *See* holiness
Sanhedrin, 28, 47, 48, 95, 170, 179
Sarah, 218
Satan, 40, 95, 146, 243, 249
Satis cognitum, 14, 94n, 95
seder, 239
Sermon on the Mount, 43, 51, 145
Simeon, 31
Simon Magus, 165
simul peccator et justus, 202
Sinai, 119, 121
    covenant of, 225
sola Scriptura, 113, 119
sower, parable of, 38
Spe salvi, 2
spirit of sonship, 205, 207
spiritual childhood, 256
spiritual reading, 155
Stein, Edith, 188
Stephen, stoning of, 170
subsistit (*LG* 8), 134–38
suffering, 138, 151, 185–87, 188, 220,
    248
    means of sanctification, 155
    of Christ, 213–14
Suffering Servant, 53
sufficient grace, 139
Sunday, 84, 171–72
supersessionism, 239

T

Talmud, 120–22
Temple, 7, 8, 33, 63, 72–74, 150, 167,
    168, 172–73, 179, 253
Ten Commandments, 22, 43, 55, 144,
    164
Tertullian, 100, 130
teshuvah, 193
Therese of Lisieux, 191–92, 256
Thomas Aquinas, 63, 66, 143, 149,
    157, 173–74, 195, 199, 208
Timothy, 100, 168
Tisha B'Av, 120
Tome of Leo I, 105
Trent, Council of. *See* Council of Trent
Trinity, 2, 71, 133, 177, 205, 255
typology, 243–45

U

universality of the Church, 53–69

V

Valentinus, 99
Vatican II. *See* Council, Second
    Vatican
Vianney, John, 186
visibility of the Church, 9, 7–18, 51,
    83, 87–88, 89
    and apostolic succession, 89, 91–94,
    135, 136
visible and invisible dimensions of the
    Church, 9, 7–18, 178
visible head of the Church, 91, 182
visible mediators, 91
visible members of the Church, 127,
    181
von Hildebrand, Dietrich, 189

W

Wojtyla, Karol, 189
woman of valor, 257
works of mercy, 9, 16, 83, 129–31
works of the flesh, 209
works of the Law, 209
works of the Spirit, 209

Z

Scripture Index

Numbering follows the RSV edition.

Old Testament

New Testament

CPSIA information can be obtained at www.ICGtesting.com
Printed in the USA
LVOW10s0738290415

436531LV00004B/4/P

9 780939 409051